surrealist poetics have foun. expression.

Henri Peyre, commenting on *Toward the Poetics of Surrealism*, says: "It will be one of the most important books on surrealism. Since the author counts among the best specialists on surrealism anywhere, the book is solidly informed, impeccable, indeed, and rests upon a vast and precise knowledge of surrealist works."

J. H. Matthews, born in Swansea, Wales, has been Professor of French at Syracuse University and editor of *Symposium: A Quarterly Journal in Modern Foreign Literatures* since 1965. He has edited a selection of stories by Guy de Maupassant (1959) as well as two special issues of *La Revue des Lettres Modernes*, and is author of *Les deux Zola* (1957) and numerous articles on nineteenth- and twentieth-century French literature. His interest in surrealism has led him to write also *An Introduction to Surrealism* (1965), *An Anthology of French Surrealist Poetry* (1966), *Surrealism and the Novel* (1966), *André Breton* (1967), *Surrealist Poetry in France* (1969), *Surrealism and Film* (1971), *Theatre in Dada and Surrealism* (1974), *Benjamin Péret* (1975), and *The Custom-House of Desire: A Half-Century of Surrealist Stories* (1975). His *Péret's Score / Vingt poèmes de Benjamin Péret* appeared in 1965, illustrated by E. F. Granell.

Toward the Poetics of Surrealism

Toward the Poetics of Surrealism

J. H. MATTHEWS

SYRACUSE UNIVERSITY PRESS   1976

Library of Congress Cataloging in Publication Data

Matthews, J   H
    Toward the poetics of surrealism.

    Includes bibliographical references.
    1. French literature—20th century—History and
criticism. 2. Surrealism—France. I. Title.
PQ307.S95M3   840'.9'0091   75-43974
ISBN 0-8156-0120-4

For GUI ROSEY

la poésie au bout des doigts

J. H. Matthews, born in Swansea, Wales, has been Professor of French at Syracuse University and editor of *Symposium: A Quarterly Journal in Modern Foreign Literatures* since 1965. He has edited a selection of stories by Guy de Maupassant (1959) as well as two special issues of *La Revue des Lettres Modernes*, and is author of *Les deux Zola* (1957) and numerous articles on nineteenth- and twentieth-century French literature. His interest in surrealism has led him to write also *An Introduction to Surrealism* (1965), *An Anthology of French Surrealist Poetry* (1966), *Surrealism and the Novel* (1966), *André Breton* (1967), *Surrealist Poetry in France* (1969), *Surrealism and Film* (1971), *Theatre in Dada and Surrealism* (1974), *Benjamin Péret* (1975), and *The Custom-House of Desire: A Half-Century of Surrealist Stories* (1975). His *Péret Score / Vingt poèmes de Benjamin Péret* appeared in 1965, illustrated by E. F. Granell.

E. F. Granell, born in La Coruña, Spain, has been a member of the surrealist movement since 1942. A political refugee, first from Spain then from Guatemala, he settled for a while in Puerto Rico, where he published *Isla cofre mítico* (1951), dedicated to Elisa and André Breton. He won the Premio Internacional Don Quijote for one of his other books, *Lo que sucedió* (1968), and took the Copley International Prize for painting in 1960. Benjamin Péret once commented, "These beings whom he introduces to us seem to have come from a world yet to be discovered. Are these forms from another time, from another place to which he is leading us? These specimens of a fauna to come—rooster-sundial, hen–sewing-machine—are somewhat evocative of those fabulous beings the first travelers recognized in America, like that paintbrush-bird ('pacho del ciello') of which Samuel Champlain offers us a picture without legs because, he says, feeding on air, it never alighted anywhere."

Contents

Preface

THE CHAPTERS that follow represent an inquiry into the nature of surrealism, carried out over a period of a dozen years, without a concerted plan and with what may be termed more accurately instinctive persistence than orderly purpose, sometimes in fact with less than full realization of where curiosity was leading.

Instead of aiming, at this point, to attain the impossible ideal of comprehensiveness, I have chosen to reconsider a few previously published articles next to other essays not printed before, in an attempt to confront a little more systematically the fascination that led me to write them. My present purpose is to illustrate some of the ways in which the term "poetics," undergoing expansion beyond conventional literary and artistic usage, can lend itself to defining the ambitions of surrealism and the ways in which these ambitions have been pursued on the broadest scale. In so doing, I hope to contribute to dissipating some of the confusion that, half a century and more since André Breton published his *Manifesto of Surrealism*, still impedes recognition and full acknowledgment of the significance and scope of a movement that has had an unparalleled impact upon creative expression and upon cultural history in our time.

The following articles, noted below in chronological order according to date of publication, have found their way into this book, revised, expanded, or otherwise modified. My grateful thanks go to the editors of the journals and magazines cited for permission to reprint material that originally appeared in the periodicals mentioned.

"Huysmans et les Surréalistes," *Bulletin de la Société J.-K. Huysmans* (1961); "Zola et les Surréalistes," *Les Cahiers naturalistes* (1963); "Apollinaire devant les Surréalistes," *La Revue des Lettres Modernes* (1964); "Du Cinéma comme Langage surréaliste," *Etudes cinématographiques* (1965); "The Right Person for Surrealism," *Yale French Studies* ['The House of Sade'] (1965); "Intelligence in the Service of Surrealism: André Breton's *Anthologie de l'Humour noir*," *Books Abroad* (1967); "Back to *Les Champs magnétiques*," *Books Abroad* (1968); "Surrealism, Politics and Poetry," *Mosaic* (1969); "GRADIVA—ou la jambe artificielle," *Gradiva* (1971); "The Goon Show: it all depends on where you're standing," *Surrealist Trans-formaCtion* (1973); "Chapeaux bas!" *Gradiva* (1974); "Fifty Years Later: *The Manifesto of Surrealism*," *Twentieth Century Literature* (1975); "Spectacle and Poetry: Surrealism in Theatre and Cinema," *The Journal of General Education* (1975).

Two essays are borrowed from *Symposium:* "Romanticism Taken by the Tail" (1969) and "Paul Nougé: Intellect, Subversion, and Poetic Language" (1970).

Quotations from Spike Milligan's *The Goon Show Scripts* appear by permission of the Woburn Press, London.

JHM

Fayetteville, New York
Winter 1975

Toward the Poetics of Surrealism

Introduction

I N 1937, a new surrealist gallery called Gradiva opened in
Paris. The occasion was marked by the appearance of a
tract signed by the gallery's director, André Breton, affirming the "non-value" of certain concrete elements mentioned
in a description taken from a story by the Hungarian novelist Alexandre Marai. Without categorically asserting as
much, Breton's text gives us to understand that he prized
the latent value of things far more than their manifest content. For this reason, evidently, he named his gallery after
the heroine of a tale by W. Jensen, brought to the attention
of surrealists in France by Freud's analysis of the story in
his *The Interpretation of Dreams.*

In surrealist parlance, the distinction between latent
and manifest content is all-important. The former is associated with imaginative freedom. On the other hand, the
latter betokens the depressing consequences of a utilitarian
principle diametrically opposed to the pleasure principle
governing imaginative activity. Looking back to our own
childhood we readily appreciate what is involved here.

Any child can testify, in a way that Breton surely
would have appreciated, to the inexplicable attraction, the
latent appeal, of objects which, to an adult, appear mani-

1

festly intended for some purpose that escapes children entirely. I recall that, as long as parental patience would allow, I used to stand in front of shop windows displaying trusses, surgical belts, artificial limbs, and so on. . . But with time, as surrealists have noted with deep regret, a child's glance loses its freshness, its capacity for stimulating wonder. Little by little, the ugly, sadly shameful aspect of things that had held my attention before now began to impress itself upon me. I would stop no longer in front of certain windows that at one time held so much fascination. Henceforth I would be able to see in the items they showed only the vulgarly utilitarian aspect of things. It took a quarter of a century or so for Luis Buñuel to reawaken with his film *Tristana* memories that had remained confused or more or less deliberately put out of mind since childhood.

Thrown carelessly on a sofa, the artificial leg Tristana refuses to wear is a disturbing sight. The stocking and shoe, put on to grant it a more natural appearance, serve now to give it a disconcerting air, make it look aggressively *unassimilable*. Designed for a purpose from which detachment has separated it, Tristana's artificial limb appears to exist *for itself*, not as a substitute for something else, and quite apart from the function in which, while it is in use, so far as we notice it at all, we see the reason for its presence.

Breton shared with his fellow surrealists the firm belief that a sense of the utilitarian is one of the crippling weaknesses of the reasoning mind. He taught that by divesting ourselves of this sense, we arrive more easily at establishing fruitful relationships with everyday objects and, naturally, with less-than-familiar objects that common sense presses us to assign a functional role in a world forever ruled by habit and routine. Stripped of the label identifying their use, even the most commonplace of things can signal to us, sometimes with remarkable precision. Visitors to Breton's Gradiva Gallery could not enter without becoming aware of the two larger-than-life human figures Marcel Duchamp had cut in the glass door.[1] Just as those visitors were made conscious of Duchamp's silhouette by the necessity to pass through it, so we find ourselves more keenly responsive than before to the outline of this or that object when we see it in unwonted perspective. This is because affective response brings us into contact with daily routine in a manner that renders it necessary to us in an entirely new way.

Cut off from the body to which it belongs—amputation brutally creating abnormal conditions—a woman's leg, some might think, is in danger of losing its erotic significance. But if this were not simplifying matters, then there would be nothing to say of the physical transformations to which Hans Bellmer submits his doll, or of the luminous canvases painted by Pierre Molinier.[2] Anyone who has imagined the lighthouse modeled on the leg of the king's favorite—a noteworthy *allumeuse* indeed[3]—which provides André Pieyre de Mandiargues with the subject of some verses in his *Incongruités monumentales,* will be ready to admit that, upon occasion anyway, meaning comes to us from unsuspected and even rationally inconceivable sources.[4] Whether or not we incline to Freudian interpretation like Breton and other surrealists, admitting as Breton does that we are dealing with "a most obscure necessity" means acknowledging at the same time being confronted with something emerging dramatically from darkness into light to prove that an exchange of inestimable value can take place between man and the world about him.

As Breton reminds us of it when, for his own purposes, he limits the meaning Jensen gives Gradiva Rediviva Zoë Bertgang, the significance of Gradiva—She Who Moves Forward—involves advancement beyond conventional utilitarianism and customary limitations in favor of poetic liberation. Essentially, the latter reflects the movement from latent to manifest, replacement of "non-value" by values subjectively grasped. To the extent that certain found objects prompt us to look at them from this angle rather than another, it is thanks to chance, apparently, that poetic liberation is effected in its purest form. But if we are content to accept the restrictive limits imposed by the accidental, without ever offering material things the assistance they can find only in man, our power of self-determination will never cease to be severely limited. We shall have to be satisfied, always, with being passive witnesses. We shall find ourselves inescapably at the mercy of a material universe we alone of all the creatures on earth have the possibility of dominating, if only we are willing and able to take advantage of the rights and privileges guaranteed by imagination. We shall have to confine ourselves, then, to assembling and drawing stimulus and comfort from documents relatively few in number. These are suggestive documents, it is true, but of a strictly external character, like the photograph of a human arm protruding from the open belly of a dead crocodile to be seen in one of the later surrealist magazines.[5]

An artificial limb may be considered doubly attractive. In creating it, man rivals nature. More important still, he exceeds nature, in making a detachable human limb. Only our idea of the utilitarian and a certain aesthetic sense to which all surrealists are quite impervious stand between us and replacing an amputated arm by a handmade leg, a custom-made one, as the genius of American commercialism terms it. Utilitarianism loses its power of restraint, though, while generally regarded aesthetic values are shown to be altogether too presumptuous, when we see Tristana take off her leg and advance, a Buñuelian Gradiva, to the window where she will expose herself, a one-legged nude, to an adolescent whose inordinately long visits to the toilet must be ascribed, presumably, to what Havelock Ellis' *Studies in the Psychology of Sex* recommends we term auto-eroticism. True, the boy is horror-stricken at what he sees after signalling to Tristana to open her robe. Only too clearly, he proves incapable of appreciating the beauty of the mutilated woman. But, while *he* draws back to hide in the bushes, *she* wears a dazzling smile of serenity.

The value with which surrealism can invest an artificial object does not depend exclusively on the faithful resemblance it bears to what it imitates. On the contrary, its value resides elsewhere. The manufactured article evidences a marvelous capacity for allowing itself to be diverted from its original destination, so as to exert its appeal through the role it now plays in an act of defiance aimed at the utilitarian principle, at good sense, and at aesthetic predispositions. So far as an object of this kind turns away from its supposed destination, taking us somewhere different as it ignores its designated purpose, it is dear to the surrealist. In its external resemblance to whatever we thought it intended to imitate, it lets us see nothing other than a trap set to snare the rational mind. Lying peacefully on the sofa, Tristana's artificial leg does not conceal from sight the straps presumably meant to hold it in place beneath her skirt. We are all the more sensitive, therefore, to their gratuitousness in a situation that lets us see the leg horizontal, not vertical. In short, these straps undergo a displacement similar to the one bringing a sewing machine and an umbrella into confrontation on a dissecting table set up by Lautréamont.[6]

What matters, surrealists contend, is provoking a displacement that will have the effect of setting off the trap in such a manner as to incite the imagination, momentarily snared by the anti-rational, to free itself at all cost. This is why the dissecting table, on which an unprecedented surgical operation seems imminent—an operation implicating both the masculine element (the umbrella) and the feminine element (the sewing machine[7])—can suggest to surrealist readers of Lautréamont the marriage bed.[8] As for the sofa on which Tristana's artificial limb rests, its shape is like that of the one drawn by Salvador Dalí in 1936. Playing on the sense of *lips*, Dalí called it "The Lips of Mae West," later incorporating it into his portrait of Miss West, and later still modeling a shocking-pink sofa upon it, for his friend Edward James. Dalí's sofa, we notice, is quite different from the lips visible in "A l'Heure de l'Observatoire—Les Amoureux," painted by May Ray, creator of an unidentifiable object (possibly a sewing machine, covered with a blanket and tied with rope) titled "L'Enigme d'Isidore Ducasse" (1920). In the American artist's painting, we are denied hope of touching the enigmatic lips floating inaccessibly above an indistinct landscape, at once a menace and a fascination. Dalí's labial sofa invites our touch, with its promise of possession and return to the womb. The scabrous element, in which André Breton saluted a profoundly subversive force,[9] plays the role of *agent provocateur* here, just as it does in the Buñuelian image of the artificial leg, metamorphosed into a detached member, in danger of being swallowed by the welcoming lips of the sofa in the drawing-room of Tristana's guardian's home.

The leg lying passively in the drawing-room puts us in mind of the snow shovel that once hung in Marcel Duchamp's New York apartment. Suspended above the floor, the shovel can no longer (or perhaps cannot yet) be put to its normal use. Neither can the detached leg. The shovel (a word of feminine gender in French) in the apartment of a man who gave his own creative identity a feminine name, Rrose Sélavy (= *Eros c'est la vie* ["Eros is life"]), bears a premonitory title, "En Avance du Bras cassé" ("In Advance of the Broken Arm"[10]), whereas the leg shown us by Buñuel remains modestly anonymous. All the same, both find in the immobility imposed upon them the condition that places them in an interrogative void. And this is a void that only poetic imagination can fill.

Whether the surrealist benefits from a sometimes all-too-fragile ignorance regarding the designated purpose of objects (like so many of those André Breton brought back from his frequent trips to the Paris flea market), or whether he practices more or less intentionally a mode of deformation that takes away from things close at hand their drably utilitarian character, the important thing is this: his imagination succeeds in moving outside limits commonly imposed and generally accepted. If it proves necessary to substitute for a flesh-and-blood leg an artificial one that, at first, seems to work less efficiently, so much the worse, or so much the better: Gradiva advances no less surely toward the beauty that constitutes the value of things.

What in fact is the nature of the new beauty to which surrealists the world over are devoted? How and where have its characteristic features emerged, and with what consequences for surrealist creative activity? These are among the questions to which replies may be sought by way of an examination of the poetics of surrealism.

The Nineteenth-Century Heritage

Long after he had parted company with the surrealists, Louis Aragon declared: "The merit of surrealism is to have, after reaching a certain polemical point in the discussion taking place at that time and which bore the name 'Dada,' a certain polemical point in its negativity, to have proclaimed the broadening of poetic domains into the past as well as in the present, to have brought light to bear upon those domains, trained new spotlights upon works and men in danger of sinking into oblivion, neglect, lack of understanding, ignorance."[1] Seen from the perspective adopted by Aragon, surrealism emerges as "at the same time an exploration of poetic domains in process of being lost and of others being created before our eyes" (p. 22).

Now one could scarcely argue that, had it not been for the surrealists, two of the dominant forms of nineteenth-century literature would have sunk from sight, never to be remembered again. All the same, in looking back to romanticism and to naturalism, surrealism did fulfill a noteworthy function in reestablishing contact with the past, after Dada had made every effort to cut off the present from what had gone before and to ignore the future.

To see in true perspective both Aragon's assertion

and the role which surrealists consciously assumed, we have to bear in mind, for example, that, as Aragon stresses (p. 17), some of the first surrealists were inclined initially to evaluate the romantics on the basis of what they had been taught in school. It was upon this basis, certainly, that Benjamin Péret awarded Victor Hugo the lowest possible score (−20) on an agreed scale, only to revise the figure to +20 after hearing unfamiliar selected poems, read for his benefit by Aragon and André Breton. Hence the claim advanced by Aragon at the end of 1963 is a proud one: "It was the surrealists who really made romanticism known, I mean in its essence, and not reduced to pedagogical outlines. That is something it seems has been forgotten. Who, if not the surrealists, has done full justice to Pétrus Borel, Xavier Forneret, Alphonse Rabbe, Aloysius Bertrand, Philothée O'Neddy and, at the forefront of romanticism, Lautréamont?" (p. 18).[2]

Of course, it would be a falsification to suggest, as Louis Aragon comes close to doing, that the surrealists' return to the past was motivated by altruism alone. Surrealists, by and large, have never denied the principle of historical continuity, have never seen themselves or sought to present themselves as occupying some sort of a vacuum. On the contrary, they have insisted over and over again that the instincts from which surrealism takes strength are timeless, and they have taken pleasure in drawing attention to evidence in the art and literature of the past that supports this contention. From the first, surrealists looked backward for selfish or at least self-centered reasons, for what they might find by way of proof that others before them had shared or could have sympathized with their inclinations and aspirations. If this had not been the case, then asking how romanticism and naturalism appear from the vantage point of surrealism would bring a sense of accomplishment only to the literary historian.

Precisely because surrealists seek an echo of their own questions and look for answers in accord with those that have their approval, their interrogation of nineteenth-century literature provides a valid starting point, if by no means the only possible one, for an inquiry into the nature of surrealist poetics.

Nowhere do we find among surrealist writings a text, comparable with Paul Eluard's essay on Charles Baudelaire, shall we say, having as its purpose examination of the nature of romanticism or of naturalism in relation to surrealist ideals.[3] Generally speaking, such comments as we do come across appear incidentally, illustrating an argument, exemplifying this idea or that, or again, if the writer happens to be André Breton, as the author curiously follows the intricacies of his own thinking. And yet, cumulatively, these remarks are brought into focus under the pull of two preoccupations shared by all surrealists: the place of imagination in creative endeavor and the treatment to be reserved for reality in that endeavor. The fact that neither of these preoccupations can find expression unless some attention goes to the other makes the posture of the romantic writer and that of the naturalist novelist equally fascinating to anyone dedicated to the cause of surrealism.

ROMANTICISM
So far as the earliest surrealists had models before them when they first began to write, these bore witness to the vogue of the literary style dominant in France during the years prior to the 1914–18 war: Symbolism. Benjamin Péret had made the discovery of poetry through a volume of Stéphane Mallarmé's verse, found on a railroad station bench, while he was between trains. André Breton had published a few Symbolist poems. Roger Vitrac's first published book was a collection of Symbolist verse, *Le Faune noir*. However, revulsion for outdated literary attitudes which, from the end of the war, brought into the ranks of Dada several young men who subsequently would form the core of the surrealist movement, soon stripped Symbolism of any value

in their eyes. Breton was to transcribe Lautréamont's *Poésies* from the only known copy, deposited in the French National Library, for publication (in March and June of 1919) in the anti-literary magazine ironically titled *Littérature*, that he co-edited with Aragon and Philippe Soupault. The dedication with which he did so is indicative of an excitement Symbolism was no longer capable of generating in him and in his friends, but could come still, apparently, from certain pre-Symbolist poetic texts.

Aragon has allowed us to see already that some of those writers whom manuals of literary history invite us to regard as among the major figures of romantic poetry in France had little appeal for surrealists. Indeed, the list of authors he has provided shows that, discovering romanticism, surrealists were drawn with least resistance to romantic poetry in its frenetic forms. The languorous verse of Lamartine left them indifferent, as did the earnest philosophizing of Vigny. Instead, they responded most readily to romanticism taken to its exacerbated stage. From the first, they praised Pétrus Borel, while the Larousse dictionary called him "an eccentric *littérateur*" who "thought himself a poet," author of *Madame Putiphar*, "a fevered, senseless novel." The mode of expression to be found in the writings Théophile Dondey published under the name of Philothée O'Neddy ("who created some stir about 1830," as *The Oxford Companion to French Literature* magnanimously reports) appeared all the more attractive because, undisciplined by good taste or social conformity, such writings evidenced little or no inclination on their author's part to submit to reasonable restraint. In short, the surrealists turned naturally and enthusiastically to those poets who, by and large, are treated in the official history of romanticism as minor figures, and in whose publications more than one literary critic would be tempted to see the very caricature of romanticism as he understands it.

This is something that needs to be understood if we are to give due weight to an outburst, which some readers may well treat as an ill-considered aside, in André Breton's

Second Manifeste du Surréalisme, originally published in the last issue of the very first surrealist magazine, *La Révolution surréaliste* (December 1929) and printed separately in 1930:

> But at the hour when the public powers in France are preparing to celebrate grotesquely the centenary of romanticism, *we* say that this romanticism of which we are quite willing, historically, to be considered today as the tail, *but then such a prehensile tail,* in its very essence even in 1930 resides entirely in denial of those powers and those celebrations, that to have had a hundred years' existence for romanticism is to be young, that what has been called wrongly its heroic period cannot be considered anything but the first cry of an infant only just beginning to make its desires known through us and which, if one admits that what was thought before it—"classically" —was good, incontestably wishes *nothing but evil.*[4]

At a time when, if we are to believe Maurice Nadeau,[5] surrealism had already passed through its own *période héroïque,* Breton evidently could not forego the opportunity to protest against governmental and academic interference in one of several areas where surrealists, asserting prerogatives which non-surrealists may feel entitled to deny, find it impertinent.

It would be naive to deny that there is an air of opportunism in the declaration on romanticism we encounter in Breton's second surrealist manifesto. But this is only to the good. The promoter of surrealism in France may not yet have told us anything really new about romanticism. He has already begun, though, to tell us something important about surrealism, and this is something having to do with more than the evolution of literary ideas and attitudes. The interesting thing about Breton's remarks is not simply the willingness shown by a leading surrealist to acknowledge surrealism to be the heir to romanticism. For this, after all, is something we feel confident we could figure out for ourselves, without undue effort. What really matters is that, beginning to direct our attention to romanticism from a

certain angle, and preparing us to review its accomplish-
ments in a certain perspective, Breton's second manifesto
extends its readers an invitation to infer from the surrealists' interpretation of romanticism some important characteristics of surrealism itself. Accepting Breton's invitation,
we become aware of deeper issues than those treated in
J.-D. Maublanc's study of the romantics' anticipation of
surrealist themes.[6] Attentive now to some of the implications of these issues, we understand better the causes to
which must be attributed the special complexion that Breton
and other surrealists give romantic ideals.

What follows is in the nature of an outline proposal
for an expedition yet to be undertaken. As such, it will be
devoted to formulating a tentative plan of operation. The
latter is intended to direct explorations in the most promising directions, so as to eliminate the risks of pursuing accessory or distracting aims, and to guarantee as far as possible that the main objectives are reached and pertinent
results are reported coherently.

We must begin by admitting that no road map at
present in our hands will be of assistance to anyone setting
out in the direction to which Breton calls us, so that we can
establish what may be learned about surrealist poetic ambitions from surrealist reaction to romanticism. Our first
need, therefore, will be a reliable compass. Apparently foreseeing this requirement, Breton has shown us where we
may look for one. This he did when intimating that the
spirit of romanticism, expressed through surrealism, may
be equated with a certain wish or desire. On the expedition we propose to undertake, our compass will be desire.

Some will surely balk at this Prudhommesque turn
of phrase, that they are being asked to countenance nevertheless. At best, they may say, one could speak of setting
one's compass by desire. Certainly, borrowing the alternative phrase they recommend would provide us with a useful
introduction to discussion of the valuable image of magnetic

attraction which, as Julien Gracq has demonstrated,[7] can be put to very good use when one is defining the appeal exerted in our time by the personality of André Breton and by surrealist ambitions to which he lent the authority of his voice. However, we can concede this without entirely discrediting a metaphor that proves its usefulness in a different way. For it reminds us we are surveying new territory, in which it can permit us to handle some of the problems posed by surrealism in a manner that Gracq did not envision.

We can agree that everyone *knows* desire is no more a compass than the saber about which Monnier's Joseph Prudhomme declared, proudly, that it was the finest day in his life was in fact a day. It is not just a matter, though, of answering logical objections with the assertion that we are free, nevertheless, to avail ourselves of a right claimed for all by André Breton in his *Introduction au Discours sur le Peu de Réalité:* the right to challenge the mediocrity of the universe by means of our power of enunciation. Still less is it a question of arguing that anyone may emulate the man to whom Breton paid this supreme tribute in the *Manifesto of Surrealism:* "Desnos *speaks surrealist* at will" (p. 44). Rather, we should consider what benefits come from identifying the characteristics and role of desire, as surrealists refer to it. It will be possible, then, to recognize how useful an instrument desire can be to anyone setting out to establish the significance of romanticism for surrealism. The desire-compass becomes so essential a part of his equipment that he must consult it frequently, before he changes direction in his inquiry as well as after.

One effect of proceeding desire-compass in hand is self-evident. At once the perspective of our inquiry becomes essentially historical, its function being to illustrate how, after the event, the expression of romantic literary attitudes lends itself to interpretation in the light of surrealist goals. True, the method proposed here would appear, by the same token, to have at least one serious defect, resulting from the adoption of chronological sequence. All the evidence assembled has to be detached from one context, for scrutiny in another. Yet no one will contest that there can be little hope of proving that even one romantic writer, however misunderstood in his lifetime, cherished the hope of earning, a half-century or so after his death, the commendation of a group—Dalí's view of time as "the delirious surrealist dimension *par excellence*" notwithstanding—whose existence he had no means of foreseeing, and less interest in speculating upon. Far more to the point is some consideration of the ways in which surrealists have been stimulated to approve or disapprove, when looking back to romanticism. The basis of discussion, consequently, is not what one, or several, or all the romantics really wanted to do, but what the surrealists have felt entitled to interpret, from the evidence coming down to us, as signifying coincidence of the romantic viewpoint with their own. Bearing this prime purpose in mind, we come to see that the word *desire* can do even more than help the investigator find where he is. In fact, its use postulates the creation of a surrealist object, invented for the occasion: a compass which is also a special kind of thermometer. What pleasure André Breton would have derived from finding such an object, during his patient explorations of the Paris flea market!

The non-surrealist explorer who has been persuaded to take along the desire-compass-thermometer into romantic terrain may be forgiven if he suspects, at first, he has been inveigled. Finding its use unfamiliar, initially, its weight annoyingly burdensome, and its care a real nuisance, he may feel disposed to wait only until he has rounded the first bend to drop it by the wayside. No doubt he expects, now travelling lighter, to advance more quickly without it. He has been encouraged to jettison this curious object—which he willingly admits may be attractive to a surrealist, but regards as rather embarrassing to normal people like us—because he has noticed one thing straight away. Certain signposts stand before him. Clearly marked, they beckon him on. Moreover, they stand in prominent positions; sometimes, indeed, exactly where he would expect to find them, even without a compass. Breton erected the first of these *poteaux indicateurs,* when he wrote in his *Manifeste du Surréalisme* of 1924:

> For me, if I had lived in 1820, for me the "bloody nun," mine not to spare that cunning, commonplace "Let us dissimulate" about which the parodical Cuisin speaks, mine, mine to cover in gigantic metaphors, as he says, all the phases of the "Silver Disc." For today I think of a *castle,* half of which is not necessarily in ruins; this castle belongs to me, I see it in a rustic setting, not far from Paris. Its outbuildings stretch forever, and as for its interior, it has been terribly restored, so as to leave nothing to be desired under the heading of comfort. (pp. 29–30)

There is nothing notably suspicious about the information these words supply. No one would begrudge Breton his preference for comfort in an ideal castle, renovated by desire. The fascination with castles to be found imaged in Breton's writings obviously owes much to romantic influence. It seems to require no excuse, to call for no involved explanation. Even if it did, in his case, there is ample proof that others associated with, or admired by, the surrealists have come under the charm of the castle. What is more, they see the castle, just as the romantics did, as a privileged locale. In Julien Gracq's novel *Au Château d'Argol* and also in Maurice Fourré's *Tête-de-Nègre,* the castle presents a background for an experience to which surrealist imagination lends special meaning.[8] "What is the novel," Gracq's rhetorical question runs pertinently, "if not lived off desire?"[9] As for Benjamin Péret, the introduction to his *Anthologie des Mythes, Légendes et Contes populaires d'Amérique* carries a paragraph, offered in lieu of a definition of the marvelous which, all his life, Péret adamantly declined to supply:

> I think of the dolls of the Hopi Indians of New Mexico, whose heads sometimes schematically represent a medieval castle. It is into this castle that I'm going to try to get. There aren't any doors and its walls have the thickness of a

thousand centuries. It isn't in ruins as one would be tempted to believe. Since romanticism, its tumbledown walls have risen up again, restored like rubies, but just as hard as those gems, they have, now that I bump my head against them, all the clarity of the ruby. Now they move aside like the tall grass at the passage of a cautious deer, now by the phenomenon of osmosis, I am on the inside, giving off the glow of an aurora borealis. . . . Although I am apparently alone, a crowd blindly obedient to me surrounds me. These are creatures less distinct than a speck of dust in a ray of sunlight. In their heads of root, their will-o'-the-wisp eyes move about in all directions and their twelve wings equipped with claws allow them to move with the rapidity of the lightning they bring in their wake. Out of my hand they eat the eyes from peacock feathers and if I press them between thumb and index finger, I mold a cigarette that, between the feet of a suit of armor, quickly assumes the shape of the first artichoke.[10]

It is deceptively reassuring to discover one does not need to set one's course by desire, in order to arrive at the region where the *château* enjoys special prestige among the surrealists. There seems little cause for alarm, at any rate. Does not the impressive bulk of the castle tower rise from the English Gothic novels to provide an unmistakable landmark? No sooner has the explorer reached the encouraging conclusion that he was right, after all, in deciding there would be no need for a compass he never did have much faith in, than he is obliged to notice something else. In the Gothic tower stands Matthew Gregory Lewis' monk, Ambrosio, who cries to Matilda, "Stay, then, enchantress! stay for my destruction."

If still too far away to hear Ambrosio clearly, the explorer need feel no anxiety, so long as he has come suitably prepared. He has only to take from his pocket his copy of Péret's *Anthologie de l'Amour sublime,* to be able to read the very extract from *The Monk* in which Lewis reports Ambrosio's words. This gives him the additional advantage of observing what significance Péret as a leading theoretician of surrealism, attaches to Ambrosio's confession of illicit love. So he will be reliably informed of the importance in surrealism of the free expression of desire. And he will be left in no doubt about the value surrealists attribute to the circumstances under which desire finds privileged expression in the castle. For Péret insists, "This is why Lewis has his characters move about in a marvelous world, fantastic and deadly, for lack of being able to show that all the marvelous bursts forth from love to crown it with the red glow of fire or of permanent rainbow."[11] The explorer will have no call to read any further—provided, that is, his preparations have been thorough enough to acquaint him with what Péret meant by *sublime love* and what Breton termed *mad love;* especially if he has taken the added precaution of consulting Pierre Mabille's *Le Miroir du Merveilleux* about the meaning of the *marvelous* in surrealism.[12]

The important thing is, of course, that the presence of the person who inspires Ambrosio's passion, Matilda, supplies *The Monk* with its "*élan lyrique,*" to borrow the phrase Breton uses in *Nadja.* Unless we can agree upon this, we shall never appreciate fully how unsatisfactory it is to try merely to catalog the points of contact between surrealist writing and romantic or proto-romantic literature. More to our purpose is attempting to determine the degree of importance surrealists give moments when, under particularly favorable circumstances, a coincidence really does occur between the themes to which they return, sometimes quite obsessively, and those romanticism appears to have rendered banal and threadbare. Thus, if he has discarded his compass, thinking to have stumbled upon terrain only too familiar to him—and so hardly worth looking at attentively—the explorer will find his efforts noticeably restricted. When examining landmarks he believes he has seen quite enough of in the past, he is in serious danger of not giving due care, of failing to see how necessary they are to orient him, as he readies himself for the next stage in his journey. The risk is all the greater at this point because, as the fact that he has been tempted to discard his compass testifies, he has not accustomed himself, yet, to looking at it when he wants to check the temperature.

Molded by ambitions and stresses to which the surrealist viewpoint gives definition, surrealist commentary sets the compass by surrealist aspirations, and calibrates the thermometer accordingly. If this were not so, then significant features of surrealist poetic practice would have to be taken as proof that important inspirational sources in romanticism are in imminent danger of drying up. The consequences would be productions devoid of interest, not to say distinctly depressing. Surrealism would have no prospect but to adopt and if possible adapt inherited clichés, of which romanticism sometimes is accused of having left all too wide a selection. In other words, so as to be able to see matters as surrealists see them, we must be especially attentive to remarks like the following from Breton's first surrealist manifesto: "The spirit of *demoralization* has elected domicile in the castle, and it is with this spirit that we are dealing every time it is a matter of our relations with our fellow men, but the doors are always open and one does not begin by 'thanking' society, you know" (pp. 30–31). Or again we should listen to the comments of Eluard: "The noblest of desires is the desire to combat all the obstacles placed by bourgeois society before realization of man's vital desires, as much those of his body as those of his imagination, these two categories being, it must be added, almost always closely intermingled and determine one another."[13] Is it not fair to say—pending fuller expansion of the meaning of the word *demoralization* as, for example, analysis of the surrealist concept of *black humor* will make this available to us—that, when we hear words like Breton's and Eluard's, our compass-thermometer begins to function like some sophisticated hearing aid, of unprecedented design?

Without hesitation, the reaction of some readers to this leading question will be categorically negative. They would reply that the ridiculous instrument in which they are being asked to place their faith has proved itself, now, to be what they suspected all along: a hindrance, rather than a help. From the beginning, they have sensed that the proposal of an historical perspective really concealed an attempt to delude and take unfair advantage of the unwary. With representative surrealist texts before them, they feel sure they can prove scrutiny of selected romantic materials in the context of surrealism to be of little purpose, in the end, since it leads predictably to distortion of the evidence. Yet that is the whole point. In reality, distortion does not have to be accepted as an unavoidable though regrettable risk. On the contrary, it deserves to be recognized for what it is: the key to the whole process by which surrealists see in certain romantic ideals and postures proof that the romantics—more exactly, those among the romantics who have their confidence—were precursors in whose work they are delighted to hear their own aspirations clamor for attention. Here, in fact, distortion necessarily results from the manner in which, following the guidance offered in surrealist writing, we must sift evidence, before viewing what we retain from the angle recommended in surrealism. Under the conditions that now apply, distortion places before us a firm stepping-stone to the understanding we wish to reach.

To be sure, it takes no longer than a moment to recognize that, as it is used by Breton and his companions in the surrealist venture, in order to establish links between romantic ambition and their own, the word *desire* is as arbitrary in its application as it is tendentious as a term of reference for romantic ideals in literature. Eluard could entitle an essay "Du Désir" while still confessing, "The point is that passion for me represents such a sum total of desires, in quality as well as quantity, that it is very often difficult for me to identify it with the simple concept of desire. The desire to be happy, to be unhappy, to identify another with oneself; to lose one's personality, to outlive oneself, to die, etc., . . . everything that makes up passion results in my overestimating it too much to have a clear idea of it." Quick as they would be to insist upon this weakness, the critics who complain most loudly are not so prompt to admit they themselves have read comments like Breton's, Eluard's, or Péret's just long enough to be convinced that a surrealist's evaluation of what he has read (or seen) is biased. Apparently, then, protest against the surrealist's right to speak his mind rests upon denial of his privilege to react openly on the practical plane of sympathy or antipathy. In any case, it is clear that too few critics have bothered to read the things this or that surrealist has had to say about the work of others (or about his own for that matter) with sufficient care to probe the motives underlying his statements. Far too many of them neglect to notice that, if they genuinely wish to give surrealism a fair hearing, what counts, in the final analysis, is not that surrealists *too* appreciate Baudelaire, for example, but where and why a surrealist's reading of Baudelaire's work differs from their own, so telling us more about surrealist preoccupations in poetry than it promised to contribute to the non-surrealist's appreciation of Baudelairian verse.

There is no secret here, and no paradox. Surrealists have never attempted to conceal their prejudices. Intentionally, the statements reproduced above have been drawn from some of the most accessible of surrealist theoretical texts, most of them anyway, so as to demonstrate the truth of the following. The application of surrealist poetic ambitions has always rested firmly upon a basis of judgment that deliberately and—so all surrealists would assert—necessarily sets matters on another plane from the one where conventional critical modes offer appraisal. Hence anyone who has not grasped the full implication of what Breton had in mind, when he referred to the "esprit de *démoralisation*" fundamental to surrealism would be well advised to turn to a page in the *Manifeste du Surréalisme*, to read something that all the writings of Péret confirm:

> The marvelous is not the same in every period; it participates in some obscure way in a sort of general revelation of which only details come down to us: these are romantic *ruins*, the modern *mannequin* or any other symbol suitable to stirring human sensibility for a time. Within this framework, that

makes us smile, there is always portrayed, however, human disquiet for which there is no remedy, and this is why I take the marvelous into consideration, why I judge this framework to be inseparable from some productions of genius, which are affected by it more painfully than the others. (p. 29)

Clearly, Breton expects no one intent upon penetrating the meaning with which surrealism invests romantic images of the *château* to disregard the hint given here. As he sees it, this image cannot be examined in isolation; otherwise its evocative power is unduly limited, perhaps even deprived altogether of the force it has for the surrealist imagination. To situate it appropriately in relation to surrealist ideals in poetry, one must begin by placing it next to some of the images surrealists find compelling; for instance the image of the *mannequin*, as captured in May Ray's photographs of the surrealist *mannequins* on display during the 1938 international surrealist exhibition in Paris.[14] It would do no harm, naturally, to avail oneself of the assistance afforded by an article of René Crevel's, published in *Minotaure*, four years earlier,[15] to say nothing of the parellels which the naturalist descriptions of Zola will help bring to mind shortly.

It would be surprising if no one questioned Breton's right to demand we consider some of the key images of romanticism in conjunction with images more readily associated with the surrealist outlook. Provoked to protest by Breton's tactic, certain readers will incline to challenge the existence of really meaningful continuity between romantic ideals and surrealist effort. Although they may feel quite justified in doing this, they deny themselves in the process the opportunity to examine a phenomenon not manifest solely in the context we have chosen for an examination of its operation. They miss the chance to observe an exemplary effect of the passage of time upon literary ideas and ideals. Erosion takes place, beyond a doubt; but so does a noteworthy amount of refinement. Seen from one angle, forces in literature appear to lose outline, under the test of time. Yet from another, they take on clearer definition. It is specious to affirm that, because time has passed over them, these aspirations have surrendered their identity. It is no less so to say the only way to protect them from distortion is to preserve them in such a way as to shield them from the ravages of time. When all is said and done, the surrealists have the distinction of being the only organized group, anywhere in the twentieth century, large enough and unified enough in their aims to compare with the nineteenth-century romantics. And they are the only ones to have left testimony to their convictions comparable in range and richness with the legacy of romanticism. More than this, they are the only major association united in poetic endeavor to have admitted their awareness of historical continuity, situating some of their own positions by reference to coordinates supplied by romantic practice and impulse.

Because the word *desire* not only helps us to hear what a surrealist hears, when he listens to romanticism, but even promises to let us hear—so far as we are willing and able to do this—*as he does*, it assists us in defining surrealist imperatives, as romanticism has contributed to giving these meaning and direction. And yet this is exactly where difficulties confront us and seem to promise disappointment. Surrealist commentary on romanticism highlights the concept of desire well enough. What it does far less satisfactorily is give shape and meaning to this concept, provide truly illuminating, concrete instances which, with real confidence, we may regard as exemplifying desire as surrealists recurrently speak of it. Even in its supposedly least elusive form, that of sexual passion, desire appears but inadequately defined within romantic writing, when we compare the latter with surrealist mad love, as Breton discusses it in his *L'Amour fou*, or with *l'amour sublime*, as examined in Péret's anthology. The interpretations surrealists are liable to place on the word "desire" are no less varied, in one circumstance or another, than those they place on the word "dream." Just as failure awaits anyone who reads into *rêve* one sense only—that of oneiric experience —so too it lies in wait for those who identify *désir* exclusively with the possessive instinct expressed through sexual yearning. The very equivocal nature of some of the examples mentioned above is a reminder that acquaintance with surrealism will have taught us nothing if it has not made us see in dreaming and desiring really two aspects of the same motivating impulse in surrealists: to possess more than man's situation in this world guarantees him, and to see what he does not yet possess—by means of poetic action.

If then surrealism is, as a statement in the *Manifeste du Surréalisme* and the title of a play by Pablo Picasso[16] combine to suggest, romanticism taken by the tail, it would be a serious error to believe that desire is to be regarded as the only thread one can follow through the labyrinthine ways of surrealist theory, to say nothing of the more demanding task of finding one's bearings among poetic texts inspired by that theory. After tracing signs of desire, we might take up and seek guidance from the theme of dreams. All it takes, after all, is willingness to accept dreaming as a compass, that is also Ariadne's thread. . .

NATURALISM

Both romanticism and surrealism attribute importance to imaginative freedom and to individual fulfillment in the face of oppressive forces, emanating directly from a society that places its values in a particularly depressing form of materialism. If we look no farther than this, we become aware of some fundamental points of agreement which predispose us to find surrealists sympathetic to romantic poetic idealism. On the other hand, the very parallels which suggest—even to someone having no more than a nodding acquaintance with surrealist ambitions through poetry—that the surrealists' aspirations are not wholly comprehensible unless their debt to romanticism has been taken into account, would seem to indicate something else too: that surrealism is not only without indebtedness to naturalism but quite without sympathy where naturalist literature is concerned. To such a person, and perhaps even more to some-

one whose interest in surrealism has prompted him to in-
quire a little farther into its nature, it comes as a surprise
to find the following declaration in André Breton's *Les Vases
communicants*, published in 1932: "I, on the other hand,
like the naturalist writers a lot: pessimism apart—they are
really too pessimistic—I consider they are the only ones to
have turned to account a situation like that one [Breton has
been talking of a banal incident, such as we all encounter
incessantly in life—on this occasion, accompanying a girl he
finds attractive to the pork butcher's]. I find them, on the
average, much more poetic than the Symbolists who, during
the same period, were trying to stupefy the public with their
more or less rhythmic lucubrations."[17] Breton's statement is
offered parenthetically, it is true, but with full enough development to include a brief word of praise for the Goncourt
brothers, Huysmans, Zola, and even Robert Caze. His words
seem to send us back to Aragon, whose comment upon surrealism as an exploration of poetic domains ends with a firm
assurance, to which it now becomes necessary to give serious
attention: "reality was everywhere for us, even at the moment when and in the place where we seemed to deny it."[18]

All the same, one cannot but wonder whether André
Breton's attitude had changed by 1932, or whether his judgments on realistic representation through novelistic form
betray some unaccountable inconsistencies. It appears ad-
missible, all right, that, displaying a surprisingly close acquaintance with the work of J.-K. Huysmans, Breton should
allude on one occasion to the Huysmans tale *Sac au dos*,
"one of the masterpieces of naturalism," so as to give an
idea of his own state of mind, at age eighteen: "Well, all it
needed was to transpose that a little, to keep it a little less
close to the ground, to give an idea of the mood of certain
young men, including myself, whom the 1914 war had just
torn from all their aspirations, to throw them into a sewer
of blood, stupidity and mud."[19] If one finds oneself inclined
to treat the aptness of the analogy drawn in *Entretiens* as an
excuse for Breton's reference to one of the stories in *Les
Soirées de Médan*, this is because his willingness to cite

Huysmans seems in flagrant contradiction with everything he has had to say about realism in the first manifesto, where we are told that "the trial of the realist attitude needs to be conducted, after the materialist attitude" (p. 18). In fact, materialism fared better in the 1924 *Manifeste du Surréalisme* than did realism. Whereas he acknowledged the former to be compatible with a certain "elevation in thought," Breton condemned the realist attitude, founded on positivism, as "hostile to all intellectual and moral progress." Confessing his horror of it, he blamed realism for inspiring the "ridiculous books" and "insulting plays" of the day. In short, he found realism guilty of "flattering the public in its lowest tastes: clarity bordering on stupidity, the life of dogs" (pp. 18-19).

Are we to infer, then, that André Breton drew a distinction between realism, to be rejected *in toto*, and naturalism, credited with producing other masterpieces as well as *Sac au dos?* This convenient explanation becomes dubious indeed, once we have read the following comment in the first surrealist manifesto: "One consequence of this state of affairs, in literature, for example, is the abundance of novels. Everyone goes to it with his little 'observation.'" Ridiculing the informational style affected almost exclusively in the novel form, as exemplified in a descriptive passage drawn from Dostoevsky's *Crime and Punishment*, Breton goes on to argue that novelists have only limited ambitions: "The circumstantial character, pointlessly peculiar, of each of their notations, leads me to believe they are having fun at my expense" (p. 19).

One essential step is required, before Breton can speak further about Huysmans, without appearing to fall victim to self-contradiction. It is no surprise to see him take this step, four years after publishing his *Manifesto of Surrealism*, in a 1928 book called *Nadja*: "How far I set him apart, is there any need to say so, from all the empiricists of the novel who claim to put on stage characters distinct from themselves and present them, physically, mentally, in their own way, for the purposes of a cause we prefer not to know."[20] This hardly looks like a promising point of departure for an examination of Breton's supposedly indulgent approach to the naturalist novel, but at least it encourages us to clear the ground, so to speak, by considering how he felt about J.-K. Huysmans.

The fact of the matter is that Huysmans' name recurred with unexpected frequency in Breton's conversation and writings. In his *Entretiens* with André Parinaud, for instance, he did not omit to emphasize that the meetings of the early Parisian surrealists in the Rue du Château took place in "that district unforgettably described by Huysmans in *Les Soeurs Vatard*" (p. 143), one of the most determinedly naturalistic of Huysmans' novels, one that receives additional praise from Breton in the context of an essay on the painting of Yves Tanguy[21] as well as in "Limites non-Frontières du Surréalisme," which appeared in translation in Herbert Read's compendium *Surrealism* (1936) and reaffirmed that Huysmans impressed Breton as the incontestable master of French naturalism. In Breton's *Anthologie de l'Humour noir* Huysmans is said to have risen to "the heights of inspiration" in *En Rade.*[22] What is the opinion, though, of other surrealists? Was Breton's admiration for Huysmans merely a personal quirk, with no serious significance?

True, the name of Huysmans is unaccountably absent from the *Dictionnaire abrégé du Surréalisme*, edited in 1938 by Breton and Paul Eluard, although, among others, the following are cited: Arnim, Baudelaire, Forneret, Grabbe, Lautréamont, "Monk" Lewis, Lichtenberg, Nerval, Novalis, Maturin, Ann Radcliffe, and Sade. However, before long the surrealist group in France made amends in one of their postwar magazines, when conducting an inquiry under the title *Ouvrez-Vous?*[23] Would you open your door to . . . ? It was a matter, essentially, of saying which among a list of creative personalities were the acceptable ones. In the case of Balzac and Stendhal, about half the responses proved to be negative. Péret, for instance, would be willing to let Balzac in, "but rather grudgingly." Breton, on the other hand, was categorical: "No (chaos)." As for Stendhal, Gérard Legrand would have opened his door only "out of irony," while Anne Seghers would have done the same thing "out of politeness." Responses like these, quite consistent with surrealism's reservations about realism, first voiced in the *Manifesto of Surrealism*, are in marked contrast with those relating to Huysmans, favorable in almost every instance. Indeed, three of the respondents only were opposed to admitting him, none of them with any show of hard feelings: Legrand ("No, fear of depression"), José Pierre ("No, with complete cordiality"), and Bernard Roger ("No, in deference to the ladies").

By and large, respect for Huysmans finds expression among surrealists of all generations, in fundamental agreement between their outlook upon the world and his. If we seek to establish where that agreement lies, we shall find ourselves approaching it with least delay when we start exploring a domain apparently far removed from that of the novel: painting.

Readers of Huysmans' best-known book, *A Rebours*, will know that at the top of the list of painters admired by that novel's hero, des Esseintes, stood Gustave Moreau. Des Esseintes, we are told, "wanted, for the delectation of his mind and the joy of his eyes, some suggestive works, casting him into an unknown world, unveiling to him the trail of new conjectures, rocking his nervous system with erudite hysteria, with complicated nightmares, with nonchalant and agonizing visions."[24] He found what he wanted, not only in Moreau but also in Redon, a few of whose works he owned —drawings which "leaped, for the most part, beyond the limits of painting, innovating a very special form of the fantastic, a fantastic of sickness and delirium" (p. 95). Breton's commentary is apposite here: "From the mythical symbolism of Moreau to the synthetic symbolism of Gauguin or the oneiric form in Redon, the transition is ensured by Mallarmé and Huysmans."[25] In *L'Art magique* he presents Moreau as "the hermit who called forth the special *Appari-*

tion of which des Esseintes spoke highly." According to Breton, Moreau remains "the great misunderstood figure" in the official history of painting (p. 212). Defended nevertheless by Huysmans, he is defended also in the 1924 manifesto, where he is cited as a precursor of surrealism.

To Breton, speaking yet again in *L'Art magique*, the reasons why Moreau has been neglected are obvious: "It was inevitable that the attitude of Gustave Moreau, clinging to 'all the casement windows from which one cold-shoulders life' (let us take this to mean, external life on which the others feed their minds), should earn him, from most painters of the *tangible* an hostility that still continues but which, in large measure, is compensated by the delight of poets" (p. 36). There is a distinct echo of these words in *A Rebours*, where des Esseintes "had resolved not to bring into his sanctuary larvae of repugnance or regrets; therefore he had wanted subtle exquisite painting, bathed in ancient dreams, in the corruption of antiquity, far from our mores, far from our days" (p. 83).

Naturally, *Ouvrez-Vous?* gives due attention to Moreau, whom all the respondents find congenial. Wolfgang Paalen, in fact, shows himself ready to admit the nineteenth-century painter because of his "kinship of mind with Huysmans." Meanwhile Huysmans commands respect among surrealists as an exceptionally perspicacious art critic, ranked in Breton's *L'Art magique* beside Baudelaire, Apollinaire, and Alfred Jarry. In comparison with these four, later critics are, in Breton's estimation, almost always "journalists in whom 'general ideas' give rise to a terror as lively as does the spontaneity of profound impressions" (p. 45). More than this, through his admiration for Moreau, Huysmans betrays a sensibility and tastes with which surrealists find themselves in clear sympathy, and which permit us to trace the origins of their affection for his novels.

If J.-K. Huysmans found favor with André Breton as early as 1913, this was because from as far back as then the future author of the surrealist manifestoes liked, as he was to put it in *Entretiens*, "what poetry and art have produced that is most *rare*" (p. 11). Hence his early admiration for Moreau, Huysmans, and Mallarmé, of whom he is generally less critical than of the other Symbolist poets: "You cannot know how important it was for me to get close to those among men who then continued that tradition." When in *Nadja* he later had occasion to mention Georgio de Chirico, one of the most potent influences upon surrealist painting, he would confide:

> So far as I am concerned, more important still than meeting certain dispositions of objects is for the mind seems to me to be the disposition of a mind toward certain objects, a disposition of these two kinds governs on its own all forms of the sensibility. Thus I find between myself and Huysmans, the Huysmans of *En Rade* and *Là-Bas*, so much agreement over the ways of appreciating everything that presents itself, of choosing with the partiality of despair among the things that exist, that if unfortunately I have been able to know him only through his work, he is perhaps the least unfamiliar of my friends.

Moreover, Breton goes on to remark, "But also has he not done more than anyone else to take to its farthest point this necessary *vital* discrimination between the life-belt, in appearance so fragile, and the dizzying apparatus of forces that conspire to make us sink and drown?" (pp. 15–16).

Breton shares with us in *Nadja*, then, his appreciation of Huysmans' particularly refined sensibility. André Breton, who lived his life, far more than is commonly realized, under the recurrent threat of debilitating boredom analogous to that weariness with life which the French romantics called *ennui*, writes here that Huysmans "has shared with me that vibrant boredom which almost every sight caused in him; no one before has known how, if not to make me witness the great awakening of the mechanical over the ravaged terrain of conscious possibilities, then at least to convince me humanly of its absolute fatality and of the uselessness of seeking ways out for myself" (p. 16).

By a curious paradox, it was the painter of the *ennui* of everyday existence that caught and held the attention of the surrealists in Huysmans. Firstly, this was so because his honesty compelled him to record his frustrations (in *En Ménage* as in the much better-known *A Vau l'Eau*) communicating them to his readers on the tacit assumption that their susceptibilities are just like his own. And he certainly finds a ready listener in Breton, who cries in *Nadja*:

> How grateful I am to him for informing me, without care for the effect to be produced, of all that concerns him, of all that takes possession of him in his hours of worst distress, outside his distress, for not, like so many poets, 'singing' this distress absurdly, but patiently enumerating for me, in the shadows, a few little involuntary reasons that he still can find for being, he does not quite know why, the one who is speaking! (p. 16)

The force of these words will not be lost on those familiar with the question preoccupying Breton throughout *Nadja*—an account of how he himself lived, over a period of several months in 1926—and to which a prefatory note in the revised edition (1963) gives special prominence: what justifies the act of writing?

All the same, we may continue to wonder why, as a painter of the aggravating *petitesses* of daily living, J.-K. Huysmans should have escaped censure from the surrealists, who ignore altogether the writings of a Duranty, shall we say, or, not to wander outside the formal limits of the naturalist novel, those of Henry Céard or Léon Hennique. It is true enough that, as we shall have occasion to notice shortly, Huysmans earns the affection of surrealists by practicing, during the time of his association with naturalism, a form of humor, without equivalent in the novels of the rest of the Médan group, in which Breton was to detect without delay unmistakable signs of *l'humour noir*. Yet this fact does not entirely answer the question still hanging over Huysmans' work. To progress further, we have to refer once again to

Nadja. Here Huysmans is described as "the object of one of those perpetual solicitations that seem to come from outside, and immobilize us for a few seconds in front of one of those fortuitous arrangements, of a more or less new character, to which it seems that by questioning ourselves thoroughly we should find the secret in ourselves" (p. 19).

To be sure, Breton does not delay opening his account of his first meeting with the mysterious Nadja long enough to supply an example illustrating what he has just told us about Huysmans. Nevertheless, we take his meaning: Huysmans is credited with having known how to appreciate the value of the chance revelations that existence, however humdrum, can bring. He is credited, in other words, with having been admirably sensitive to the appeal of the unexpected, the unwonted, *l'insolite* which, from one end to the other, inspires one of the key texts of the first decade of active surrealism, Aragon's *Le Paysan de Paris* (1926). It was, indeed, his gift for detecting the *insolite* that qualified Huysmans for the title of poet, in the surrealist sense of the term.

Thus, writing in the second major surrealist magazine, Tristan Tzara placed Huysmans next to Charles Cros and Germain Nouveau, when making this appeal: "Let us situate them in their place, in the most up-to-date position, that of necessity was theirs in different domains, but in which the relationship of poetry-means-of-expression to poetry-activity-of-the-mind tends to take on definition to the advantage of the latter and prepares us this way for the release of forces that will become decisive."[26] To the surrealist, it goes without saying, Huysmans is a poet—"It is perfectly well known today," observed Tzara, "that one can be a poet without having written a single verse"—while his contemporary Paul Verlaine is not, if we are to believe *Ouvrez-Vous?*, where every respondent slams the door in Verlaine's face.

Breton had no time in *Nadja* to furnish even one example representative of the poetic vision released under the impact upon an especially receptive sensibility like Huysmans' of a "solicitation" from outside, extended by beneficent chance, Can we not find an example for ourselves, though? For instance, the following seems to fulfill quite well the conditions Breton has laid down:

> But what could be glimpsed from everywhere, from the embankments, the bridges, the windows, was, on the horizon, on the bare wall of a six-story building, in the Ile Saint-Louis, a giant gray frock-coat, painted in fresco, in profile, with its left sleeve bent at the elbow, as if the garment had retained the attitude and fullness of a body, now disappeared. This monumental piece of advertising took on, in the sunlight, above the ant's nest of pedestrians, extraordinary importance.

This descriptive detail is very reminiscent of what we find in Robert Desnos' surrealist novel *La Liberté ou l'Amour!* (1927), where "from the top of a building Bébé Cadum, magnificently lit up, announces new times" and is "the attentive witness to events of which the streets, let us hope so, will be the stage."[27] Fairness recommends, though, that we admit that the frock-coat does not come down from its wall to play a role in narrative incident, as the advertisement for Cadum soap does. It obliges us to admit something else too: the extract that has served us as an example comes not from a novel by J.-K. Huysmans, but from one by Emile Zola: *Son Excellence Eugène Rougon*, among the earlier works in his Rougon-Macquart series.

All in all, when it comes down to offering proof of his appreciation of naturalist literature, André Breton's writings limit evidence to allusions to the works of J.-K. Huysmans, whose outlook, we cannot fail to notice, seems to correspond best to surrealist ideals when *A Rebours* begins giving expression to the *decadent* side of his creative personality. Hence the remark made by a leading surrealist painter, in an interview: "During a period of solitude, Huysmans with his need, his desire for evasion, has helped me a lot."[28] Cer-

tainly, it is the Huysmans of *A Rebours* and *En Rade* whom
Breton placed on the same level as Baudelaire, Rimbaud, and
Lautréamont in his *Second Manifeste du Surréalisme:*

> But see of what admirable and perverse insinuation a certain
> number of altogether modern works have shown themselves
> capable, the very ones of which the least we can say is that
> there reigns in them a particularly unhealthy air: Baudelaire,
> Rimbaud, . . . Huysmans, Lautréamont, to confine myself to
> poetry. Let us not be afraid to make this insalubrity a law. It
> must not be possible to say we have not done everything to
> reduce to nothing that stupid illusion of happiness and *entente*
> which it will be the glory of the XIXth century to have de-
> nounced. Certainly, we have not ceased to love fanatically
> those rays of sunshine full of miasmas. (p. 184)

Huysmans tells us des Esseintes wants to "break with the
irritating memories of his past life" (p. 87), just like the central figure in René Crevel's *Etes-vous fous?*[29] In *A Rebours*
des Esseintes shares with surrealists, too, a need to "escape
from the horrible reality of existence, to go beyond the con-
fines of thought, to feel his way, without ever arriving at a
certainty, in the mist of the beyond of art" (p. 145). And his
conduct, lending the title of Huysmans' novel its full significance, shows des Esseintes to be seeking to create for himself
a mode of existence that tends to "detain itself in dreams"
(p. 261), thanks principally to imagination—which he sees
as "easily able to make up for the vulgar reality of facts" (p.
50)—seconded by the ability to "abstract oneself sufficiently
to bring on hallucination and to be able to substitute the
dream of reality for reality itself" (p. 51).

 Not for a moment could such an attitude fail to impress Breton, who was to write in his *Point du Jour* (1934),
"Everything, in the end, depends on our power of voluntary
hallucination." However, while *A Rebours* lends the strongest possible support to Huysmans' claim to rank among the
poets surrealists revere, it bids us observe a sensibility in
retreat from reality and so does nothing to enrich our understanding of why naturalism in the novel appeared to Breton

to have more poetic virtue than Symbolism in verse. That Zola's novels promise assistance in this direction makes it all the more surprising that Breton seems to have been reluctant to call upon Zola to provide illustrations, in his defense of naturalism.

Zola's name is not mentioned in *Ouvrez-Vous?*, any more than Flaubert's or the Goncourts'. Was this omission simply accidental? To find out, I once wrote to several surrealists for their opinion of Zola. One only replied to my question: "I should be very happy to know the general outline of your talk on Zola and the surrealists, all the more so because I've never been able to appreciate that author; perhaps he has been badly served by the dazzling proximity of the Huysmans of *En Rade* and *A Rebours*." One senses an impulse to be courteous. For it seems very likely that, even had Huysmans not been his contemporary and, for a time, his disciple in naturalist practice, Zola's reputation would have suffered, among the surrealists, by reason of a theory of literature devoid of value, according to their standards. Moreover, while Huysmans surely would have attracted their attention, even had he written no novels, being a perceptive art critic and the interpreter of Moreau and Redon, Zola's defense of Manet would have done no more than relieve surrealists of any qualm of conscience about their limited acquaintance with his work. Yet in spite of all that militates against their acceptance of Zola, the parallel between the naturalist view of reality and the surrealist can be seen nowhere so clearly as when we examine the Rougon-Macquart novels.

Wherever we look in Zola's *Les Rougon-Macquart: histoire naturelle et sociale d'une famille sous le Second Empire*, we find him sensitive to "la lumière moderne de l'insolite" so appealing to surrealists. Thus in *Nana* we come across a typically surrealist fetish-object ("And so we had," Aragon reminds us,[30] "sorts of modern fetishes, signs and objects")—a glove:[31] "in the bedaubed disorder of shop signs, an enormous scarlet glove, in the distance, seemed to be a bloody hand, severed and attached by a yellow cuff."[32]

And whose is the phrase, "the modern light of the un-wonted"? It is not Zola's but Aragon's, coming from *Le Paysan de Paris*, which affords a few interesting parallels when we are considering Zola's descriptions.

> First they were captivated by a complicated arrangement: up above, umbrellas, laid aslant, seemed to form the roof of a rustic hut; below, silk stockings, hung from rods, displayed the rounded outline of calves, some sprinkled with roses, others in every shade, black net, red ones with embroidered clocks, flesh-colored ones with a satiny texture having the softness of a blonde's skin; finally, on the sheets covering the shelves, gloves were laid out symmetrically, with their fingers stretched, their narrow Byzantine virgin's palm, that stiff and as though adolescent grace of women's clothing not yet worn.

Everyone familiar with Zola's work knows this passage from *Au Bonheur des Dames*.[33] What about this other paragraph, though?

> And what can I say about the display of sponges that completes this shop, born at the end of the romantic period, when *Les Burgraves* was hissed, and haunted castles were left abandoned? Sponges in bottles, sponges left free, with a texture more changeable than the wind, with a texture more changeable than that of the skin of women, extra-fine like a serviette made of bee's nest, or porous like the sonorous grottoes of the sea where tritons helmeted with green sea-weed stretch their limbs, sponges that swell under the an-noyance of water.

As we soon see, when we read a little farther, this is not, as possibly it might seem to be, an unpublished page of Zola's, but the work of another writer altogether: "I know a man who loved sponges. I never have the habit of using that word lightly. This man, then, *loved* sponges." We have now left *Au Bonheur des Dames* for *Le Paysan de Paris*,[34] whose author receives warm praise in Breton's *Entretiens* (pp. 38–39) for demonstrating a remarkable facility, when it comes to uncovering the *insolite*. And yet, in moving on from a naturalist text to a surrealist one, we have encountered no sudden significant change, either in content or in imagery. Where Zola speaks of Octave Mouret's department store, Aragon's attention goes also to a shop selling walking sticks in the Passage de l'Opéra, which he liked to explore. And in Aragon's 1924 description of the Passage, a favorite haunt of the early surrealists, we find a phrase that seems to have come straight out of Zola's description of Au Bonheur des Dames: "an art of panoply in space" (p. 27).

Surely the most important thing to notice here is this: in one of the classic texts of surrealism, Louis Aragon betrays no more inclination to turn away from reality than the leader of French naturalism. In other words, commenting upon the evidence presented above, as it was offered in the form of a lecture, one listener at least revealed he had missed the point entirely, when he affirmed, "But the surrealists seek to obliterate the everyday universe so as to bring in the *insolite*. Zola synthesizes the two universes." His remark is worth citing only because it led to an exchange involving comments by the surrealists Jacques Brunius and E. L. T. Mesens:

> BRUNIUS: The surrealists have not tried to substitute the *insolite* for the real: this is the superficial side of their movement. They have a broader view of the real than Zola's, which is natural; they came later, they've lived through the crisis of rationalism, and they've revised the values that were Zola's.
> BERVEILLERS: Let's not speak of the *insolite* if the word bothers you, but of the singular, the strange.
> MESENS: The irrational.
> BRUNIUS: To the extent that Zola is a poet, he would not have accepted his own rationalist theories.[35]

There exists, indisputably, another point of contact between surrealism and naturalism, as evidenced in the writings of Aragon and Zola. However, this is one we must approach circumspectly, if we are to respect the preferences of both parties, despite the invitation we have the impression of being extended when Aragon writes in *Le Paysan de Paris* of his "vertige du moderne" (p. 141). We can proceed safely only so long as we bear in mind that, if Zola too felt the dizzying attraction of modernity, the points of comparison claiming our attention, when we look at his novels alongside Aragon's text, by no means exhaust the meaning of *le moderne* in surrealism. For Aragon and the other young men who during the early twenties, after seeing their hope in Dada cheated, were seeking a more satisfying outlet for their creative needs, *le moderne* could be grasped only in relation to the *esprit nouveau* of Apollinaire and that vague intuition which, prefacing his *Le Libertinage* (1924)—published fully six months before the *Manifeste du Surréalisme*—Louis Aragon called *le mouvement flou*.[36]

With due regard for these reservations, we may advance our understanding of how naturalism anticipates surrealism by way of an examination of a number of descriptions—among the most typical, incidentally, in *Les Rougon-Macquart*—which foreshadow Aragon's handling of objective reality in *Le Paysan de Paris*. In fact, we have no need, really, to quote some of the best-known passages from Zola's work (the description of the Paris markets in *Le Ventre de Paris*, that of the mine in *Germinal*, or the evocation of the locomotive in *La Bête humaine*, let us say), when we have Aragon to summarize for us: "The concrete has no other expression than poetry." Indeed, Aragon might have been thinking of these very descriptions when he wrote in *Le Paysan de Paris:*

> All the fauna of imaginations, of their marine vegetation, as though through hair of shadows is lost and perpetuated in the ill-lit zones of human activity. . . . The door of mystery, human weakness, opens, and here we are in the realms of shadow. . . . Where the most equivocal activity of living people is carried on, the inanimate sometimes takes on a reflection of their most secret motives: our cities are thus peopled with misunderstood sphinxes that do not halt the daydreaming passerby, if he does not turn his meditative absentmindedness in their direction, that do not ask him fate-

ful questions. But if he knows how to divine them, this wise man, then let him question them, it is still his own depths that, thanks to these faceless monsters, he is going to plumb once more. The modern light of the unwonted, that is what is going to hold his attention henceforth. (p. 18)

Another poet with strong affinities with surrealism, Jean Malrieu, has expressed the same thought more succinctly: "To describe is to describe oneself. Why measure oneself by the scale of things, if it is not to find what comes before choice?"[37]

There is a paradox here, well enough known to those whose judgment of Zola finds general acceptance, but of whom Breton wrote in his second surrealist manifesto that they "can conceive of nothing beyond foul reporting, monumental masonry and drawings on prison walls, those who know only how to jiggle the specter of Zola before our eyes, Zola whom they *do research on* without succeeding in taking anything from him . . ." (p. 189): Emile Zola confidently defined the history of the novel in the last third of the nineteenth century as that of "the collapse of imagination," and yet could have signed this confession, taken from *Le Paysan de Paris:* "Reason, reason, oh abstract phantom of the waking hours, already I've driven you out of my dreams, here I am at the point where they are going to commingle with apparent realities: there is no longer any place here except for me" (p. 11). Indeed the question asked by Aragon is just as pertinent to assessment of Zola's achievement as it is to surrealism's: "Knowledge gained by reason, can that for an instant oppose knowledge gained from the senses?" (p. 11). For it is Zola who, both in his preparatory notes for *L'Argent* and in the text of that novel, likens the Stock Exchange in Paris to an enigmatic, frightening sphinx:

> Passersby would turn their heads, in desire for and fear of what took place there, the mystery of financial transactions which few French brains can fathom, sudden ruin, sudden fortune that could not be explained, in that wild gesturing and barbaric shouting.[38]

The Stock Market in *L'Argent* "beats like a human heart" in the district where it is located, giving the same impression as the Paris market, the Halles, whose "colossal breathing, still heavy with yesterday's indigestion," is audible to the hero of *Le Ventre de Paris*.[39] As for the coal mine in *Germinal*, its presentation is faithful to the following notation in Zola's work sheets: "Take up again the heavy, labored breathing, choking, painful."[40] Aragon might have been thinking of Zola, then, when he wrote in *Le Paysan de Paris*:

> The spirit of worship, dispersing in the dust, has deserted the sacred places. But there are other places that prosper among men, other places where men occupy themselves without a care with their life of mystery, and which little by little become aware of a profound religion. Divinity does not inhabit them yet. It takes form in them, it is a new divinity, precipitated in these modern Epheses like, at the bottom of a glass, metal displaced by acid; it is life that here makes this poetic divinity appear, which a thousand people will pass without seeing and which, all of a sudden, becomes palpable, and terribly haunting, to those who just once have maladroitly glimpsed them. (p. 17)

While the haunting presence of the mine in *Germinal* and the department store in *Au Bonheur des Dames* illustrates Aragon's statement perfectly well, Zola's depiction of the somber fate of those whose lives are ruled by the Voreux or whose livelihood is threatened by the Bonheur des Dames seems at the opposite pole from Aragon's celebration of modernity in *Le Paysan de Paris*:

> Gaudily painted with English words and words of new invention, with a single long flexible arm, a luminous faceless head, one foot and a belly with a calibrated wheel, gas pumps sometimes have the air of gods of Egypt or those of cannibal peoples who worship only war. Oh Texaco motor oil, Eco, Shell, great inscriptions of human potential! soon we shall be crossing ourselves before your fountains, and the youngest

among us will perish for having gazed upon their nymphs in
naphtha. (p. 143).

However, Zola's view of the world about him was not exclusively depressing. Descriptions of various displays in the
Paris markets—salads among them—prove as much. And,
after all, Gervaise Macquart's terror before the brandy still
in *L'Assommoir* or the terror experienced by those living in
the same district as the Bonheur des Dames puts us in mind
of Aragon's description of Parisian department stores as
"great modern wild beasts," lying in wait for women (p. 50)
and even of the hair dryer "with its snake's neck" and similar "sly instruments" said to be "ready to bite, all slaves of
steel that will revolt one day" (p. 51).

The important factor, of course, is that in Zola's writing as much as in Aragon's we find evidence to support the
following declaration in *Le Paysan de Paris*: "Make no mistake about it: imagination never goes unpaid, it is already
the formidable beginning of a realization" (p. 165). We have
only to look into a window of the Bonheur des Dames to
see this:

> The rounded bosoms of the dummies [*mannequins*] made the
> material swell out, the ample hips exaggerated the slimness of
> the waist, the missing heads were replaced by large tickets,
> attached by a pin to the red bunting of the neck; while mir-
> rors, one each side of the window, by a calculated effect,
> reflected and multiplied them endlessly, populated the street
> with those beautiful women for sale, carrying prices in large
> figures, in place of their heads. (p. 711)

The surrealist elements in this passage speak eloquently for
themselves. We find here the mirror play for which, following Lewis Carroll, the surrealists have always shown affection, as Desnos does in *La Liberté ou l'Amour!* where the
hotel room in which the Corsaire Sanglot and Louise Lame
find sanctuary becomes "the poetic place where . . . the

mirror liberates menacing and autonomous characters" (p. 26). Above all, the principal figures in the scene Zola depicts appear to be related to the heroine of Max Ernst's novel in collages, *La Femme 100 Têtes [The Hundred Headless Woman]*, and kin to the Grande Mannequin, subject of René Crevel's article in the fifth number of *Minotaure*, "that Antigone who knows, to adorn herself, how to arrange Oedipean complexities in very sensual smiles" (p. 18). It is thanks to the Grande Mannequin, Crevel assures us, that "her fatherly material can live a life as full as that of her own body," a body so perfect that "she does not always bother to take with her, in her peregrinations, a head, arms, legs." Crevel completes his description of the Grande Mannequin, by the way, with this phrase that brings to mind the famous white display, the "chanson du blanc," as Zola calls it, in *Au Bonheur des Dames:* "At her approach old rags find youth and life once again."

Indeed the parallel is closer still. Readers of Zola will find quite familiar the evocation of the department store where Crevel's Grande Mannequin is to be found as "architecture halfway between vegetal and animal, halfway between that which fades and that which bleeds" (p. 18). Crevel's phrase reads in fact like a summary of Zola's description of the Bonheur des Dames, part building, part machine, part colossal ogre. And what about Crevel's reference to department stores, during white sales, as "markets of flesh, kilometers of flesh offering themselves to the desires of the Grande Mannequin"? Does it not find fuller development in *Au Bonheur des Dames*, where sales are said to attract "a whole crowd brutal with covetous desire," where the material on display is described as "breathing with the breath of temptation" and the *mannequins* appear to have become erotically animated (pp. 719–20)?[41]

Certain pages of Zola's, like those in *Au Bonheur des Dames* devoted to "apotheoses of half-dressed *mannequins*," anticipate the animism of the universe in metamorphosis, dear to surrealists. Like the latter, Zola tried to communicate his impression of the fundamental forces that rule human existence. Thus the anthropomorphic landscapes of Salvador Dalí, or better still André Masson, are evocative of the descriptions which bring to life the landscape, outside and inside the garden, the Paradou, in *La Faute de l'abbé Mouret.*

This is where comparison of Zola's descriptions with surrealist ones and with analogous surrealist creations is most instructive. One can hardly say that Masson's anthropomorphic landscapes, brought to life by eroticism, picture objectively observed reality. Nor can one claim, either, that Zola's depiction of external reality ignores the world about him. Despite his grave assertion of faith in the real world, Zola's novels testify to the frequency with which he left the highway of representative realism for the byways of the curious, the strange, and the unwonted. In consequence, while it has become a truism that the naturalist novel is hedged about by confining theoretical limitations, it is no less a commonplace of literary history that Emile Zola, promoter of naturalism in France, was far from being the cold observer of facts and phenomena he wished to be. Indeed, examination of his documentary notes would greatly enrich the harvest of effects of the kind we have been gathering.

Zola sought to limit the contribution of subjective imagination, which he saw as weakening the scientific truth of his picture of reality, trying to control imagination's interference by means of the documentary method—by close attentiveness to external reality. The irony of his situation, therefore, was that the more he looked, in the process of documenting himself, the more the act of observing nourished his imagination. This is why by adopting an approach diametrically opposed to that of Huysmans—whose sense of the oppressiveness of reality led him to write *En Rade*—Zola arrived as a sense of the real no less imaginatively liberative.

Self-styled *"clerk of the court,"* Emile Zola found himself using his "notes taken from life," against his firmest aesthetic convictions, to redefine reality in terms peculiarly his own. Fully aware of what he felt to be his weakness, he spoke of being "rotten to the marrow with romanticism." To a considerable extent this weakness appears, in the perspective of surrealism, the saving grace of Zola's naturalism. For the consequences of his quite instinctive quarrel with the objective truth of observable reality are to be seen in his descriptions of the familiar world that offer the closest analogy with the surrealist viewpoint.

Beyond question, when he resorted to documentation (close inspection of objective reality) as a brake to imagination, Emile Zola was paying imagination unwilling tribute. Thus, to the degree that he can be regarded as a proto-surrealist writer, he was a distinctly and uncomfortably reluctant one. However, the example set in his novels is a salutary warning to those who, seeing surrealism as ever in conflict with the reality principle, remain indifferent to the etymological force of the word *surréalisme*, which alludes to a higher sense of realisms and persuaded Herbert Read to propose, as its English equivalent, the word *superrealism*.[42]

Zola arrived at some of the most memorably personal of his evocations of the world about him by a method born of the earnest wish to look at reality attentively and render it faithfully. His practice, therefore, raised the question of naturalism's achievement above the level where one must speak of a theory voluntarily submitting accomplishment to measurement by comparison with external reality. Thus in Zola, as in Huysmans, the objective world serves as a sounding board for the creative sensibility, so providing the necessary stimulus for creative activity. It was the surrealist Benjamin Péret who spoke in one of his stories ("La Maladie No. 9") of "passing to the other side of the eye." Among the nineteenth-century novelists mesmerized by physical reality, it was Zola, though, who showed most impressively how this could be done. His trite definition of the novel as "a corner of creation seen through a temperament" yielded significant effects. For in the perspective of surrealism's revolt against

oppressive aspects of the world about us, Zola's signal service is to have demonstrated that reality can neither resist
temperament nor dampen its fire. In 1953, the surrealist
painter Max Ernst published a volume reproducing certain
pictures he had painted in the Nevada desert in 1946, accompanied by texts. Ernst called his book *Sept Microbes vus à
travers un Tempérament*.

The legacy left to surrealism by romanticism and
naturalism has nothing noteworthy to do with literary form.
It transcends form, in fact, to the point where, for example,
the surrealists' declared aversion to the novel as a literary
genre ceases to be one of the pertinent factors governing
response. Nor is it, exactly, a legacy that can be assessed
with any degree of accuracy under the heading of subject
matter, as opposed to form. Instead, what surrealists were
to find in two of the most vital literary movements of
nineteenth-century Europe was evidence of a distinctive
sensitivity, manifesting itself unequivocally and excitingly
through characteristic relationships entertained with respect
to objective reality.

It would be unjust to all the romantics who find favor
with the surrealists to argue that desire, as surrealist aspirations have identified its presence in their work, is of a
monotonously uniform nature. And it would be just as unfair to contend that, in naturalist writing, Zola's depiction
of objects, of things physically present in contemporary
society, stands out because, erroneously, it is presumed to
take its tonality from frustrated sexual urges. It would be
futile indeed, and quite ridiculous, to try to limit too closely
the character of desire, as reflected in romantic and naturalist
writing, or to see it in one light exclusively. Anyway, that
is not the important thing. What matters, really, is this: to
the extent that romanticism and naturalism evidence significant affinities with the surrealist way of looking at the world,
they do so on the level of affective reaction. In disregard of
theoretical argumentation, the latter treats external reality

not as hostile and impermeable to subjective influence, but as capable of lending itself productively, and without resistance, to appropriation by the creative sensibility, as being, in other words, susceptible to imaginative assimilation without which, surrealists believe, poetic action is impossible.

The Emergence of Surrealism

Whoever, after appearing in the magazine *Littérature* in 1919, *Les Champs magnétiques* came out in 1920 over the signatures of André Breton and Philippe Soupault, only three hundred copies were printed. Reprinting *Les Champs magnétiques* in 1967, the Parisian house of Gallimard at last placed before a wide audience a text more talked about than read, a book about which Breton had written fifteen years earlier, in his *Entretiens*, "Incontestably, that was the first *surrealist* (and by no means Dada) work, since it was the fruit of the first systematic application of automatic writing" (p. 56).

Historian of Dada, Michel Sanouillet has seen fit to contest this assertion. Defending the thesis that there is nothing to be found in surrealism that cannot be found earlier in Dada, he remarks, "If affirming that *The Magnetic Fields* constituted the first surrealist work is as legitimate as seeing in *The Flowers of Evil* the first Symbolist text, to claim that the book is 'by no means Dada' is a questionable assumption, automatic writing being a mode of expression perfectly in keeping with the Dada spirit and, as we have seen, generally practiced in its unrefined form by the protagonists of the Movement since 1916."[1] The first part of

Sanouillet's statement seems to have been devised to conjure up a red herring—unsuccessfully, of course, since no comment of Baudelaire's has come down to us relating *Les Fleurs du Mal* to Symbolism. The second part, meanwhile, betrays a bias with which *Les Champs magnétiques* itself invites us to take issue.

No one, least of all André Breton, would question that the discovery of automatic writing came before the baptism of surrealism. Indeed Breton does not date the inception of surrealism from the use of the automatic method, in *Entretiens*, but from its systematic application. In choosing to pass over the adjective that Breton carefully uses, Sanouillet falsifies perspectives, so as to make it easier for himself to defend an argument that really is of little pertinence and would call for no mention here, if it were not for the lesson it has to teach. Following Breton's lead, we experience less reluctance to accept the evidence of historical chronology. After all, more to the point than the observations of a literary historian busily defending his territory is the viewpoint of the authors of *Les Champs magnétiques* themselves concerning the verbal experimentation their text exemplifies. There is no deep secret here, by the way, since Soupault has explained clearly enough: "At that period, while André Breton and I were not yet baptised surrealists, we wanted first of all to give ourselves over to experiments. These led us to consider poetry as a liberation, as the possibility (perhaps the only one) of giving the mind a freedom we had known only in our dreams and of setting us free from the whole machinery of logic."[2]

Reflecting upon the aspirations shared by Breton and Soupault, as mirrored in these words, we come to understand better how important the revelation of the extended practice of automatic writing appeared to them to be, in 1919. Neither writer, we recall, was engaged at that time in an organized program expressive of an attitude toward literature, although their magazine *Littérature* had been founded in a spirit of protest and inquiry. In fact, it was their eagerness to find and turn to account a program that might lead them away from conventional poetic expression that made them respond so readily to Dada's message of iconoclasm and revolt.

Evidence of enthusiasm for Dada, taking a form one is entitled to characterize as naive, is to be found in letters written by Breton in 1919 to a leading Dadaist in Zurich, Tristan Tzara.[3] "It is to you that my eyes turn today," cried Breton on January 22. Only two days later, he was asking, "Will you trust me; I am prepared to like you." On February 18, he confessed, "I am tempted to write to you as I do to no one else," adding, "So far as my feelings go I am as close to you as one can be." By March 2 he was writing, "Your poems are marvelous. I thank you first of all in my own name. Of all the living poets you are the one who moves me most." April 4 saw the following declaration of community of purpose: "If there are no doubt a few less things that disgust me, because I am younger, I tend like you only to cast off my artistic prejudices, the only ones I still have." Breton brought this letter to a close with the words, "I count immeasurably on your friendship, that's all." In confirmation came another letter, dated sixteen days later ("I have a crazy confidence in you"), evoking the name of Breton's earlier idol, Jacques Vaché, destined to be mentioned again in a missive of July 2: "I think of you as I've never thought of anyone . . . except Jacques Vaché, I've said this (that is to say, before I act I almost always reach agreement with you)." According to this same letter, by the way, both Aragon and Soupault shared Breton's desire to please Tzara. "Louis Aragon has got back to Paris," Breton reported. "Not a day goes by but that he, Philippe Soupault and I speak of you: 'Tristan Tzara would like this, or . . . .'" Similarly, a letter written September 5 refers to "the place you have in Soupault's thoughts and mine," while another, dated October 7, says explicitly, "There is nothing, dear Tristan Tzara, like your letters for leading me to the end of my reflections and for bringing my plans to fruition one after the other, if that's not too much to say." This correspondence reached its climax in a letter of December 26, written just before Tzara left Zurich for Paris: "I'm waiting for you, I'm waiting only for you now."

These curiously passionate letters help us measure how profound was the shock of disappointment experienced by their author once Tzara had come to Paris and had begun organizing Dada activities there. Breton's *Entretiens* summarizes events as follows:

> The great disappointment of that time—a disappointment to many of us—came from the fact that Tzara was not as I had supposed him to be: a poet, yes, and even a great poet in his moments, certainly. But the fuss made over him in Paris seemed to have drugged him, doped him. I give this statement no polemical intent, limiting myself to translating what I felt then. He would have fun, say clever things, repeat tricks that had been well received, exercise to the best of his ability, but within an area that began to get smaller pretty soon, his personal attraction. The *1918 Dada Manifesto* had seemed to open the doors wide but we soon discovered that those doors opened onto a corridor going round in a circle. (p. 59)

In his dissatisfaction with Dada activities we see what caused André Breton to transfer his attention from Tzara's antics to the more exciting promise that *Les Champs magnétiques* had seemed to offer ("We were, André Breton and I," testified Soupault in *Profils perdus*, "enraptured" [p. 167]). As we watch the results crystallize and take form in the 1924 *Manifeste du Surréalisme*, we see better that, from the first, there existed a basic difference between Tzara and Breton, which the latter's enthusiasm for the former could not mask for long. No later than October 7, 1919, a letter of Breton's showed him to be aware of something more significant in Tzara's behavior than the mere paradox of producing literature while denying it. "The absence of a system, you say," he wrote Tzara, "is still a system, but more attractive; *I* don't find it either more attractive or more antipathetical." Even before their first meeting, Breton sensed a crucial divergence in approach which eventually made it necessary for him to draw a distinction between Dada and surrealism.

The distinction soon became clear enough to justify recognition of *Les Champs magnétiques* as the first specifically surrealist work.

The essential fact is that in Breton's mind (and in the minds of those like Soupault and Aragon who were not slow to throw in their lot with him), Dada defended a negative program, capable of exerting its appeal over them for a limited period only. Discontented with negativity, which was inimical to his nature, as it was to giving poetry new direction, Breton rejected Dada in preference for exploration of the potentialities of a discovery which, *Les Champs magnétiques* had persuaded him, opened the door on a system of positive value.

Whatever a close analysis of the text may teach us one day, with the help of the famous first copy of the original edition (bearing marginal comments by Breton, who underlined the passages for which he was responsible), no commentary must be allowed to obscure the excitement that was Breton's and Soupault's, when confronted with the revelation manifesting itself through *Les Champs magnétiques*. Nothing should be permitted to divert attention from the importance future surrealists were to attach to the discovery of a form of verbal expression in which the poetic self excitingly occupies the centre of the universe, exerting an ever-widening circle of influence.

The most accurate way to judge this influence, with least risk of falsifying the underlying motivation of surrealist endeavor, is in relation to the poetic self, as characterized by surrealist aspirations. Quite understandably, especially in the early days of experimentation by those entitled to call themselves surrealists, it appeared likely that total freedom of expression, without which the poetic self would be inhibited, could be obtained best through the practice of verbal or pictorial automatism. In time, a broader perspective began to make its needs felt, demanding that reality be handled in ways automatism alone could not guarantee. It was only to be expected, therefore, that, with time, the promise of automatic practices should lose something of the attraction they had held originally. Yet at no time during the long history of surrealist activity was *Les Champs magnétiques* to lose its prestige among participants in the movement. Never has it been denied pride of place among creative works in which poetry takes on a quality that surrealist ambitions invest with a special value we must now try to describe a little more closely.

GUILLAUME APOLLINAIRE

After explaining in his *Manifeste du Surréalisme* how he and Philippe Soupault first experimented with language freed from conscious control, in a method of composition that they found to be highly charged with poetry and which came to be known in surrealist circles as automatic writing, André Breton made the following statement:

> In homage to Guillaume Apollinaire who had just died, and who on several occasions seemed to us to have been drawn in the same direction, without for all that sacrificing to it mediocre literary devices, Soupault and I designated by the name of surrealism the new mode of expression which we had at our disposal and from which we were anxious to let our friends benefit. (p. 38)

Guillaume Apollinaire could scarcely be said to merit recognition as the only writer, recently deceased, to enjoy special favor among those young men, tired of consecrated literary techniques, who by 1924 were ready to call themselves surrealists. Alfred Jarry had died no earlier than 1907 and Jacques Vaché—an immensely important figure, in Breton's eyes at any rate—had committed suicide in 1919. However, it is still Apollinaire whose influence, carefully delimited in scope, it is true, found most immediate and most prominent acknowledgment at the time when the surrealist movement was launched formally. For this reason, no doubt, it is customary to associate Apollinaire's name with the birth of surrealism, as though doing so called for no reservations of any kind,[4] as though, shall we say, the seed of surrealism had been sown in verses like his "Lundi rue Christine." And yet, to appreciate in which direction the surrealists were starting out at the beginning of the twenties, and for what reasons, we must give attention not only to the breadth of Apollinaire's unquestionable influence upon their poetic activity, but also to those limits beyond which Guillaume Apollinaire ceased to be a guide for surrealist exploration.

Anyone asking himself the important question which continues to face us, that of the immediate origins of surrealism, does not take long to notice that three of the very first surrealists, Aragon, Breton, and Soupault, all of whom may be credited with speaking knowledgeably, have testified warmly to their admiration for and indebtedness to Apollinaire.

Although Soupault was not to remain a surrealist for long, his affection for Apollinaire continued unabated. Almost forty years after the first surrealist manifesto appeared he had not ceased to see Apollinaire as "a daring poet, the most daring poet of his day." This evaluation, in *Profils perdus* (p. 9), is reiterated: "a great poet" (p. 13), "an inspired poet" (p. 14). What had interested him, Philippe Soupault now claimed, was the future: "To me the real Apollinaire was the one who wrote: *'Allons plus vite nom de Dieu/ Allons plus vite'*" (pp. 11–12). Yet Soupault was careful not to suggest that Apollinaire had sought to initiate any literary movement: "Guillaume Apollinaire did not want to be the leader of a school (he told me so himself). He was rather what he himself called a signal rocket" (pp. 10–11). By no means blind to certain weaknesses in Apollinaire— notably his craving for recognition and his erudition— Soupault still saw him in the most favorable light:

> It is none the less true that he was the one who offered the young poets of his day the chance "to go more quickly and farther" as he so ardently wished and claimed.

It is above all because of this offer that our debt to
him is considerable. (pp. 14–15)

One noteworthy feature of Philippe Soupault's tribute to Apollinaire is that nowhere does it allude directly to
the part played by Apollinaire in giving vitality to the spirit
of surrealism. Cautiously advanced in general terms, when
they go beyond the range of personal reminiscence, Soupault's reasons for admiring Apollinaire tell us nothing,
overtly, about his influence upon those for whom the name
surrealists soon would be the only fitting designation. If we
are looking for a more open confession of this nature, we
have to turn elsewhere.

Soupault first met Apollinaire when he was seven-
teen, in 1914. Breton, meanwhile, did not get to know him
until 1916.[5] It was, then, in Apollinaire's apartment that
Breton made Soupault's acquaintance: "the elective admiration we both felt for him had been the basis on which we
were brought together," *Entretiens* points out (p. 35). Louis
Aragon, on the other hand, remained at first relatively
unimpressed, preferring Jules Romains's *Odes et Prières*
to Apollinaire's *Alcools*. At the beginning something of
a heretic in the eyes of his friends Breton and Soupault,
Aragon was to abjure his errors before long. In March of
1918 he published a warm review of *Les Mamelles de
Tirésias* in *SIC*, expressing admiration for Apollinaire again
the following year, in an issue of the same magazine dedicated to the poet's memory. Later, writing in *Paris-Journal*
on November 30, 1923, he declared, "Apollinaire never
wrote anything that was not admirable." Later still, looking back during his *Entretiens avec Francis Crémieux*, he
was to refer to "the man who influenced us all the most at
that period": "Apollinaire, the man of modernism" (p. 21).

True, Apollinaire's ideas on the role of the modern
in poetry and the application of these ideas in his own work
no more completely exhausted the concept of the modern in
surrealism than did Zola's practice in his novels. All the

same, the example set by Guillaume Apollinaire offered a welcome and timely release from the stifling influences of discredited literary theories and their consequences. Setting aside for the moment certain reservations they felt about Apollinaire's essay "L'Esprit nouveau et les Poètes," we appreciate that, though the ideas expressed therein—to say nothing of the elements those ideas led him to introduce into his own verse—from a comfortable distance may appear dated, one cannot ignore the appeal such an essay would hold for young men who, while still compulsively drawn to poetry, found no savor any more in the aesthetic refinements of Symbolism.

Despite condemnation by Jacques Vaché, who could not forgive the author of *Le Poète assassiné* for contributing to *La Baïonnette*, and who disrupted the first performance of *Les Mamelles de Tirésias*, brandishing a revolver, the early surrealists acknowledged Apollinaire to be a poet of the first rank. Indeed, their respect for him brought with it unexpected indulgence for those texts in which he wrote in praise of war. Thus in an article on *Calligrammes* that appeared in the first number of *L'Esprit nouveau* in 1920, Aragon could write: "To speak to us of the very thing we abominated and to charm us by means of the worst realities, the *tour de force* is scarcely believable. That voice in the night: *Ah Dieu que la guerre est jolie/Avec sec chants ses longs loisirs*, did it revolt enough the serious men who considered tragic an adventure in which they risked after all only their lives."

All this Soupault might have taken the trouble to point out, had he not found it best to forget his surrealist past, except when it was to his advantage to do so.[6] For Philippe Soupault's own contribution to surrealism, as Breton evaluated it in his *Entretiens*, lay in an "acute sense of the modern (or what at that time we called 'modern,' without concealing from ourselves what was unstable about that very notion)" (p. 36). Soupault's reluctance to go into this matter suggests that, if we want to see Apollinaire more clearly, in the way the earliest surrealists saw him, we cannot do better than refer to the comments of one of their number whose recollections betray no distracting influences of the kind obviously felt by Soupault: André Breton.

Breton's testimony comes from three sources primarily: a 1917 article devoted to Apollinaire's writings in prose and verse, reprinted in his *Les Pas perdus*,[7] the introductory note to the section of his *Anthologie de l'Humour noir* devoted to Apollinaire,[8] and his memoirs, *Entretiens*. Ranging over almost fifty years, these texts all tell the same story. As *Entretiens* puts it, "He was a very great personage, in any case such as I have never seen since. Rather haggard, it is true. Lyricism personified" (p. 23). At age twenty-one, looking forward in his adulatory article of 1917 to the time when those close to Apollinaire would share with others their memories of him, Breton declared, "To have known him will be considered a rare blessing" (p. 25). And indeed, as we can see, his own remarks on Apollinaire, during radio interviews taking place thirty-five years later, still bear witness to fervent admiration.

Breton's article in *Les Pas perdus* gives Apollinaire ungrudging credit for pursuing a supremely important goal: "the reinvention of poetry" (p. 38). The *Anthologie de l'Humour noir* places him "at the crossroads of all routes" (p. 409). From the first Breton admired in him the author of "La Chanson du Mal-Aimé," of "Zone," of "L'Emigrant de Landor Road," and of "Le Musicien de Saint-Merry." *Entretiens* presents Apollinaire as "the champion of the *event-poem*," that is to say "the apostle of that conception which demands of each new poem that it be a total reorganization of the means at its author's disposal, that it follow its own adventure outside paths already laid down, in disregard for gains realized in the past" (p. 23).

The magnetism of Apollinaire, the man no less than the poet, did not blind Breton and his friends to some implications of "L'Esprit nouveau et les Poètes" that conflicted with their own aspirations. While still responsive to aspects of Apollinaire's proposals in his celebrated article from the *Mercure de France*, which seemed to be of a positive nature, they shared certain objections, summarized in these terms in Breton's *Entretiens:*

> If we found it good to see him confirm that in poetry and art "surprise is the great new stimulus" and insist upon "a liberty of unimaginable opulence," we were disturbed by the concern he showed for renewing contact with "the critical spirit" of the classics, which seemed to us terribly limiting, as well as with their "sense of duty" which we considered debatable, in any case out-of-date and, anyway, out of the question. The wish to situate the debate on the national and even the nationalist plane ("France," said Apollinaire, "custodian of the whole secret of civilization . . .") seemed to us even more inadmissible. We could not accept, any more, the sight of art humiliated before science. We deplored above all that "the new spirit" conceived in this fashion should try to place reliance on external artifice (typographical and otherwise): lyrical means properly so-called were neither taken farther nor renewed. (p. 44)

This said, the evidence available to us nevertheless testifies to the birth, among the early surrealists, of a legend in which Guillaume Apollinaire held a privileged place. "He is," wrote Breton in 1917, "among those one loves enough not to picture their future history" (p. 45).

As a young man, Breton evidently felt more at liberty than he did later to ignore history. All the same, he could not expect history to stand still. Legends, after all, are susceptible to change—at least they readily undergo modification under conditions imposed by the changing perspectives of passing time. It is interesting, then, to see how participants in the surrealist venture, separated by time from the fascinating presence of Apollinaire, were to view his work and its significance with respect to their own ambitions. Such an inquiry has more then anecdotal interest. For when we address ourselves to the question of Apollinaire's reputation among surrealists who did not share the rare privilege of knowing him as Aragon, Breton and Soupault did, we come closer to estimating the significance of the first *Manifeste*, as seen from within the surrealist group.

All the poets with whom we are concerned now joined the surrealist cause at various times after surrealism was launched. They all rallied to the flag run up by Breton, so publicly declaring their acceptance of an ethic and an attitude toward poetry that could be accused no longer of evidencing any ambiguity. Surrealism already had begun to take its characteristic orientation, one Apollinaire certainly had helped to indicate. Already, before their arrival, surrealism had its exalting legend in which the name of Apollinaire figured next to those of Lautréamont, Jarry, and so on. Thus, with due regard for individual peculiarities, the testimony provided by these later recruits allows us to gauge to what extent changing attitudes toward Apollinaire call for revision in that legend.

Where modulations are to be observed, these may be detected with least delay when we follow a chronological order: judgments expressed by a writer who came to know surrealism in the decade following the appearance of the *Manifeste du Surréalisme* preceding those of a few poets who responded to surrealism's call during the forties. These, in turn, come before those joining surrealist activities from about 1950 onward. This means commencing with Jehan Mayoux.

When Jehan Mayoux became a surrealist in 1932, Apollinaire was still, for most of the older members in the Paris group, a *presence*. The fervent enthusiasm of those who had known Apollinaire personally, at an impressionable age, still could be felt. Questioned about what Apollinaire meant to him, Mayoux replied: "Apollinaire? an important personage. For me, the first contact with modern poetry. For this reason I cannot say he has had no influence upon me; it very quickly became one with that of the surrealists (whom I read before I knew them). If it can be felt in the little I've written, I know nothing of it." We can see here how Apollinaire's influence came to be transmitted from the first-generation surrealists to a representative of the second generation. To Mayoux, Apollinaire is still present; but his presence takes on a very special character. And so, if Mayoux could bow before Apollinaire the modern poet, he was to see virtue in that poet's work when considering it in the perspective of surrealism. The first-generation surrealists had borrowed from Apollinaire whatever seemed useful and pertinent. They admired features of his writing seemingly in accord with their own ambitions or appearing to cast light on these. The second-generation recruits therefore had every reason to view Apollinaire through surrealism. This was already, in other words, a para-surrealist Apollinaire whom they came to know, a writer whose ambiguities and complexities, the very image of his eclectic mind, they found it easy to ignore to the advantage of "le poète moderne" whose preoccupations took him in somewhat the same direction as surrealism was going.

This way of looking at Apollinaire's work was not peculiar to those who joined surrealism in the thirties. It influenced also the approach of certain persons recruited in the forties. Among these we may cite Jean-Louis Bédouin, to whom the revelation of surrealism came only after the end of the Second World War. This, by the way, was the very time when he made the discovery of Apollinaire's poetic universe:

> The discovery of Guillaume Apollinaire is linked for me with that of surrealism, and specifically with my association with André Breton. In a manner no doubt subjective, it was through the latter that I sometimes had a fleeting impression of getting close—against all possibility—to the man who was Apollinaire, and it is from such lightning flashes that I recognize best, even today, the legendary character of that personage. "To have known him will be considered a rare blessing," Breton has written. So far as I am concerned, that is

strictly true—and I should add that it sometimes has seemed to me that I was not far from benefiting, in my turn, from that blessing.

No clearer statement is needed to make us feel the magic of Apollinaire's name, within surrealism. In fact, Bédouin gladly acknowledges how powerful that magic can be:

> In the circumstances, it would be very difficult for me to "situate" Apollinaire objectively. I prefer to abandon myself to that feeling I had when very young [born in 1929, Bédouin would have been seventeen in 1946]: he was the *enchanter*, he had really enchanted modern poetry, and, for this reason, we had a common cause.

Conscious of this enchantment and aware too that it had been safeguarded by surrealism's legend, Bédouin asks a question no less essential in his case than in Mayoux's: "Is that influence? Then of what sort of influence should we speak? Certainly not of a *literary* influence. The greatest poems of Apollinaire are not necessarily the most daring ones from the formal point of view of prosody. No, I believe, in this case, in a sort of more subtle influence, more important, that has to do with the capacity he had for making us *marvel* (his famous maxim: 'J'émerveille')."

So far as Bédouin's words may be said to have a representative value, they indicate that within the surrealist movement Apollinaire's long-term influence is comparable with that of Rimbaud, whom surrealists have sought to follow as *inquiéteur*. The need to disturb and disrupt, one of the most stimulating aspects of Rimbaud's message, goes naturally, in surrealist poetic practice, with exploration of the world of the marvelous. Hence, so far as Apollinaire's example is concerned, anyway, the following conclusion seems to Bédouin mandatory:

> The essential thing is that Apollinaire had at the same time a prodigious gift for verbal invention, an extraordinary sense

of the image, never-failing intellectual curiosity, and the capacity, like a water-diviner, for discovering palpable riches *to come*. This gift for invention, that stands out the more because linked, in his case, with aspects of certain traditonal values (most contestable ones, sometimes)—this perhaps is what I admire most in Apollinaire, and what seems to me to make up one of the fundamental aspects of his incontestable *lyric genius*.

For reasons his testimony makes plain, Bédouin may be considered representative of those who, coming to surrealism during its middle period, had no real difficulty following the example set by their elders, so responsive to a voice Breton's 1952 *Entretiens* qualifies as "prodigious" (p. 44). Bédouin's remarks therefore seem to assure us that Breton still spoke for all surrealists when, citing the celebrated maxim from "L'Esprit nouveau et les Poètes"—"La surprise est le plus grand ressort nouveau"—he declared that surrealism "not only has concurred in this opinion, but has made it an imprescriptible law" (p. 242). However, it would be unwise to conclude that Bédouin leaves nothing to be added, when we are trying to paint an accurate portrait of Apollinaire, as he appears to surrealist eyes, after 1945.

Someone else who came under the attraction of surrealism at about the same time as Bédouin is more severe. This is Claude Tarnaud, who states his position with clarity:

> We, you understand, landed right in the middle of surrealism (when I say we, I'm thinking of those of my "generation"—Bédouin, Jouffroy, Alexandrian, Jaguer, Bonnefoy, etc.), when that "movement" already had a "history"—a history we discovered in lightning abridgment and which for us had as much, if not more, importance as the texts and the testimony that illustrated it. So far as I was concerned, everything happened at the same time, a marvelous kaleidoscope, and if the adventure may have seemed, *a priori*, to carry less risks than the explorations on which those who had preceded us had launched, new vistas seemed to us to be opening up

more or less everywhere. Maps, however rudimentary they may have been, already existed, certainly, but, by reinventing them, we were able to convince ourselves we'd drawn them ourselves.

So far, there is nothing in what Tarnaud tells us to make us anticipate any radical divergence in his evaluation of Apollinaire, compared with Bédouin's, or even Mayoux's. A new note is struck only when he goes on to say:

> In this explosion of luminaries, this diorama of unimaginable and unhoped-for richness, Apollinaire, I fear, was only a secondary star. We were instinctively drawn to those whose lives had balanced more dangerously on the tip of the beam. Their "message" seemed closer to us for it meant that the game wasn't over, far from it, and that if they had withdrawn into the distance this was also so as to leave us elbow room. Let me mention, pell-mell Lautréamont (above all), Rimbaud, Jarry, Vaché, Rigaut, Cravan, Roussel (and I'm resisting the desire to add "above all" after each of them).

For Tarnaud, it is true, Apollinaire was "un initiateur primaire": "So as to point out to us that there was something else, he indicated certain vanishing points—and goodness knows what else!—one reads *Alcools* first, doesn't one? and in the stink of institutions of learning, a meteor lays down the law, suddenly. But—and here I'm selecting a chronological sequence that seems to me fairly common—the tornado named Lautréamont sweeps away these overly vague aspirations."

If the first surrealists apparently saw in the very vagueness of Apollinaire's aspirations something to attract them, finding therein, at the time when they were seeking a direction for themselves, an attitude or state of mind very close to their own, several of their successors, before whom the pathway of surrealism, already well-trodden, appeared unmistakably marked, were to feel at liberty to be less indulgent, not to say more severe, on the subject of certain aspects of Apollinaire's work, and even of his creative per-

sonality. And this occurred especially when they could not
be persuaded of Apollinaire's complete agreement with the
surrealist program he had done so much to bring to life.
This is why we hear from Tarnaud objections not yet familiar to us:

> And then Apollinaire had in some ways a damning false
> naiveté. I understand what "La Jolie Rousse" can have meant
> to Breton; I could not forgive the pleading tone! In spite of
> the admirable "Nous voulons explorer la bonté, contrée im-
> mense où tout se tait"—and the fact that I'm quoting from
> memory doesn't mean much!—Apollinaire was also the "gen-
> til poète," a sort of contemporary Villon, whose refrains
> André Billy hums in our ears, the poet who sang of sweet-
> smelling war, to whom Truffaut pays homage in his unspeak-
> able *Jules et Jim*. . . In the initiative genius, then, one smells
> classroom seats and corded velvet pants too much—classroom
> seats made later, as is fitting, into a precarious altar on which
> to sacrifice him.

Tarnaud's conclusions may be anticipated from the above:
"No, you see, I don't think Apollinaire has had a noteworthy influence on me, or on those claiming kinship with
surrealism since the last war—if there has been an influence
it made itself felt indirectly, through those who knew him
and testified to his sovereign authority. But that's already
something else."

In the perspective of surrealism, nothing summarizes
better the anticonformist attitude of Tarnaud than this final
statement:

> To finish I'd like to cite a very fine remark made to me by
> Duchamp, more than two years ago, while we were preparing
> the surrealist exhibit in New York. In front of a picture by
> Miró in which the painter had used as "background canvas"
> the portrait of a personage playing the Spanish grandee
> (bought no doubt at the flea market),[9] Duchamp tells me,
>
>> "This personage looks like Apollinaire, don't you
>> think?"
>> "Yes indeed."

"But he has a beard, Apollinaire didn't have one."
"..."
"Well, it's just because he has a beard that he looks like Apollinaire..."
And laughing into his pipe, Duchamp goes off. A pertinent conclusion?

Tarnaud endorses the view of Apollinaire, expressed by no less an influential figure than Marcel Duchamp, as at once a patriarch and a bore. One might think his evaluation too exceptional among the surrealists for serious attention if it were not that we find it echoed elsewhere, especially among those initiated into surrealism later than he.

Apollinaire had been dead for close to twenty years when Pierre Dhainaut was born in 1935. The viewpoint of such a late recruit to surrealism could not be expected to be altogether that of his elders:

> I had the good luck not to waste time and to arrive at once at what constitutes the central core of the poetry of our time, in France. It was ten years ago[10] that I read simultaneously *Alcools* and André Breton's *Poèmes*. This is why I didn't linger long over Apollinaire. I recognized his "charm"—and even more, by the way, in *L'Hérésiarque et Cie* and above all in *Le Poète assassiné*—but the meddle-with-everything side, the confusion, the warlike exaltation, the Verlaine and sentimental side made me uncomfortable, and still makes me uncomfortable. . . . Those who are my age, who discovered poetry shortly after 1950, were above all marked by the climate of surrealism.

Guy Cabanel's impression coincides exactly with Dhainaut's: "Apollinaire is for me a two-faced hero: a pioneer of the new poetic paths and a very simple-minded fellow not without humor and not without points of agreement with Douanier Rousseau, very representative of a certain period." Small wonder that, despite a politeness which, one suspects, owes something to the fact that no surrealist willingly invited

Breton's displeasure in the early sixties any more than earlier by attacking too energetically one of those he venerated, Cabanel concludes: "To tell the truth, I don't think I've come under the poet's influence: temperamental differences no doubt."

Temperamental differences there surely are. But these do not account on their own for the decline of Apollinaire's reputation, to be noted when we place the views of younger surrealists next to those expressed by the men who first strove to give surrealism a sense of purpose. Especially among poets whose fidelity to surrealist principles coincides with the final years of Breton's life, gratitude to Apollinaire is noticeably lacking as a common bond. The simple truth appears to be that the later an individual feels the attraction of surrealism, the less he needs to place reliance upon Apollinaire's example, the less guilty he is likely to feel, turning away from Apollinaire, the more natural it is for him to find inspiration in the writings of those who have preceded him in surrealism. Mayoux's debt to Péret is beyond dispute; so is Dhainaut's to Eluard. And if the poetic innovations of Cabanel are excitingly without precedent in the writings of elder surrealists, they most certainly owe nothing, either, to the works Apollinaire has left behind.

One may note, of course, that force of circumstances revitalizes legends by adapting them to current needs. In consequence, the thirties and forties tended to see the models ever before surrealist eyes immobilized in particularly significant attitudes. Thus attention shifted from the writings of Rimbaud, which could not be expected to escape some degree of contamination as a result of the attention they were receiving from outside surrealist circles, to his exemplary gesture: abandonment of literature. Thus, too, in the surrealists' estimation, the social, moral, and intellectual posture of a Vaché or a Jarry far outweighed their achievements as writers—quite limited, after all, in Vaché's case. Despite the inescapable influence of Breton, Apollinaire's legacy tended to become, more and more embarrassingly, a literary one, in which little by little the presence of artifice and the disturbing consequences of the writer's need to *please* claimed more attention than qualities that surrealists could accept without hesitation as, according to their own lights, poetic.

No more than Aragon and Soupault, apparently, did André Breton foresee that changing circumstances could strip Apollinaire gradually of an influence so deeply felt by those who had launched the surrealist movement. Today, of course, it may appear inevitable that the picture of Apollinaire should have undergone some modification, regardless of Breton's preeminence among surrealists in France right up to his death in 1966. Proof that some modification, in fact, did take place is of special interest all the same. For examination of the evidence raises a question having to do with something more important, now, than just the fate of Apollinaire's reputation in surrealism. If Apollinaire's writings have not stood the test of time, in the climate of surrealism, can we expect the text laid as the cornerstone of surrealism—the *Manifeste du Surréalisme*—to have fared any better? Does this question seem specious? We may persuade ourselves easily enough that there is no good reason to raise it: after all, from the first, Apollinaire's writings were seen, in surrealism, as providing, at most, suggestive points of departure for inquiry; Breton's manifesto, in contrast, was written to lay down a firm platform upon which the structure of surrealism would be erected. Breton's was not an external text, offering stimulating parallels, liable in time to lose their attractivness somewhat. If the first surrealist manifesto were to lose its appeal, as Apollinaire's work finally did, then, it seems, the only conclusion open to us would be that surrealism had changed direction sufficiently for the *Manifeste du Surréalisme* to have ceased being an authoritative statement about surrealist ambitions. No such dramatic reorientation has taken place over the years. Nevertheless, there is still something to be learned from asking why and in what ways the *Manifesto of Surrealism* has survived as a seminal influence upon surrealism, far beyond the frontiers of France.

Manifeste du Surréalisme

Reconsidered from a distance at once comfortable and safe,
any document of importance in the history of ideas is likely
to elicit condescension as often as admiration. *The Manifesto
of Surrealism* presents one distinguishing feature which
hardly makes it unique among documents of this nature,
yet still merits emphasis. When it appeared in 1924, it succeeded in inspiring, among critics anyway, more condescension than anything else, and continued, generally speaking, to do so for a long time. This fact lends weight to the
question with which it seems fitting to begin: Has the moment come at last, more than a half-century later, when
someone who has not participated in the surrealist venture
can feel admiration for Breton's manifesto, and even con-
fess publicly to doing so?

It is true that, as time goes by, we hear praise of surrealism voiced more and more frequently, and from various
quarters. Sometimes, though, our impression is that surrealism at last appears to have earned the right to grudging
approval because, as everyone agrees, it is not in good taste
to speak ill of the dead, but nevertheless reassuring, in some
cases, to remind ourselves of their passing. At other times,
it looks as if a number of those who confidently take upon
themselves to comment on society and the art it fosters have
made the belated discovery of surrealism's presence in the
twentieth century and are determined not to give posterity
the opportunity to condemn them for having ignored it
altogether. Then, too, there are those who, apparently bent
on smothering surrealism with their attentions, generously
credit it with having touched just about every aspect of our
lives. Into this category fall commentators who gravely cap
their tribute to surrealism as a vital force with the supposedly persuasive observation that even the gentle art of commercial advertising betrays the influence of surrealism these
days—as though the launching of the surrealist movement,
marked by the appearance of Breton's manifesto, were somewhat comparable to the discovery of electricity.

Exactly because people can get away with this sort of

thing, my guess is that the answer to the question raised a moment ago is probably negative. It is in the very nature of surrealism to draw a firm distinction between initiate and outsider. Hence we cannot appreciate the true significance of the surrealist manifesto without beginning by considering what it represents within the context of surrealist aspirations, rather than within that of art and literature, where critics feel entitled to impose their demands and occasionally manage to do so with success.

Our perspective on the *Manifeste du Surréalisme* will be a distorted one, so long as we have failed to see that Breton's purpose in writing it was to issue a call to arms, not lay down a rigid battle plan, arrogantly assumed by its author, and by those who shared his views, to be equal to the task of coping with any contingency the future might bring. An interpretation that treats the 1924 text as authority for regarding surrealism as a static rather than a dynamic phenomenon is, whether deliberately or not, twisting its meaning. The proponents of such an interpretation are guilty of grave injustice to André Breton and to the ambitions he sought to bring into focus. By the same token, anyone who seeks to discredit Breton, his manifesto, and the movement it formally launched, by the expedient of referring to the *Manifesto of Surrealism* solely with the aim of highlighting in later surrealist practice departures from theory as formulated there (one thinks, first of all no doubt, of the vexing question of the part played over the years by automatism in surrealist creative effort)—such a person is paying tribute, inadvertently to be sure, to the remarkable vitality from which surrealism has drawn strength.

The first manifesto simply marked the opening of surrealist activities according to a concerted plan, but by no means a binding one. It codified ideas that had been in gestation for up to half a decade, and it gave a sense of unified purpose to forms of protest and exploration, already tried out (in some instances within the loose framework provided by Dada in France), projected, or just anticipated. Of course, it marked, too, the opening of the surrealist hunting season, which seems likely to continue so long as there are sportsmen to be found, blessed with inaccurate aim and blank cartridges.

Although it placed immediate trust in certain modes of inquiry, invested with special prestige at that time, Breton's 1924 text by no means limited surrealist action to these directions only. Nor did it preclude additional or even quite different methods for prospecting the surreal. Indeed, displaying that noteworthy lucidity for which he has received all too little credit, André Breton himself warned against the dangers of *poncifs*—of creating a surrealist stereotype—at the very moment when, in the interest of uncovering the surreal, he was recommending that the real be approached and handled in certain ways:

> I do not believe in the early establishment of a surrealist stereotype.[11] The characteristics common to all texts of this kind, among which are those I have just cited and many others which only rigorous and grammatical analysis could make available to us, do not preclude a certain evolution in time, for surrealist prose. Coming after numerous attempts to which I have devoted myself in the last five years and most of which I indulgently judge to be extremely disordered, the short tales that make up the rest of this volume [Breton is referring to his automatic texts *Poisson soluble*] furnish me with glowing proof of this. (pp. 56–57)

One thing the *Manifesto of Surrealism* did very well, so making a serious claim on the attention of its readers in the mid-twenties, was to focus on several basic human needs, no better satisfied today than then, under the living conditions imposed by western society. At first glance it could appear that the impact made by what Breton had to say came, above all, from his proposals for meeting these needs. It takes closer acquaintance both with the manifesto itself and with the history of surrealism since 1924 to persuade us that the immediate proposals—including the much debated theory of verbal automatism—have been of less lasting influence, really, than Breton's urgent insistence that the needs these proposals were designed to help meet are legitimate, and must be recognized as such. The vigor of the first surrealist manifesto owes much to its author's conviction that these needs never can be set aside as inadmissible, that, on the contrary, each individual has the right to seek their satisfaction, together with the privilege of doing so by whatever means he deems appropriate.

The first surrealist manifesto is not a program for revolutionizing art and literature, but an appeal for a revision of human values. In other words, the treatment it has received from most commentators—more important still, the perspective in which it has been viewed from outside the surrealist circle—limits its scope to the point where its meaning is radically changed. So it is that much in the program Breton wished to outline is lost on those who know no more of his text than that it supplies a conveniently quotable definition, a few lines long:

> SURREALISM, n. Pure psychic automatism by which we propose to express, either verbally, or in writing, or in any other manner, the true functioning of thought. Thought dictated, in the absence of all control exercised by reason, outside all aesthetic and moral preoccupations.
> ENCYCL. *Philos.* Surrealism rests on belief in the higher reality of certain forms of association neglected heretofore, in the all-power of dreaming, in the disinterested play of thought. It tends to ruin definitively all other psychic mechanisms and to take their place in resolving the principal problems of life. (p. 40)

In fact, the trouble begins with this definition and, more especially, with the narrow interpretation commentators have felt entitled to place on it. The definition in Breton's manifesto, so frequently quoted (as though it says all there is to know about surrealism and as though, too, it carries its own refutation within itself) is somewhat like the tip of an iceberg. Its real value is that it marks, above the water line, the presence of something of far greater proportions beneath the surface.

There are times, indeed, when it seems especially regrettable that André Breton did not heed Mallarmé's warning about the limitations of naming things. There are certainly moments when—aggravating though the consequences would have been for so many people—one could wish that, while speaking of surrealism, Breton had refused to define it so closely, just as Péret refused to define the marvelous, even though he saw it as "the heart and nervous system of all poetry."[12] For what happens, when the *Manifeste du Surréalisme* falls into the hands of art critics and literary commentators? Bent over Breton's text, many such people give themselves up to examination of a document in which they are attentive to the "letter" of surrealism. Even those who do so in good faith seem reluctant to take the hint from Breton's statement, within the manifesto itself, that Guillaume Apollinaire, to whom he was indebted for the word *surréalisme*, possessed the "letter" of surrealism, but not its "spirit." Admitting that it might have been better to borrow from Gérard de Nerval the word *supernaturalisme* —although Breton does not mention the fact, this would have meant recognizing that surrealists wished to go a step farther than Emile Zola—Breton observed:

> It seems, indeed, that Nerval possessed to a marvelous degree *the spirit* with which we claim kinship, Apollinaire having possessed, on the other hand, only *the letter*, still imperfect, of surrealism and having proved to be powerless to give us a theoretical glimpse of it that could hold our attention. (p. 39)

In spite of all this, the message of surrealism is plainly legible. It can be read, though, only by someone willing to seek the spirit behind the letter of its definition.

Now, as Robert Champigny has demonstrated efficiently enough, the definition of surrealism consigned to

Breton's manifesto uses reasonable language in a way unreasonable.[13] Cogently argued and objectively formulated, Champigny's objections set off the fundamental difference between the language of criticism, utilized at the highest lovel of responsibility, and language as surrealism calls for its use. To Champigny, language is an instrument perfected by reason, its application reasonably governed. To Breton and those for whom he spoke in his *Manifeste du Surréalisme*, language employed only within reasonable bounds is language misapplied.

Clearly there is a paradox here from which surrealism has never escaped altogether. It is a paradox that carries a heavy penalty. This we see when the surrealist idea of poetry is confused so often with literary ideals, and then subjected to evaluation by standards in which the surrealists themselves have neither faith nor interest. Looking back from his *Second Manifesto of Surrealism*, originally published in the last issue of *La Révolution surréaliste*, André Breton was to remark, when referring to the question of social action, as seen from the perspective of surrealism:

> The problem of social action is, I make a point of returning to this and insisting upon it, but one of the forms of a more general problem that surrealism has set about raising and which is *that of human expression in all its forms*. Whoever says expression says, to begin with, language. There is no reason to be surprised, then, at seeing surrealism place itself first almost exclusively on the plane of language, nor should it be surprising to see it return to that plane, after whatever foray it may be, as though for the pleasure of behaving there as in conquered territory. (p. 183)

All the same, neither in the *Second Manifeste* nor elsewhere was Breton ever to arrive at a solution, clear and unambiguous to all, with respect to the problem of how to make the public aware of the difference between language used surrealistically and the language of literature.

It was not that Breton knowingly promoted confusion in this regard. On the contrary, some of the far-reaching consequences of the surrealist conception of language can be detected already in his manifesto of 1924, where, I have suggested, the most important features of what he has to tell us elude detection by the process of linguistic analysis to which Champigny feels fully entitled to resort. Here we face another paradox that can hardly escape notice, one which can leave us wondering whether André Breton was indulging in a hoax or whether he fell victim to his own system.

In turning to the manifesto form, regardless of whether he intended merely to follow habits encouraged by association with Dada, Breton was borrowing a mode of verbal communication that supposedly owes its persuasiveness—its very *raison d'être*—to the reasonable clarity of its dialectical presentation. Apparently, then, this is a paradox just as insurmountable as the other. All the same, there is reason to believe Breton had more success in dealing with it. More than this, when addressing himself to the problem he had created for himself, he managed to demonstrate, within the manifesto itself, that the message of surrealism owes its force to the spirit rather than the language of its definition.

True, as we watch Robert Champigny meticulously and expertly uncovering the weaknesses of Breton's logic, the abuses, if we may call them so, to which he treats deductive language, as we see Champigny lay bare certain inconsistencies to be noted in the progression of the argument upon which the very idea of surrealism appears to rest, we observe in action a rigorously reasonable mind, intent upon demolishing a structure in which it can place no credence. But if this were all there was to it, we should be left with the simple and less-than-satisfactory alternative of belief or disbelief, of blind support for Breton's ideas or rejection of them. And this means we should be either lining up behind Champigny or pretending he has never opened the *Manifeste du Surréalisme*. Confronting Breton's text and Champigny's strictures has something important to show us, however. For, when contemplating the unbridgeable distance separating the author of the surrealist manifestoes from his critic, we glimpse what André Breton really meant when he asserted, "Language has been given man so that he may make surrealist use of it" (p. 48). Without intending to do so, Champigny has done the *Manifesto of Surrealism* a valuable service.

The weaknesses reason brings to light, those all-too-evident breaks in logical sequence, are less significant as signs of dialectical inadequacy or muddy thinking than as proof that the *Manifeste du Surréalisme* was never intended to measure up to the demands of reasonable argument. Thus the excitement Breton's text is capable of generating in the mind of a surrealist is not stimulated by persuasive deduction at all. It comes directly from the spectacle of successive intuitive leaps, taken with no display of caution (there was in André Breton an odd mixture of self-importance and humility) in a direction which such a mind, tired of society and its ways (including its literary and artistic ways), already is predisposed to follow. In a very literal sense, Breton can be said to have practiced what he preached. More precisely, perhaps, he preached by example, not precept, while yet adopting a form of expression he appeared to have chosen with the relatively uncomplicated purpose of setting forth a theory.

One cannot go so far, exactly, as to say the *Manifesto of Surrealism* carries within it its own defense, or even attempts to do this. Such a contention would reduce Breton's achievement to a cleverly conceived plan, quite expertly carried out. But it does seem, nevertheless, that this is a text which—without even trying to do so—sets itself outside criticism. Generally acknowledged standards of critical appraisal do not apply here. They are struck with irrelevance. Meanwhile the appeal of the manifesto, to those it invites into the surrealist circle, is sufficiently compelling to make all reservations look superfluous.

Examined from this point of view, the first manifesto is no exception among André Breton's writings. It explores, to be sure, some of the major themes its authors and others will take up subsequently in the name of surrealism. More than this, though, it illustrates the manner in which Breton invariably will respond to these themes. Thus in the *Manifesto of Surrealism* Breton really only adopts the *posture* of someone devoted to the defense of ideas important to him, while in fact he believes these to be self-evident and incontrovertible truths that, so long as they have been firmly stated, need no supporting argument to impress the reader with their validity. In this important respect, Breton's writing in the first manifesto—the demands he makes upon language—is different in no way at all from his writing in *Les Vases communicants* (1932), shall we say, or in *L'Amour fou* (1937). Gravity, a certain weightiness—these characteristic features of his language are never called upon to serve a carefully controlled argument, painstakingly followed through. Instead, they regularly are placed at the disposal of an intuitive interpretation of human destiny, which no evidence to the contrary can either halt or cause to falter. Breton's grandly structured sentences advance imperturbably across the pages of the 1924 manifesto just as they will do, twenty years later, in *Arcane 17*.

Are we beginning to wander from the point, to lose sight of the central text that is supposed to be commanding our attention behind others which followed it? Hardly, Breton's subsequent writings enable us to place the first surrealist manifesto in the light under which surrealists view it.

Benjamin Péret, the greatest of surrealist poets, wrote comparatively little of a theoretical nature on the subject of poetry. To Péret, evidently, creation and commentary were separate activities, exerting unequal attraction. Breton, in contrast, theorized as he created, and created as he theorized—his presentation of the idea that diurnal experience and dreaming are communicating vessels in *Les Vases communicants*, for example, or his development of the concept of mad love, in *L'Amour fou*. André Breton never felt the need to draw a line between theory and practice, even in that initial formulation of basic ideas issued as a manifesto.

This is one of the most important discoveries the first surrealist manifesto has to share with those who really hear its message: the fascination of language lies in its being a less-than-adequate instrument and, at the same time, the most readily available means by which man may assert his freedom from controls, socio-political, ethical, moral, literary, and artistic. Obviously, Breton's manifesto was not the first document, nor will it be the last, to celebrate the tantalizing potential of language and its disappointing limitations. Its special value, at least for many of those it has helped draw into surrealist activity, lies in the tension it establishes between hope and despair (the fundamental tension on which surrealist effort rests, after all), in the excitement released beneath the surface of a text that, at first sight, looks to be far more indebted than it really is to the demands of reasonable discourse—and therefore, in Breton's eyes anyway, condemned to failure—and which, then, owes its magnetism to forces reasonable disputation can do nothing to invalidate.

There is, in the *Manifesto of Surrealism*, a passage that receives but limited development, and indeed seems not quite in place. This is a section where special emphasis is given the surrealist possibilities of dialog. Nothing later in the text appears to justify its presence, and Breton seems inclined to neglect to draw definite conclusions from it. What is its importance, then? It would be going too far to contend that this passage found its way into the manifesto simply because André Breton wanted to place in his reader's hands a key for opening the meaning of the *Manifeste* as a whole. Even so, his remarks on the nature of surrealist dialog do assist us in arriving at a fuller understanding of the function served by the manifesto, as seen from within the surrealist movement.

Discussing dialog, Breton tacitly admits one of the weaknesses of verbal exchange, when he acknowledges that, uttering a statement, the speaker is denied ultimate control over the effect it will produce in a listener. For that very reason, though, language possesses a capacity for exciting stimulus: the statement uttered now takes on value from the effect it has upon the listener—an effect the speaker cannot predict with complete accuracy. Each statement, in other words, is but a point of departure for response which, in its turn, offers a starting point for further response. Hence as dialog progresses, Breton intimates, so the weaknesses of language recede before its strengths. Moreover—and this is the most enlightening aspect of all in what the surrealist manifesto has to tell us about dialog—those strengths impress themselves upon us most when (as during a conversation between a mentally disturbed patient and his doctor) a statement elicits a response that is not confined within the bounds of reasonable sequence (pp. 49–50).

What this means is that Champigny's inability to enter into a dialog with Breton owes nothing at all to bad faith on his part. It is entirely predictable, because inevitable. This is not to say that the only response to his manifesto Breton would have found acceptable is an incoherent one, or that he wrote specifically for madmen. But it does mean that whatever satisfaction someone derives from the *Manifeste*, by attempting to respond to it in the language of reason, this is not the same satisfaction reserved by Breton's text for those prepared to imitate the people named therein (p. 40) as having given proof of "ABSOLUTE SURREALISM."

Since he viewed man as being, once and for all, a dreamer—stating as much in the second sentence of his *Manifesto of Surrealism*—André Breton really could not be expected to have tried to make contact with others, except in the language of dreams. There is no place for misunderstanding here, since to a surrealist the language of dreaming is that of desire seeking satisfaction, of aspiration reaching out for fulfillment. This then is the language Breton speaks most directly, both to those already committed to surrealism and to those whom his monolog in manifesto form is able to draw into fruitful unscripted dialog.

The *Manifeste du Surréalisme* continues to stand as an act of faith. It still communicates Breton's confidence in the resonance his words can find in the minds of others, in that echo which, in spite of everything, justifies reliance upon words. His trust in the future which, for him, gave meaning to what otherwise would be merely the vanity of believing one can reach a public by means of the written word, is entirely in keeping with Breton's optimistic assurance that surrealism "is what will be." Indeed, as exemplified in the first surrealist manifesto, it clarifies this affirmation, by confirming that the full flowering of surrealism is not to be sought in a statement like the *Manifesto*, but in the response it solicits.

Has reconsideration of Breton's first manifesto really done nothing more than bring us up against a truism? One writes, and André Breton freely admitted this, to find an audience. All the same, the distinctive emphasis placed on communication, effected at the extra-reasonable level that surrealism makes its own, saved Breton from self-contradiction, when publishing a manifesto while yet firmly convinced that "it is absolutely necessary to keep the public from *coming in* if one wishes to avoid confusion."[14] The public, that large majority of the reading population only too content with life in contemporary society, and with the satisfactions it provides, must be kept always at a distance: at no less a distance, incidentally, than art critics and professors of literature. To such people, the *Manifesto of Surrealism* does have something to say, naturally, because its medium is language. Yet we can be sure that, however much admiration or condescension it releases in them, their response will reflect reaction to the letter of the manifesto. To this extent, objections raised, reservations expressed, disagreements voiced appear, from the surrealist point of view, to tell more about the limitations of the reader than about the spirit of the text under scrutiny. And, as André Breton was hardly the first to point out, it is the spirit that quickeneth. . .

Let us suppose, at this point, that someone who, before opening this book, had no knowledge of surrealism has
read this far and now pauses to take stock. By no means
have all his questions about where surrealism is headed been
answered yet. He decides, therefore, that it would be wise
to check his impressions against first-hand evidence, with
the hope of clarifying them. While doing so, he happens
upon two statements that seem to be in conflict, both made
by André Breton. One is this tribute to Jacques Vaché: "But
for him, I would have been a poet." The other is the beginning of a sentence in the *Manifeste du Surréalisme:* "Poetic
surrealism, to which I am devoting this study. . . ." The sense
of contradiction precipitated by these two phrases brings
into focus several questions about the poetics of surrealism
still unresolved, although the elements of an answer to each
are in our hands already.

On June 24, 1917, Vaché attempted to sabotage the
première of *Les Mamelles de Tirésias*, which he condemned,
so Breton reports in *Les Pas Perdus* (p. 21), as "too literary."
An estimate of the degree of influence exerted by Vaché over
the young Breton can be made most accurately if we take
guidance from this sign of disapproval. To a notable extent,
the influence of Vaché, whose acquaintance Breton made at
the beginning of the year (1916) when, no more than five
months later, he was to meet Apollinaire for the first time,
takes on the characteristics of a counter-influence, when
considered beside the reputation enjoyed by Apollinaire
among the future founders of surrealism. In 1916 Breton
still entertained a conception of poetry derived from the
Symbolism of Mallarmé. Mocking the aspirations cherished
by André Breton, Jacques Vaché would introduce him, ironically, as André Salmon, at that time associate of Guillaume
Apollinaire, Max Jacob, and Pablo Picasso. Thus it was in
leading Breton to question the validity of a literary career
and, finally, to ponder the question of the usefulness of literature itself that Vaché can be said to have cured him of
wanting to be "a poet," in the Symbolist tradition. This is

why in *Entretiens* Breton will draw a highly significant parallel between Jacques Vaché and des Esseintes, in Huysmans' *A Rebours:* "His 'à rebours' was practiced under conditions of surveillance such, with such meticulousness, though, that a kind of avenging suppressed laughter, yes purely internal, would crackle in his footsteps" (p. 26).

Although none of the others involved with Breton in launching surrealism felt the influence of Vaché quite as deeply as he did, it is scarcely an exaggeration to say that, had they all been equally and earnestly attentive to what Vaché had to say, then Apollinaire would have been treated with less respect in surrealism than he enjoyed for quite some time. Certainly, it is not going too far to say that, where assessment of his literary merits was concerned, in their evaluation of Apollinaire surrealists found themselves from the very first applying criteria handed down by Vaché, via Breton. In fact, the only definite changes we have been able to detect, when asking how succeeding generations of surrealists have looked upon Apollinaire's work, are the direct consequences of an increasingly rigorous application of standards in which Vaché encouraged Breton to place his faith. Indeed, if it were not for the lessons Breton learned from observing Vaché—who refrained from all literary activity, leaving after his death only a slim collection of letters, assembled, naturally, by Breton[15]—we should have real difficulty understanding how a surrealist can deprecate in Apollinaire's writings the work of the man of letters, while yet praising their poetic quality. For, at first sight, the surrealists' distinction between poetry and literature appears to be so finely drawn as to tempt us into concluding that surrealism invests poetry with a meaning either too esoteric or too elusive for the practical purposes of identification, too private, in fact, to be of any interest outside the limits within which surrealists confine their activities.

Once we begin looking at surrealism this way, the whole question of the nature of surrealist poetics undergoes distortion. Our point of departure leads us into conducting our inquiry in the wrong directions. We end up gathering incomplete evidence, at most, and are likely to pass over some very pertinent testimony. We progress better, at all events, if we grasp the importance of a conviction underlying the writings of the first surrealists, the *Manifeste du Surréalisme* included, which has never been questioned over the years. This is the conviction that separating poetry from literature means rescuing poetry from the pernicious effects of literary tradition and ambition, freeing it so it can address itself to pressing needs which validate poetic effort. Thus the ambiguities in Apollinaire's writings which, once the magnetism of his presence had ceased to make itself felt, began drawing increasingly sharp criticism from surrealists, are significantly expressive of traditionalist respect, both for the external form of the poem and for conventionality in its content (the "Verlaine side" of Apollinaire's verse, as Dhainaut called it).

This has been the particular advantage of reviewing what surrealists have thought of Guillaume Apollinaire over the years, rather than their opinions of the work of a figure universally admired among them, and without reservation, Isidore Ducasse, Comte de Lautréamont. For in Lautréamont's *Les Chants de Maldoror* and *Poésies* no exemplary struggle is manifest between poetry and literature, as surrealists feel it imperative to differentiate the two. Hence Lautréamont continues to be not so much a signal rocket, like Apollinaire, but—to borrow the fine metaphor proposed by Baudelaire, a *phare*—a beacon, a veritable lighthouse by which the surrealist poet navigates as, disenchanted with established poetic traditions and totally without faith in respected literary models, he ventures away from the familiar coastline.[16]

It goes without saying that further evidence still is needed to substantiate the distinction surrealists draw between poetry and literature. But first we must take the preliminary step of acknowledging this distinction as having been made firmly and purposefully, from the earliest surrealist writings onward. Anyone who fails to realize this is the case must face his own reluctance to credit Breton with meaning exactly what he said, when insisting in his first manifesto that surrealists propose to express the true functioning of thought, not only verbally and in writing, but "in any other manner" as well.

A Language of Intelligent Revolt

BEFORE POETRY, as surrealists understand it, can find full and free expression, certain obstacles have to be removed. These include traditionally respected barriers which, surrealists are convinced confine it, very often to the point where it must become inaccessible to us, separating us altogether from the poetic experience. This is why, when alluding in his *Manifeste du Surréalisme* to what he termed "the true functioning of thought," André Breton tacitly questioned the value of thought, as we customarily speak of its operation. Surely, the special prestige of automatism, among first-generation surrealists especially, is that it appeared to demonstrate the feasibility of escaping the rigorous control exercised by reason over the organization of verbal statements. Automatic writing, in other words, represented one promising form of escape, expected to make possible expansion of the poetic domain well beyond the limits within which, for the most part any way, poetic practice in the past appeared to have confined itself submissively.

Automatism, dream transcription, mediumistic trance —the well-publicized paraphernalia of early surrealism—all testify eloquently to the first surrealists' eager inclination to give unreason the attention denied it by reason and to see in denial of rationality a prerequisite for at least some modes of poetic inquiry. As a result, outsiders have generalized on the basis of apparently persuasive evidence, identifying surrealism primarily, not to say exclusively, with promotion of the supposed virtues of irrationality over rationalist processes such as are taken to be typical of the scientific mode of investigation with which, from its inception, surrealism showed itself to be in violent disagreement.

Now, there seems at first little injustice in viewing surrealism from this angle. Did not a leading surrealist of the founder group refer to efforts made from time to time to draw poetry and art into the field of science, saying forcefully, "the enterprise has always failed and will fail again, because poetry and art live fully in intuition, by and for intuition, and their means of action is imagination"?[1] Indeed, Péret's comments on this subject merit longer quotation. Their essential import seems clear enough already, though. And if any doubt subsisted in our minds, we should have only to consult his poetic writings, notably his *Histoire naturelle*, to dissipate them altogether. Everything he wrote bears witness to Péret's contempt for "the deforming prism of rationalist education."[2] However, it shows too that oversimplification can deform in its way, just as much as surrealists believe reason does. *La Parole est à Péret* vigorously attacks the "artificial opposition between poetic thought and logical thought, between rational and irrational thought."[3]

This is not the moment to embark on a discussion of the special contribution made by Benjamin Péret to surrealism. It *is* the moment, however, to recognize that, when we speak of surrealism's program as taking definition in sharp opposition to scientific inquiry, we risk interpreting it as having tried to do no more than follow a trend familiar in early-twentieth-century Europe, a trend which developed naturally, even necessarily, it seems to some, after the collapse of confidence in science, fostered in late-nineteenth-century literature by contemporary philosophical thought. To do this amounts to seeing surrealist writing as scarcely more than a set of variations on the themes of Paul Bourget's

Le Disciple. Yet the surrealists are not conformists. Nor are they simply pretentious or even foolhardy *littérateurs.* We shall see in a moment that Péret's stance before logical thought was quite in keeping with surrealism's distinctive approach to experience. To begin with, let us acknowledge that, if his outlook is to prove to be representative of that of most influential surrealists, this can only be because, from the first, all surrealists shared the same ambition: to explore reality by the best means available to them, both the outer reality of the world in which we all find ourselves and the inner reality of our relationship to that world and to those we encounter there.

This is a necessary starting point for further examination of the nature and scope of surrealist poetry. For the latter cannot be delineated with any semblance of fidelity so long as we deny surrealists the right to speak of poetry as a form of investigation that nothing obliges them to circumscribe within the narrow framework of written and spoken language.

Habit and inherited assumptions induce in most of us the belief that speaking of poetry means being concerned, and exclusively concerned, with the use of language in certain more or less prescribed forms. And this prejudice survives even in the minds of those who, while gladly granting the poet the right to as much formal liberty as he may claim, yet ask of his writing that it *make sense.* The transition from habitual thinking on the subject of poetry to reflection on surrealist poetry seems to be facilitated, it is true, by the following. Aragon, Breton, and Eluard—those whose names come to mind with least delay, when most people hear surrealist poetry mentioned—all explored the potentialities of the language medium. Significantly enough, though, the name of Péret does not figure by any means on everyone's list of surrealist poets. For Péret treated language in ways which, generally speaking, find acceptance with far more difficulty than those favored by his fellow surrealists of the first generation. And because of this, his methods earned him, among the surrealists themselves, an enviable reputation as a writer possessed of unrivalled poetic qualities. The point, of course, is that, if André Breton deserves to be remembered as a major surrealist poet, then so does Benjamin Péret. So also does the painter Joan Miró, to say nothing of the film director Luis Buñuel or of Jean Arp, who was at one and the same time painter, sculptor, collagist, and artist with words.

Anyone who now finds himself resisting extension of the meaning of poetry, to the point where the title of poet may be conferred upon surrealists whose chosen or preferred medium is not that of the written word, has fallen victim to some of the most persistent fallacies current with respect to surrealist practice. One of these in particular demands our attention at this stage, the one that, fittingly, Péret has isolated for us. Until we have established how and why it represents an erroneous view of surrealism, we shall find it difficult to progress toward fuller understanding of the poetics of surrealism. This is the fallacy taking its origins in a false assumption we can summarize as follows: surrealists have always been so devoted to the irrational that they can see no merit in the rational. Thus they discard logic and are incapable of applying intelligence to solving the problems preoccupying them. Expanding upon Péret's observation in *La Parole est à Péret*, two texts especially serve to prove this assumption unfounded and give the lie to the fallacy it has generated. Written by leading exponents of surrealist theory, André Breton and Paul Nougé, who certainly had their differences regarding the best ways to advance surrealist ambitions, these publications evidence fundamental agreement through statements radically different in nature—the one a private diary, not meant for publication, the other the preface to an anthology of other men's writings—that is proof in itself of the significance for the surrealist enterprise of the posture adopted independently by the French spokesman and by the Belgian.

ANDRÉ BRETON: *Anthologie de l'Humour noir*
In an important discussion of the idea of black humor, the
surrealist Annie Le Brun gives due emphasis to the significance of an anthology André Breton first put together in
1940 and issued in its definitive form in 1966:

> However, at a time when the notion of black humor, under-
> stood within its most restricted limits, is enjoying immense
> favor, when black humor is a fashion, when we are witnessing
> inflation of the macabre joke, and as a consequence inevitable
> neutralization of the idea of black humor, it seems that . . .
> this anthology stands today, paradoxically, at the opposite
> pole from an idea of black humor circulating commercially,
> and that this book plays the role of violently contradicting
> everything that is trying to make of black humor a new kind
> of joke that sells well.[4]

Annie Le Brun spares us confusion as we head for the territory of black humor, first explored by Breton. She does so,
incidentally, while still stressing, "no doubt, it is no more
possible to define humor than poetry" (p. 100). The intention here is not to follow in her footsteps, but to consider an
underlying unifying element, concealed beneath the diversity of evidence brought together in Breton's anthology.

Following the lead of Sigmund Freud, André Breton
speaks of humor in the *Anthologie de l'Humour noir* as a
"process permitting us to brush aside reality in what is most
painful about it" (p. 360). His preference goes naturally to
those writers whose work reveals the application of this
process, having as its primary function either to express the
need to set reality aside or to express a need, no less urgent,
to break its hold. He observes apropos of Charles Cros, for
example, "The pure playfulness of certain quite fanciful
parts of his work must not make us forget a revolver is
trained in the center of some of the finest of Cros's poems"
(pp. 207–208).

Expressing his admiration for Cros, Breton remarks,
"The freshness of his intelligence is such that nothing which
is the object of desire seems to him *a priori* utopian, that he
feels less than anyone, in terms of what is, an interdict

weighing upon what *is not* (in his eyes *is not yet*)" (p. 206). At this stage, this estimate of Cros's gifts seems to suggest no more than the happy coincidence of two elements the 1924 *Manifeste du Surréalisme* might have led us to suppose that Breton and other surrealists considered mutually exclusive: desire and intelligence. Our impression that the coincidence we have noted is of no special importance appears to find support, in fact, in the admission made by Breton, while discussing Raymond Roussel in his anthology, that pure psychic automatism, in which the first manifesto placed so much faith, "does not claim to designate anything but an ultimate state which would demand of man the total loss of the logical and moral control of his acts" (p. 382). With what justification, then, can Breton commend Cros's intelligence, and approve the "mechanism of intellectual subversion" which he argues Cros, Germain Nouveau, Rimbaud, and even Verlaine contributed to developing (p. 274)? How, in short, did Breton regard intelligence, and what role did he reserve for it in the pursuit of surrealist aims? These are questions to which no book of Breton's responds quite so directly as the *Anthologie de l'Humour noir*.

At first glance, Breton's respect for Cros's intelligence presents a paradox. This paradox has its counterpart in the writings of Fourier, whom Breton was to learn to admire enough to compose an *Ode à Charles Fourier*. We find him noting in his *Anthologie:*

> The commentators most disposed to praise him and even the most enthusiastic adepts of his economic and social system have agreed in deploring in Fourier wandering thoughts and imagination, have not known what to do to conceal the "wild nonsense" in which he took pleasure, have glossed over the "fantastic and rambling" aspect of his thought, so magnificently controlled most of the time. How to explain the coexistence in one and the same mind of the most eminent rational gifts and of taste for vaticination taken to its extreme limits? (p. 85)

Of course the same kind of paradox strikes readers who feel sure Breton's preference went invariably to the irrational, when they find the *Anthologie de l'Humour noir* treating intellectual power with respect. The parallel seems close indeed, as Breton recalls how both Marx and Engels praised the nineteenth-century thinker, Fourier. We have cause to listen carefully, therefore, when Breton asks: "How did Fourier at the same time satisfy such demands and disconcert almost all those who came near him, with his vertiginous flights right into the zone of the unverifiable and the marvelous?" (p. 86).

Naturally, Breton's answer is meant to apply only to Fourier's work. We shall find it instructive, all the same.

For André Breton, the answer to the question we have heard him pose is to be sought in Fourier's proclamation of the absolute necessity to "remake human understanding and to forget what has been learned." More especially, Breton's anthology of black humor shares with us his belief that the full answer lies in the interpretation he himself places upon Fourier's program, as summarized in the phrase just cited, "which demands that we attack universal assent and that we finish with what is alleged to be 'good sense'" (pp. 87–88).[5]

We have now reached the core of the explanation Breton has to offer for the paradox of Fourier, "this brain in which hyper-lucidity and extreme rigor, on the plane of social criticism are allied, on the transcendental plane, with complete license in conjecture" (p. 89). Clearly Breton was to feel strongly the attraction exerted by the example set by Fourier's work, in which *rigueur* and *toute-licence* functioned side by side in fruitful coexistence. His unhesitating approval of the duality noticeable in Fourier draws our attention to a noteworthy trend in his own thinking. This must be clarified if we are to comprehend the significance Breton attached to black humor and the part he felt intelligence plays in its practice.

Toward the end of the preface to the *Anthologie de l'Humour noir* Breton castigates "jokes without gravity," asserting that black humor is *"par excellence* the mortal enemy of sentimentality that seems perpetually on its last legs . . . and of a certain short-term fancy, which passes itself off too often as poetry, persists very much in vain in wanting to submit the mind to its crumbling artifices" (pp. 21–22). Here is one of the major sources of a feeling of unrest that finally led Breton out of Dada when, missing the gravity it was in his nature to require, he had reached the conclusion that, among the Dadaists, he simply was marking time. More than this, Breton's statement alerts us to one of the criteria by which he judged and approved black humor. Even though it may seem so upon first encounter, black humor is never irresponsible. When selecting material for his anthology, André Breton could claim, he always bore in mind the axiom he quotes with approbation from Pierre Piobb's *Les Mystères des Dieux:* "There is nothing that intelligent humor cannot dissolve in a roar of laughter."

Whereas blindly habitual respect for reason will never cease to appear to surrealists an impediment, intelligence assumes in surrealist practice the value of an instrument, readily available for breaking down the barriers erected by rationality, convention, and educated response. In this connection, the special form of intelligence represented by humor lends itself admirably to serving the cause of surrealism. Nevertheless, the surrealist needs to evoke a higher intelligence, Breton asserts. Without this, humor will remain incapable of effecting the liberation surrealists may demand of it. Therefore those wishing to evaluate black humor correctly and to appreciate its potential benefits for surrealists will progress only very slowly until they understand that, when referring to a higher intelligence, Breton postulates the dissociation of intelligent activity from rationality.

Breton starts out from this assumption: in the world that black humor makes its target, we should be wrong to suppose the existence of fundamental and natural agreement between intelligence and reason. Accordingly, intelligence takes on value when and where it ceases to operate in confirmation of reason's teachings. Only when viewed from the angle Breton recommends can intelligence be seen as capable of taking on the task for which he finds it to be so well suited. This, it goes without saying, is the task of which he is speaking when he commends Hegel. To be sure, André Breton sees black humor as an advance beyond Hegelian objective humor. All the same, he insists, "One can however consider that Hegel has made humor take a decisive step forward into the domain of cognition when reaching the concept of an *objective humor*" (p. 16). Breton's basis for evaluation has become clear enough, now, to leave us in no doubt regarding the origins of his disdain for *la plaisanterie sans gravité*, as we find him praising Léon-Pierre Quint's book *Le Comte de Lautréamont et Dieu* for presenting humor as *"a higher revolt of the mind"* (p. 16).

At this point, the coincidence of *connaissance*—in its dual sense of knowledge and cognition—with *révolte* calls for consideration. Let us start with a comment of Breton's, prompted by some critic's remark that Jonathan Swift "provokes laughter, but without sharing in it." Breton observes in his *Anthologie*, "It is precisely on these terms that humor, in the sense in which we understand it, can externalize the sublime element that according to Freud is inherent in it and transcend the forms of the comic" (p. 26). It is not difficult to see how, in Breton's estimation, transcendence of the purely comic elements is effected in black humor only when one takes advantage of a kind of distance (the convenient French word is *distanciation*) which, as the case of Swift demonstrates, is guaranteed by exercise of a detachment best obtained when the writer has recourse to intelligence. But what is the nature of this transcendence?

Surrealists attach supreme importance to poetic intuition because they believe it to be of a nature to anticipate relationships that the rationalist's view of the world prevents him from perceiving. And so, by the standards set in surrealism, one of the main functions of the poet is to "make cognition take a step forward." It is plain that use of the word "knowledge" goes in surrealist thinking with categorical denial of the demands of reason and of its pretension to delimit not only the known but the knowable. Thus the knowledge to which surrealists aspire reaches out beyond the known toward the hoped for, the *desired*.

In surrealism, then, the function of intelligence, as Breton saw it, is to recognize what has been discovered by means that reason is incapable of admitting. Through use of intelligence, man can expect the practice of black humor to achieve, more effectively and with less delay, the act of surmounting the real. As the *Anthologie de l'Humour noir* speaks of it, transcendence is distinguished by the exercise of intelligence outside the limits to which reason, as it normally controls the operation of intelligent thought, would have us submit. Preaching that the surreal is a higher perception of the real, Breton looked upon utilization of a higher intelligence as the practical means to transform our perception of what experience brings us. Bearing in mind the peculiar resonance which, from *Les Pas perdus* onward, the word *connaissance* has in surrealist statements of purpose, and remembering also how the language of alchemy has left its mark on the vocabulary of Breton and his associates, we cannot but be struck by this remarkable appeal to intelligence, called upon to work against an ordered universe of rational proportions.

In the context presented by Breton's anthology, the role reserved by surrealism for a higher intelligence complements that of poetic intuition. This is why we hear Breton remarking, on the ideas of the Marquis de Sade, "It took nothing less than the will shown by true analysis to extend, by surmounting all prejudices, the field of human knowledge to bring out the fundamental aspirations of his thought" (p. 51). Born of the intelligence in which Breton placed his faith, the aspirations finding expression in Sade's writings result in material significantly defined in the *Anthologie* as "ground favorable to a mutation of life" (p. 64).

Rather than embark at this stage upon an inquiry into Sade's reputation in surrealist circles, let us merely note this. When he speaks of Sade in the *Anthologie de l'Humour noir*, the invocation of intelligence in Breton's effort to surmount what he terms, out of deference to Freud, "the accidents of the *ego*" is no more in doubt, he is convinced, than in the writings of Georg-Christoph Lichtenberg: "*To believe or not to believe*, this dilemma has never been debated in a more pathetic manner, with greater genius, than by a man endowed to a supreme degree with the sense of intellectual quality as Lichtenberg was" (p. 71). And it is Lichtenberg whom Breton credits with having formulated a "special kind of interrogation on the plane of cognition" (p. 72).

It is noteworthy that Breton links Lichtenberg's mode of interrogation with his role as "the very prophet of *chance*, of that chance about which Max Ernst will say that it is the 'master of humor'" (p. 74). Mention of chance here pinpoints the confluence of intelligence and humor, since humor is now located in recognition of the appropriateness of some juxtaposition effected by chance, or in acknowledging the validity of the rationally inappropriate nature of this same juxtaposition. Now we see intelligence act out its fruitful accessory role: produced while reasonable objection is suspended, the gratuitous encounter brought about by chance (verbally in certain surrealist poetic images, or, since Breton has referred to Ernst, in the surrealist pictorial collage) requires the intervention of intelligence before the liberating value of the encounter can be acknowledged and appreciated to the full.

At this stage, intelligence serves to testify to the fact that transcendence of normal rational associations indeed has taken place, by identifying the suitability to surrealism's aims of the phenomenon released by chance. We may go so far as to view the process of setting mundane reality aside —a process to which every surrealist has dedicated himself —as incomplete until its achievements have survived the test of intelligent appraisal.

This, at all events, is what may be inferred from Breton's estimate of Xavier Forneret. "Let us observe," he writes, "that one would attempt in vain to do the author of

Sans titre a disservice, by alleging he was more or less unconscious of or without responsibility for the echoes he
awakens in the impartial and attentive reader, this man who
placed his book under the invocation of this phrase by Para-
celsus: 'Often there is nothing above, everything is beneath,
search'" (p. 165). These remarks on "the Unknown Man of
Romanticism," as Breton calls him, propose a solution to the
conflict that surrealists realize full well results from confrontation of the pleasure principle with the restrictive demands of the so-called real world, at the center of the surrealist's predicament. For Breton alludes discreetly to a form
of intelligence that he evidently considers capable of providing the key to the higher law of which Jean Arp spoke so
frequently.

Breton does not claim the solution in question is attained easily. Nor does he contend it is reached in every
instance. For in dissociating intelligence from reason man
runs a terrible risk, from which several of the authors represented in the *Anthologie de l'Humour noir* failed to escape. The bitter irony of their situation is summed up in
Breton's reference to Baudelaire's "intellectual enfeeble-
ment" and to the "atrocious lucidity" with which Swift
followed the progress of his own mental decline.

When, on the other hand, the humorous resolution
of the conflict between desire and material circumstance is
successfully attained, Breton indicates, it is thanks to the
beneficent intervention of intelligence. Thus the work of
Lewis Carroll provides an excellent example of the satisfactory achievement of release through humor. As Breton
sees it:

> "Nonsense" in Lewis Carroll takes its importance from the
> fact that it constitutes for him the vital solution to a profound
> contradiction between acceptance of faith and exercise of rea-
> son, on one hand; on the other hand, between acute poetic
> consciousness and rigorous professional duties. The special
> characteristic of this solution is that it goes with an objective

> solution, which happens to be of a poetic order: the mind,
> brought up against any kind of difficulty, can find an ideal
> solution in the absurd. (pp. 183–84)

The absurd mentioned here has nothing to do with the form of literature popular in the period between publication of the first edition of Breton's anthology and appearance of the definitive edition. When he refers to the absurd, Breton is looking in a different direction altogether from the one leading to the philosophy of the absurd: "Complaisance where the absurd is concerned opens once again to man the mysterious kingdom where children live. The *play* of childhood, as a lost means for conciliating action and reverie with a view to organic satisfaction, beginning with simple 'word play,' finds itself in this way rehabilitated and dignified." And what is the result? "A systematic recuperation" powerful enough to "threaten the severe and inert world in which it is prescribed that we live."

Perhaps his notes on Carroll take André Breton farthest in describing the use of intelligence deliberately directed against the thought processes with which we usually associate its activity. The "recuperation" sought in surrealism becomes systematic, by this fact endowing intelligence with a poetic role in making it "threaten" the very world it normally persuades us to accept as immutable. "One cannot deny," declares Breton, "that, in Alice's eyes a world of inadvertence, inconsequence and, in a word, of the unsuitable gravitates vertiginously at the centre of the true" (pp. 184–85). Needless to say, surrealists are predisposed to take special delight in the contribution made by intelligence in provoking the fascination of vertigo. "All those who retain a sense of revolt," Breton concludes, "will recognize in Lewis Carroll the first instructor they had when they stayed away from school" (p. 185).

In black humor, intelligence conducts us through two stages of experience, first by casting doubt upon the stability of the real, then by affirming, or at least testifying to, the existence of something beyond the control of contingent reality—hence the importance Breton attaches to the work of yet another nineteenth-century writer, Villiers de l'Isle-Adam. Here, he argues:

> a fundamental doubt lays siege to the reality principle, tending to make the presented forms of life lose the despotic character they generally assume, in such a manner that human existence is grasped in its continual becoming. This strictly Hegelian attitude on Villiers's part cannot fail to bring with it a certain disaffection with regard to his own time, to upset the philosophical equilibrium to the advantage of what does not exist in the present. Past and future monopolize all the intellectual faculties and faculties for feeling in the poet, detached from the immediate spectacle. They are two quite transparent philters, from the moment when one ceases to let oneself be hypnotized by the muddy precipitate that makes up the world of today. (p. 197)

Breton's suggestion in the preface to the *Anthologie de l'Humour noir* that black humor is "a *higher revolt of the mind*" (p. 16) is no empty phrase. This is why the whole volume rests upon a "preoccupation with the so to speak atmospheric conditions in which the mysterious exchange of humorous pleasure between men can operate" (p. 12). Villiers de l'Isle-Adam shared this preoccupation. So too did J.-K. Huysmans, whose spokesman des Esseintes admired Villiers profoundly.

It is no surprise to find in the *Anthologie* texts taken from *En Ménage* and from *En Rade*. For Huysmans' sense of humor was evidenced in an interview with J.-K. Huysmans published over the signature of A. Meunier, who was none other than Huysmans himself. Noting in himself "an inexplicable amalgam of refined Parisian and Dutch painter," Huysmans went on to mention also "a pinch of black humor and of rough English comedy" that could be detected in his novels up to and including *A Rebours*. Citing these phrases, Breton goes on to argue that right up to 1892, when *En Route* began taking Huysmans in a direction no surrealist would care to follow, this form of humor seems to have been, for Huysmans, "the very condition for maintaining his mental appetite" (p. 247).

In a way, Huysmans may be said to have followed the example set by Villiers de l'Isle-Adam, whom he praises in *A Rebours* in these terms: "in Villiers's temperament another corner, very differently sharp, very differently clear, existed, a corner of black jokes and ferocious raillery." This puts des Esseintes in mind of Swift (p. 239) and helps us understand the humor of *En Ménage*, as characterized in Breton's anthology of black humor:

> By the excess of somber shades in his painting, by attaining and going beyond what is customary from a certain critical point in distressing situations, by minute, acute prefiguration of the blighted hopes brought, in his eyes, in the most banal alternatives, by any option, he achieves this paradoxical result of releasing in us the pleasure principle. External realities systematically presented from their most petty angle, the most aggressive one, the one that wounds most, demand of Huysmans' reader constant vital energy, undermined by accumulation of daily cares of which he is all at once made too aware. (pp. 247–48)

Here, then, lies the originality of Huysmans, as it appears in the context of the *Anthologie de l'Humour noir:* he "seems to surrender, himself, the benefit of humorous pleasure," so giving us the impression that it is reserved "exclusively for us," as the author, always apparently overwhelmed by his miseries, gives us "the illusion of gaining an advantage over him."

There is something the writings of Villiers de l'Isle-Adam and J.-K. Huysmans illustrate particularly well: the use of intelligence permits us to cast doubt upon the premises of the real, and reaffirms the principle of human experience as *devenir*, "in its continual becoming." This is the principle surrealists promote energetically, in their resistance to the hypnotic stasis of the rational. Time loses its prerogatives, as past and present are perceived as standing in the same relationship to one another as the two communicating vessels of sleeping and waking, examined in Breton's *Les Vases communicants*. What is required—and Breton clearly believed it guaranteed—by the use of intelligence is a glance rendered quite innocent of past associations. This explains why emphasis falls repeatedly in the *Anthologie de l'Humour noir* upon the pitiless scrutiny of the utilitarian that surrealists can expect of intelligence. Hence, consideration of the work of Lautréamont leads Breton to comment, "An absolutely virgin eye is on the lookout for the scientific improvement of the world, goes further than the consciously utilitarian character of this improvement, situates it with all the rest in the very light of the apocalypse" (p. 228).

Challenging the stasis of a world conceived in accordance with the dictates of utility, Breton returns to the theme of mutation to announce, apropos of Lautréamont's writings, "It is all over with the limits within which words used to be able to enter into relationship with words, things with things. A principle of perpetual mutation has taken hold of objects, as of ideas, tending toward their total deliverance which implies that of mankind" (p. 229). In this respect, the language of Lautréamont is at one and the same time "a solvent" and "a germinative plasma," both of unequalled power. The implication, obviously, is that Lautréamont's approach to the word as "un *recommencement*" produces results similar in effect to those obtainable by appeal to chance through pictorial collage, or through automatic writing, as the *Manifeste du Surréalisme* called for its practice.

Affirming that verbal automatism entered French poetry with Tristan Corbière's *Amours jaunes*, Breton writes in his anthology, "Corbière must be the first in point of time to have let himself be carried on the wave of words which, outside all conscious direction, breaks each second in our ears and which the majority of men hold back by means of the dike of immediate sense" (p. 266). The surrealist function of intelligence, in these circumstances, is to turn attention away from the immediate meanings of words (as of everything else released by creative imagination), in order to direct it to the significance that gushes forth once the dike of the utilitarian has been breached. And so André Breton betrays no uneasiness, when discussing the "flagrant discord" between generally accepted ideas and certain affirmations to be found in the books of Jean-Pierre Brisset, for instance, or in the paintings of Douanier Rousseau.

To Breton, it is simply a matter of noting that, in cases such as these, black humor ceases to be the privilege of the author and becomes instead the privilege of his public: "entirely a humor of *reception* (as opposed to the humor of *emission* on the part of most of the authors who interest us)" (p. 308). What now counts above all is the manner in which, for example, Raymond Roussel, resorting to a purely mechanical mode of word play—resulting in something Roussel himself called "sorts of *equations of facts*"—then found himself obliged to solve his equations *logically*, within narratives structured upon bases owing their very existence to unquestioning appeal to chance.

As Breton speaks of it in the *Anthologie de l'Humour noir*, Roussel's method is characterized by the following significant pattern: "The greatest arbitrariness having been introduced into the literary subject, it was a matter of dissipating it, of making it disappear by a succession of passes in which the rational constantly limits and tempers the irrational" (p. 383). Evidently then Roussel's approach merits attention no less than Francis Picabia's: "Picabia," Breton stresses, "was the first to understand that all ways of bringing words together, without exception, are permissible and that their poetic virtue is all the greater, the more they appear gratuitous or irritating at first sight" (p. 402). In both cases, intelligence furnishes confirmation of poetic intuition. When, discussing Picabia, Breton speaks of "the *superego* that acts like a condenser of light, like armor facing the inside" (422), he intimates that the kind of defense offered by humor represents an intelligent estimate of the human situation and a form of *dépassement*, a way of going farther that cannot come in total absence of conscious intent. There can be no doubt, therefore, that Breton identified use of intelligence with fulfillment of the self. His assessment of Kafka tells us as much: "No work militates so much against admitting a souvereign principle outside the person thinking" (p. 441). His judgment of Duchamp reflects the same view: "Marcel Duchamp is surely the most intelligent and (for many people) the most embarrassing man of this first half of the twentieth century" (p. 468). His tribute to Duchamp is especially revealing in its assertion: "What is in question is complete profound initiation into the most modern way of feeling, of which humor offers itself in this work as the implicit condition" (p. 469).

The initiation in which the capital contribution made by Duchamp is warmly acknowledged in the *Anthologie de l'Humour noir* could not be effected without assistance from intelligence of a kind Breton finds in the writings of Benjamin Péret. Crediting Péret with enviable success in liberating language, Breton traces his success to a quite remarkable *"detachment"* (p. 505). Guaranteed by the control of intelligence, the detachment that released Péret from respect for habitual relationships, normally inculcated and approved by conventional reality, has its equivalent in Breton's estimation, in the surrealist painting of Dalí, whose paranoiac-critical activity allowed him during the thirties to "be half-judge half-interested party in the case brought against reality by pleasure" (p. 537). In the equilibrium existing in Dalí's surrealist canvases between "the lyrical state founded on pure intuition" and "the speculative state founded on reflection" Breton asks us to admire the activity of an "intelligence of the very first order" which, he bids us note, excels in "rationalizing by degrees the distance covered" (p. 537). Without the "methodical work of organization, of exploitation," carried out by intelligence upon elements supplied by paranoia, Breton argues, Dalí could not have succeeded in a task tending to "reduce progressively that which is hostile about daily life and to overcome this hostility *on the universal scale*" (p. 538).

PAUL NOUGÉ: *Journal*
Nowhere outside France does the history of surrealism date
from so far back as in Belgium, where the exchange of ideas
with Parisian surrealists has never suffered from disadvantages created by language differences. And yet—except of
course for that of René Magritte in painting—the contribution made by Belgians to surrealist endeavor has not been
given its full weight. Significantly, the French surrealist
Jean-Louis Bédouin devotes just one indecisive page to Belgium, in his *Vingt Ans de Surréalisme (1930–1950)*, while
reserving a whole chapter to Martinique, and dividing another between the United States and Latin America. Regarded in French surrealist circles as the companion volume
to Breton's *Entretiens* (which covers the period 1913–52),
Bédouin's history grants nine times as much space to England in the thirties as to Belgium from the twenties onward.
   If we examine the three anthologies of surrealist
poetry published under the editorship of French surrealist
writers, we find Belgium poorly represented. When assembling his *Petite Anthologie du Surréalisme* in 1934, Georges
Hugnet deemed it necessary to acknowledge among Belgian
surrealists only E. L. T. Mesens and Paul Nougé. In *La Poesia
surrealista francese*, published in 1959, Benjamin Péret included no Belgian except Mesens. Five years later, recognizing both Mesens and Nougé is his *La Poésie surréaliste*,
Bédouin added but one more Belgian name, that of Achille
Chavée. It was left to an Argentinian surrealist, Aldo Pelle-
grini, to provide Belgian surrealism with adequate representation. His *Antología de la poesía surrealista en lengua
francese* (1962) takes into account the work of Chavée, Co-
linet, Havrenne, Lecomte, Mesens, Nougé, and Scutenaire.
When finally a Belgian, Christian Bussy, undertook to offer
a faithful image of surrealist poetic activity in Belgium, his
anthology did not find a publisher in his own country. It
appeared, ironically, in Paris in 1972.
   Outlined in a discussion between Bussy and Marcel
Mariën, serving as a preface to the former's anthology, the
distinguishing characteristics of surrealism in Belgium still

have not been examined in detail.[6] One thing is clear enough already, though. From the mid-twenties onward, a divergent conception of how surrealism operates gave rise to a drama that accounts in no small measure for the neglect of Belgian surrealism by French surrealists. It explains, for instance, why Péret, the supreme practitioner of verbal automatism, left Nougé out of his *La Poesia surrealista francese*. Refusing to bow to the authority exercised in France by Breton, Belgian surrealists have always gone their own way.[7] This is all the more reason, then, to notice how Nougé's ideas complement Breton's in one important respect, and aim to bring about comparable results.

On June 19, 1941, Paul Nougé noted in his private diary his "distrust in any appeal to motives of feeling, sentimental motives," adding, "I am terribly, wretchedly perhaps—an intellectual. *A position, a habit or a mannerism to be submitted to critical examination.*"[8] If Nougé really continued to be unaware of the sources of his intellectualism into his forties (he was born a year earlier than Breton, in 1895), his surrealist friends were more sure than he on this score. André Souris for instance has affirmed, "Nougé was fascinated by Valéry's thinking, and I think one cannot define his attitude without referring to the principle that is at the center of Valéry's work, according to which it is more important to be acquainted with the process of creation than to give oneself up to it instinctively."[9] Alluding to Valéry's *Monsieur Teste* which, incidentally much impressed the young Breton, Marcel Lecomte has called Paul Nougé "a sort of Monsieur Teste": "He is a Valéryan intelligence, with a taste for power too, and belief in the decisive virtue of revolution, of social revolution as well."[10] What concerns us, primarily, is Lecomte's assurance that, so far as Nougé was concerned, "at first there was in him already the notion of intelligence considered as a means of exploration and explosion: intelligence conceived as being capable of provoking a back-wash, subversion."

Fascination with the writings of Paul Valéry, which obviously lasted longer in his case than in Breton's, is visible on more than one page of Nougé's *Journal*, as it was reflected in his gesture earlier, upon becoming acquainted with Valéry's work, of destroying all he had written previously. It does not call for mention in the present context as the foundation of a study of literary influence, but rather as evidence pointing to a significant phenomenon. In Nougé we see a surrealist who, so as to handle the problems raised by the act of poetic creation, called upon his intellect.

Surrealism's chief spokesman in Brussels, Paul Nougé once spoke of his *inquiétude* in the following terms:

> And the first effort I must try to make is to give this disquiet the form and weight that in their turn would give me a hold over it. And as the only means at my disposal are means that come from the intelligence (I cannot honestly trust myself to something belonging to another layer of the mind) so as to allow myself to apply these means I must therefore substitute for an amorphous state an intellectual being, a *problem* or a series of *problems* which result therefrom, which are on the plane of intelligence the irradiation of this state of disquiet, which are its intellectual equivalent.

This statement, dating from 1928,[11] is not a sign of some passing phase. Nougé's *Journal* again shows him defining his essential characteristic, on June 18, 1941, as "never to lose control, never any abandon, spontaneity . . ." (p. 25). Two days later we hear him speaking of his major preoccupation in terms of "a *becoming aware* as wide and as precise as possible" (p. 27). Elsewhere the same year Nougé made a comparable confession: "To feel oneself at the highest point of lucidity, of agility and to feign weightiness, the confusion of dotage, to feel the person you are speaking to, your friend, is taking advantage of this; to articulate embarrassed words on the most mundane subject possible, while I penetrate it, goose it, judge it, smile—I know of no more refined pleasure."[12]

The statement just cited is an important indication of the direction Nougé always sought to follow as a poet. "Indeed," he admitted on another occasion, "I consider myself to be an action rather than a person, an action for which I feel myself partially responsible and which I try by all the means in my power to render more effective."[13] Raising again the ambiguous question, "Qui suis-je" (meaning both "Who am I?" and "Whom am I following?"), with which Breton opened *Nadja*, Paul Nougé went on to assert, "I look upon this question as null and void, for I know it to be basically insoluble. In which direction would it draw me, toward what mirage, what terror, what sterile comprehension." Thus dissociating himself from the kind of surrealist quest undertaken in *Nadja*, Nougé intimated that he was heading in a somewhat different direction: "But I know it is given me to act and the limits of my action, its extent which is perhaps laughable, is not to be a subject for rancor. It exists, that is enough, on condition I turn it to the best account I am allowed to invent."

Reading these last words, we gain a better understanding of an obscure passage in Breton's *Second Manifeste du Surréalisme*, where we find, "*I should rather like it*, wrote Nougé recently, *if those among us whose names are beginning to make something of a mark were to erase them*" (p. 211). With characteristic hauteur, Breton continues, "Without knowing exactly of whom he is thinking . . . ," omitting to explain that the sentence he has quoted is taken from a letter written him by Nougé, where the words "erase them" are underlined and followed by this prediction: "They would gain a freedom from which much can still be hoped."[14] According to Mariën's interview, as reported in Bussy's *L'Accent grave*, it was Breton Paul Nougé had in mind and suspected of being still too devoted to literature to meet the standards of those with whom Nougé himself had been associated in founding the magazine *Distances* in Brussels.[15] Be that as it may, Nougé's discussion with Christian Bussy regarding his collaboration on *Distances* runs as follows in *L'Accent grave:*

C. B. To you, what does "keeping one's distance" mean?

P. N. Avoiding getting mixed up in that "art for art's sake" production we condemned completely.

C. B. This was also safeguarding one's freedom?

P. N. Safeguarding also one's freedom.

C. N. In the surrealist mind, liberty and revolt are the same thing.

P. N. Necessarily!

Despite his reluctance to follow Breton's lead, then, it is evident that Nougé was a long way from attempting to give surrealism in Belgium a radically different orientation from the one it was taking in France.

Confirming in 1941 that he regarded liberty as "no doubt the great conquest of the surrealists," Nougé expressed this belief: "One would be giving up once and for all that fine word liberty, if one did not imagine that for some people it represents, quite simply, *a certain possibility for detachment*. One has only to suppose the 'Tremble, carcass. . .' extended to the intellectual domain."[16] In his opinion, liberty is bought at the price of detachment. This is its guarantee, we infer from a text of his called "La dernière Apparition": "The thoughts that come to him, and perhaps that are mine also, keep their distance, create for us a very pure empty space in which all things perhaps become possible—or have been possible."[17] Another text, dating from 1927, nearly twenty years earlier, insisted, "Surprise does not always come to us from the revelation of a thing entirely unforeseen, but again from the distance to be noted subsequently between the thing we had imagined and the object that presents itself to us."[18] A fuller explanation is to be found among Nougé's second series of *Fragments:* "I write, I have always written for someone who is much more intelligent than I, much more sensitive than I, much more. . . Of whom I am afraid. And who does not exist." This statement permits us to come closer to comprehending how he

saw his function as a surrealist writer relying upon his intellect.

First, it disposes of those features that made the practice of literature for literature's sake as abhorrent to Nougé
as to the next surrealist:

> The deception of language, of writing, no longer
> leaves room for doubt. Hence a whole series of problems, a
> density of doubts, which would not fail, if one were to pay
> them no heed, to corrupt infinitely shifting reality once and
> for all. One must, under penalty of death, make short work
> of these questions that have no echo, of sincerity, of agree-
> ment, among other unsubstantial meats.

Then it shows that Nougé was not the least intimidated by
his task as a writer who found himself obliged to recognize
the inadequacies of language; on the contrary, he hoped to
turn these very inadequacies to advantage:

> I like this flagrant disproportion between writing and
> the person manifesting it. Is it not fully time to treat as it
> deserves that mediocre inclination which leads us to reduce,
> to the scale of everyday man, the written objects that depend
> but very little upon him? What a wretched character this
> traveler brings back to us. And yet. . .
> No, though, at the very most I shall be allowed to
> note the inequality here.[19]

In Nougé's case, realization of the limitations of language—recognition of how limited is the writer's control
over the words he uses—is the starting point for an approach to verbal poetry to be found, rather unexpectedly,
in his essay on chess. Here the following remarks appear
under the heading "Les Echecs, la Poésie":

> There have been writers who used words in a very
> special fashion. They really thought themselves the masters,
> they were free to exercise complete domination over lan-
> guage. It was in their power to retain only certain of the

properties of words, setting aside so to speak the others. . . .
They did not seem to suspect that a revolt of language was
possible. . . .

    In truth, if words allow themselves to be handled, it
is with the help of infinite carefulness. One has to welcome
them, listen to them before asking any service of them. Words
are living things closely involved with human life. Let someone try to retain certain "properties" to the detriment of the
others, and they immediately take their revenge.[20]

The Valéryan tendency of the ambition at which Nougé's
remarks hint is clear enough in this conclusion: "It is time
to recall that there is today another way of understanding
poetry." It is attested also by his admission in response to
Bussy's question, "Why do you write?" that he did so, "in
the Valéryan sense of the word, to 'charm,' that is to say to
influence and therefore act upon the eventual reader."

    However, to the extent that he wanted to act upon
his readers and yet refused to do so through adoption of the
confessional mode ("Artless or disguised, confession is not
my strong hand," we read in the first series of *Fragments*),
or through the emotional enticements he associated with
literary devices, Paul Nougé established a distinctive relationship with his public, designed to take him farther in the
direction important to him than Paul Valéry was interested
in going. In one of his first-series *Fragments*, he confides:

> What it pleases me to give you, what really concerns you, I
> intend that this be the very thing I direct at you, *against you*,
> on which I count to lead you where I should like to see you
> and toward which I am advancing with you.
>
>   If I were not convinced of accomplishing a step of
> this kind at once, I would give up, and I would not just for
> pleasure run the risk of shutting myself up in a prison of
> words, of defining myself.

Manipulation of reader response to his private satisfaction was much less Nougé's preoccupation than challenging it ("*against you*"), with beneficial results. "Why do I

happen to write," he asks himself in *Histoire de ne pas rire*, "why do I imagine one writes with a certain degree of pertinence? Well, to put the reader out, to trouble his habits, small and big, to *turn him over to himself*" (p. 127). The ambition that motivated Nougé's writing was not so much the hope of dominating his audience as of achieving the following aims: "Let us take best advantage of what could be ours. Let man go where he has never been, experience what he has never experienced, think what he has never thought, be what he has never been. He must be helped, we must provoke this mental exaltation and this crisis, let us create bewildering objects."

It may seem that such poetic surrealist objects as Nougé would have liked to see created can be produced better by painters than by writers—after all, Nougé made these proposals within the framework of an essay entitled *René Magritte ou les Images défendues*.[21] Yet the role of objects like these is no different from that of words to Nougé, who never ceased treating language as a subversive agent. Thus his comments are relevant to poetry on the broad scale by which surrealist endeavor is measured, as he goes on to remark, "But where will the object find this subversive quality? As we have seen: in its capacity for occupying human consciousness to the point of drying up the monotonous ebb and flow, to the point of forcing the mind to invent the means for setting it aside." And so, whether he was speaking of the writer, the painter, or even the chess player, Nougé saw matters in the same light. In *Notes sur les Echecs* he observed:

> And again: the player at the chess table, the least one can do is to suppose him to be an opponent.
> But the supposed reader must be first of all an opponent. An opponent before being beaten. (p. 85)

Paul Nougé's approach to the language of poetry did even more, leading him to a discovery mentioned in his *Histoire de ne pas rire*:

But it will be noticed perhaps too that this conception of literature seems to banish the "naive" resources of language and to divert it from its so-called spontaneous ends; that this fairly exclusive cult of subversive intention, of traps set, of machination; that all this that seems to lead assuredly to the most artificial and skimped constructions, forces us, as soon as it is applied, into a paradoxical discovery. The writer finds himself thrown into total freedom.

And one notices at this very moment that it was the blind cult of spontaneity, of unrestricted "expression" that bound this writer almost inevitably to the worst mental servitude. (p. 130)

Not only do we see here that Nougé would never have been content with slavish imitation of Valéry, but we can appreciate why, writing in his *Journal* on July 4, 1941, he declared intelligence "must have a *mordancy*. It *attacks* a problem" and is "a claw that shatters as it scratches." And we see, too, how Nougé was led to reflect upon "a *projective poetry* that really *opens* the imagination."

Examining the idea of "une *poésie de projet*" we come to appreciate better what lay behind Nougé's plea for the creation of "des objets bouleversants." In *Histoire de ne pas rire*, a 1930 text called "La Lumière, l'Ombre et la Proie" defines the true nature of the object in this fashion: "it owes its existence to the act of our mind that invents it." This is to say that, according to Nougé, "The *reality* of an object will depend closely upon the attributes with which our imagination has invested it, upon the number, the complexity of these attributes and upon the manner in which the invented complex finds its way into the whole pre-existing in us and existing in the minds of our fellow men." Going further, Nougé argues:

One may notice also that the more powerful the reality of an object, the more successful this reality has been, the greater are the chances too of being able to extend it by means of a new reality, to enrich it or to turn it upside down [*bouleverser*] so as to draw a new reality from it.

Where we touch upon one of the reasons for placing confidence in poetic activity as in scientific activity, both, by different approaches, applied to inventing new objects. (p. 87)[22]

As he bids us note, here we detect "the characteristic trait of the mind" which was, for Nougé, "action." It is "an *act* of our mind that gives the object a *meaning*" (p. 89). Believing this, in a text called "Exprimer," written in 1928 and reprinted in *Histoire de ne pas rire*, he argued against reduction of art to the level of *"a means of communication"* resting upon the assumption that art can produce only what "already existed fully formed before it" (p. 62).

A little later, in 1932, Nougé wrote a tract entitled "La Poésie transfigurée," occasioned by the legal proceedings instituted in France against Louis Aragon for his inflammatory poem *Front rouge*. In this text, countersigned by Magritte, Souris, and E. L. T. Mesens, Nougé spoke of "poetry's intrinsic value of human provocation, its immediate quality as summation bringing with it, *in the manner* of a challenge, an insult, a palpably adequate *response*." In this sense, of course, no distinction needs to be drawn between poetry and painting. In fact, Nougé sees the same essential problem in both: "It is a matter of getting chance on one's side by going through calculation as far as calculation can take one. Thereafter begins the adventure that must compromise us as it compromises those to whom we are addressing ourselves."[23] Thus throughout his life Nougé's preoccupation remained unchanged. As he expressed it in his "Réflexions à Voix basse" on April 20, 1925, "The distrust inspired in us by writing does not fail to be mixed in a curious fashion with a feeling of the qualities we must acknowledge it has. There is no doubt that it has a singular aptitude for keeping us in that zone fertile in dangers, in renewed peril, the only one in which we can hope to live."[24]

In his *Journal* Nougé makes a remark, dated June 18, 1941, which helps us understand how distrust of language, born of the realization that the intellect cannot dominate it entirely, caused him, strange as it may seem, to place his confidence in words, so making him a poet: "The circumstances, the mediocre circumstances of my life, have been such that everything of value I have done has always been so under the sign of *subversion*, of felonious action." Noting in his *René Magritte ou les Images défendues*, "the object, separated by some mysterious operation from the weighty universe to which it still belonged a moment ago, the strangely *unfettered* object sets about living at the whim of days and of sleep," Nougé reveals why he decided to "Be content, once and for all, with what is not known." To do otherwise, would be to fall victim to the "enticement of clarity, of coherence, of clearsightedness or of a certain persuasive tone"—that is, to a conception of poetry having but one disastrous result: "being reduced to the limited exercise of a sort of handicraft the frontiers of which are recognized in advance." Far better, in his opinion, is adoption of the perspective recommended among his first-series *Fragments:* "What to hope for, what to undertake if not the formation of some object that can do without us?" Thus the image—verbal or pictorial, it makes no difference—must be defended (*défendue*) for the very reason that it appears, to common sense, to be forbidden (*défendue*).

During an interview with Christian Bussy, Marcel Mariën, who stressed the special nature of Nougé's poetic aspirations, called him "one of the most extraordinary specialists in a field still uncommon: that of intellectual liberty, in other words of liberty of mind vis-à-vis the world and oneself." Indeed, Paul Nougé did not take long to realize that, "In order to stop the mind's movement, it is essential to stop the mind." This observation in his second-series *Fragments* prepares us for the following comment on something we have heard him call *la poésie de projet* and now, in his *Journal*, under the date June 11, 1941, he calls *la poésie projective:*

The underlying theorem of *projective poetry* is the following: what are the elements of a poetic form that can be deformed with impunity by means of a metaphor while letting poetic coherence subsist?

In other words: *what are the limits of formal causality?*

The point made here, with the utmost consistency, is this: "Now, there is no thought that is not an action in process of being accomplished." Whether, as on that occasion he was writing (in 1930) of "Le Problème de la Sincérité," or whether he was delivering a lecture to mark an exhibition of Magritte's paintings and a performance of Souris' music, Nougé did not vary in his attitude: "we shall not give up what we consider to be essential to the mind: a certain power of deliberate action."[25]

His *Conférence de Charleroi* explains that "our desire is to place ourselves entirely at the service of the mind's possibilities," claiming that "the mind proceeds by bewildering inventions." "Inventions bouleversantes" give rise to "objets bouleversants" in which Nougé placed his faith as a surrealist. More than this, they confirm the mind's capacity for precipitating the unforeseen, in which he saw special poetic virtue:

The mind is nourished on our risks and our defects, as on our victories.

And the latter themselves, humble or discreet, of which we should be tempted to take no notice, are perhaps destined to have infinite repercussions.

But here, all anticipation is specious, for there could be no question of solving a problem the terms of which, every moment, offer to escape you. . .

The certainty remains nevertheless that the mind exists only with the help of a limitless adventure, with ceaselessly renewed movements and perspectives, in which the dangers we discern and which, every moment, threaten to make it take a sharp turn, are also, if we refuse to bow to them, the firmest guarantees of the only victories that still tempt us.

According to Souris' statement to Bussy, reported in *L'Accent grave*, Nougé "had come to conceive the possibility of constructing sorts of word machines whose every effect he imagined he could foresee entirely. He was a sort of nominalist, as they would say in a philosophy class, in this sense that, to him, the word was the thing itself. The word was not the signifier of something signified, but constituted in itself an object capable of the biggest deflagrations." There was a time, Souris reports, when "all it took was for him to write the word 'blood' to have the feeling, the certainty, that the reader would be soaked with the matter represented by that word." Borrowing the language of commercial publicity, Nougé would write, for example, "Your ears are listening to you, your eyes are spying on you, run, your hands are going to catch you," persuaded, Souris assured Christian Bussy, that these words had "a magic power, bewildering qualities, an irreversible power of metamorphosis." And he would write lines like the following:

> Ma bouche qui bouge
> devant vous
> n'est pas habitée de paroles
> ordinaires
> Ma bouche ce soir est habitée
> de paroles qui ne sont
> pas à moi
> de paroles qui ne sont pas des
> chansons ni des charmes
> mais des balles de fusil
> reflets d'épées
> et je suis attachée aux paroles de ma bouche
> comme une langue de feu
> au souffle exterminateur
>
> Allons—où croyez-vous être?[26]

> [My mouth that moves
> before you
> is not inhabited by ordinary
> words

My mouth this evening is inhabited
by words that are
not mine
by words that are not
songs or charms
but rifle bullets
the glint of swords
and I am attached to the words of my mouth
like a tongue of fire
to exterminating breath

Come now—where do you think you are?]

Convinced that, more than any other human activity, poetry "gives rise, with the help of language, to stupefying misunderstandings,"[27] Nougé felt it pertinent to ask, not where we are, but where we think we are. Thus for him the word *liberté* had a special application, when he wrote, "One can establish to begin with that it is the liberty surrealists have retained vis-à-vis the means *turned to account* in every domain that has proved to be singularly fruitful."[28] We realize this when we hear him go on to assert, "Surrealism has tended less to degrade traditional means of expression than to confer equal dignity on all means of expression, to revise the very notion of expression and to attempt a complete generalization of it." In his view, therefore, surrealism is not simply the enjoyment of freedom from imposed or inherited aesthetic or technical restraints; it is the promotion of methods calculated to guarantee language its own freedom of action. His approach to poetic language rests upon the conviction that "groups of words, shreds of language," retain the power to "engender a movement or sketch a movement in a direction almost always unforeseeable with respect to the language from which they have been separated."[29] Hence the method advocated is the one mentioned in his "Notes sur la Poésie": "We put language and forms to a use different from their habitual functions in order to devote them to new missions." And the rewards? We find a hint of these in the following verses from his poem "L'Ecriture simplifiée":

> Au revers des saisons et des regards avides
> les mains qui se promènent aux pentes de la nuit
> se gantent de rumeurs de visions et de signes.
>
> Une vaste maison bourdonnante de songes
> et les tuiles du toit s'envolent dans l'air pur
> et les songes touffus se déplient et s'élèvent
> et la rumeur des mains se promène au travers
>
> d'un monde qui s'accroît au gré des mots divers.
>
> [On the reverse of seasons and greedy eyes
> hands running over the slopes of the night
> slip on gloves of distant murmurs of visions and signs.
>
> A vast house buzzing with dreams
> and the tiles of the roof fly off in the pure air
> and involved dreams unfold and rise up
> and the distant murmur of hands runs through
>
> a world that increases in size as diverse words please.]

Words are not the repository of recollected feelings or past experiences. That is to say, they are not to be used to look backward. Nougé indicated as much when speaking of them as "objects." Written language treated as an object, he explained in the section called "Le Langage" in his "Notes sur la Poésie," is "capable at every moment of *making sense*, but an object *detached from the person using it* to the point where it becomes possible under certain conditions to treat it as a material object, matter for modification, for experimentation." Language, the end of "Notes sur la Poésie" assures us, becomes "an object suitable for provoking, in the person submitted to it, certain states, certain thoughts or certain ideas, and makes use of them as an object modifiable after the manner of a material object (by adjunction, suppression, interpolation, deflection, etc.) with the sole pur-

pose of producing a certain effect, foreseen, adumbrated—
or simply considered to be unforeseeable."

Small wonder Nougé can be heard celebrating, in
"L'Ecriture simplifiée," "The beautiful mental skein we shall
not be able to unwind." Small wonder he can be heard in
"Les fausses Transparences" drawing attention to the "false
transparencies" that "take advantage of your inattentive
eye," and pointing in "Des Merveilles équivoques" to "those
ambiguous marvels" that "move about in our changing discourse." In his opinion, "To think a thing is to question it
upon what is essential and specific about it." Hence, he went
on to explain in *René Magritte ou les Images défendues*, this
means "bringing it *under question* again, with all the precision of which the mind is capable." Furthermore, "It
means expecting of it an answer that will modify the relationships between this object and the rest of the universe
and with ourselves, an answer that will cast light upon it
at the same time as it enlightens us." In short, "To think
an object is to act upon it"—that is, Nougé has already
given us to understand, to be a poet: in the same context
the metaphor is defined as "a wish in the mind that what
it expresses will exist in complete reality, and further, as the
belief, the moment it is expressed, in that reality." To put it
simply, "one really knows only what one invents."

Basic to the argument just summarized is something
Nougé's *Journal*, in an entry dated June 10, 1941, calls "a
dynamic theory of changing the scale of *objects*, in terms of
a desire, a will for action," a theory that prompted him to
comment, eight days later, "We must in fact move on from
the reign of the image to the reign of action," and to oppose
"poetry of enticement" with "poetry of anger." He insisted,
"The sentence must become a diagram of angry motives."
His aim was to provoke "psychic explosions" by means
other than those of "pedantic phonetics." Hence this remark: "One might as well say that the explosion does not
have to do with syllables but with semantics, rather." When

one thinks of Desnos, of Vitrac, or of Leiris (who turned the word *causalité,* which we have heard Nougé employ, into *cause-alitée* ["cause confined to its bed"]), and when one recalls, further, that Breton claimed the great poets to be "auditives," rather than visionaries,[30] it is not difficult to see where the originality of Nougé's recommendations lies.

And yet the intellectual approach proposed by Nougé in placing his faith in semantic explosions is not really different from the approach commended in Breton's *Anthologie de l'Humour noir.* Marcel Mariën, who assembled the poetic texts of *L'Expérience continue,* has pointed out that his friend "gave special attention to the capacity words have for saying something for themselves, therefore something more than is meant by the thought moving them around, this something else being always more or less ambiguous, by the very circumstances of language." This remark in *L'Accent grave* finds support in Nougé's own statement regarding the principle underlying his *Subversion des Images,* a collection of disquieting photographic images: "It is a matter of giving people and objects a function, a use different from the habitual."[31] The subversive principle remained the same, for him, whether it was applied to photography, to language, or to painting. The interesting thing is that Nougé sought to apply this principle by means he strove to keep discreet. His essay on Magritte speaks of an "intervention as trivial as it is decisive" and of "that almost ideal situation in which the thing hoped for would be born, through the introduction of a single comma, from a page of writing; from a canvas of complex painting through the action of a single stroke of black ink."

Paul Nougé's *Clarisse Juranville* demonstrates that he was not content to confine his attention to the level of theory, when considering how the intervention interesting to him might be effected. Mlle Clarisse Juranville was the author of a drill-book on verb forms, *La Conjugaison enseignée par la pratique,* a Larousse school manual that brought together "Textes suivis renfermant des Verbes de même terminaison, Devoirs d'invention, Dictées, Permutations, Conjugaison de tous les verbes présentant des difficultés." Borrowing her name as well as her textbook, Nougé derived from the latter a series of poetic texts by the very method of intervention he had discussed with reference to Magritte:

J'ai dérangé les objets que renferment les maisons
j'ai fait mes préparatifs de départ et pris toutes les précautions

Chanterais-je si vous m'en priiez?
Trouverais-je vous m'aimiez?

Vous pleurez un oiseau mort.[32]

[I have disturbed the objects contained in the houses
I have made my preparations to leave and taken every precaution

Would I sing if you asked me?
Would I find if you loved me?

You weep for a dead bird.]

Later, employing an analogous technique, Nougé would write "Un Miroir exemplaire de Maupassant,"[33] from which comes the following extract, where it is easy to detect fragments from Maupassant's stories "A Cheval" and "L'Aventure de Walter Schnaffs":

A la sortie de la mairie
le vieux fut entouré
interrogé
Hector Gribelin avait été
élevé en province
le bateau a été jeté à l'ouest
la prison fut ouverte
et
Walter Schnaffs
jeté dedans
Le paysan resta suffoqué
Walter Schnaffs demeura immobile
Tout redevint muet et calme

[Leaving the townhall
the old man was surrounded
questioned
Hector Gribelin had been
brought up in the provinces
the boat has been driven in a westerly direction
the prison was opened
and
Walter Schnaffs
thrown in
The peasant was choking
Walter Schnaffs remained still
Everything became quiet and calm once again]

June 13, 1941, was to find Nougé still reflecting, in his *Journal*, "Study closely the experiment consisting in 'cutting up' a so-called prosaic phrase to transform it into a poem. And the same experiment in reverse. This must lead toward concrete considerations on the conditions and nature of the poem," and concluding, "it is by studying the *deformation of images* that we shall find *the measure of poetic imagination*." Almost two years later, he was considering going even further. Now, noting among certain "propositions" attractive to him "the poetic experiment suggested by the palimpsest," he jotted down, on May 22, 1943, "Write a poem composed of two or three texts more or less distant from one another, but after the manner of juxtalinear translations." On another occasion the language of mathematics suggested to him a method of poetic creation: "The deformation of images must designate, in a strictly mathematical manner, the metaphorical *group*." And again, citing the phrase "l'accouplement long, chaste et hideux," he commented on "The vertiginous psychoanalytical differential of the two associated words 'chaste and hideous,'" emphasizing "the application, here, of the mathematical sense of differential."[34] At yet another moment, he was devising a game in which participants would be furnished with playing cards on which fragments of sentences were printed.[35] But whatever he was doing, Paul Nougé made plain to the at-

tentive reader that he considered intellectualism valueless to
surrealists, unless it serves as a subversive means to poetic
ends that he knew no better way to attain:

L'
intérieur de votre tête
n'est pas cette
MASSE
GRISE et BLANCHE
que l'on vous a dite

c'est un
PAYSAGE
de SOURCES et de BRANCHES
une
MAISON de FEU
mieux encore
la
VILLE MIRACULEUSE
qu'il vous plaira
d'
INVENTER[36]

[The
inside of your head
isn't that
GRAY and WHITE
MASS
you've been told

it's a
COUNTRYSIDE
of SPRINGS and BRANCHES
a
HOUSE of FIRE
better yet
the
MIRACULOUS CITY
you'll be pleased
to
INVENT]

4

Subversion and Revolution

HERE IS NO DENYING that, in an anthology of texts illustrating black humor, André Breton found himself discussing language more than anything else. Similarly, reflecting throughout his career on his vocation as a poet, Paul
Nougé found himself speaking most of the time of poetry
as a way of handling words. Yet at no time, in his *Journal*
or elsewhere, did Nougé contend that the province of poetry
was the medium of spoken language alone. Nor did Breton
argue that only through words can the intelligence governing black humor find faithful expression. In his *Anthologie
de l'Humour noir*, excluding reference to the paintings of
Dalí and Picasso while alluding to their writings, Breton was
doing no more than accept the limitations imposed by his
undertaking. Not once, in that volume or outside it, did he
ever suggest that verbal language is the only acceptable medium, or even the best one, for intelligent poetic communication. Nougé's preoccupation with his own function as a
writer never blinded him to the importance of the parallel
role of René Magritte as painter. His essays on Magritte's
painting—among the most valuable and illuminating ever
written on the subject—prove conclusively that we have no
excuse for believing Nougé looked upon the poetic creative

act, approached intellectually, as necessarily circumscribed within the limits of spoken or written language.

A reading of Nougé's public and private reflections,[1] like an examination of Breton's *Anthologie de l'Humour noir*, does something more important than merely show that intelligence receives wider recognition among surrealists than might be anticipated. Breton and Nougé both demonstrated *how* intelligence earns the respect it is granted in surrealism. In doing so, they showed a certain type of intellectualism to be totally consistent with surrealist activity.

Transcender, dépasser, surmonter: the verbs that Breton represents as applicable *à l'échelle universelle* are surely among those that recur most often, not only when he is talking of intelligence at the service of surrealism, but also when other surrealists are discussing their common aims and the means by which they pursue their ambitions. The presence of verbs like these in the *Anthologie de l'Humour noir* indicates that, when ascribing intelligence a very necessary role in surrealism's program of revolt, Breton was not unfaithful in any way to the principles that had led him to publish, let us say, *Qu'est-ce que le Surréalisme?* in 1934. The reason then that Breton's anthology warrants attention, in preference to other writings of his from the same period, is that this compilation does something vitally important. It does not simply reiterate what we have learned from earlier texts, but gives special prominence to one feature of the surrealist program that needs to be understood before certain aspects of surrealist poetry can be appreciated.

The form of humor to which judicious use of intelligence lends particular meaning, this *"révolte supérieure de l'esprit,"* is, as Annie Le Brun has taken care to insist in her essay "L'Humour noir," "subversion in its pure state" (p. 108). It is in its subversive force that humor gives unity to the extracts assembled in Breton's volume. And it is in its subversive role that intelligence, as Breton speaks of it, complements intellect, as Nougé repeatedly talks of it, intellect, to borrow Lecomte's phrase, "capable of provoking a backwash, subversion." Each in his own way, André Breton and

Paul Nougé looked upon intelligence as a weapon to be used with telling effect, in surrealism's struggle with established reality, in its effort to subvert rational preconceptions, habitual assumptions, commonsense conclusions, and everything else that appears to provide a firm basis for a mode of reality that surrealists find disappointing and frustrating. The things we learn from Breton's anthology and from Nougé's diary, once alerted to the vitality of the subversive principle, place us in a better position to appreciate how necessary it is to broaden and deepen our understanding of the poetics of surrealism by way of examination of subversion as surrealists refer to its operation. We can begin such an examination with consideration of the surrealists' reasons for feeling and expressing admiration for one of the most notorious writers of all time, D. A. F. Sade.

The Marquis de Sade

In 1949 André Breton prefaced a collection of stories by Jean Ferry with an extended essay from which the following statement is taken:

> For my part, I honor more than ever today, because they are so rare, works electrified by the need for subversion that alone is capable of showing the capacity of individual resistance opposed to general domestication. On condition of course that the means placed at the disposal of subversion are up to its level, poverty of means being of a nature to compromise it radically. In the face of present-day strangulation of "revolutionary" ideas by those very people who claim for themselves the monopoly of these ideas, the subjection of these ideas to a rule than cannot be broken and that stays their growth, the historical chances that these ideas will be corrupted and the certainty of seeing them put forward by people who share them not at all but, in the strange period we live in, find real material advantages in them, subversion, as it is practiced in art in particular, remains the great reservoir of new strength, it alone today can claim to assume to the fullest extent human protest against absurdity, inertia and flagrant injustice in every form.[2]

Just ten years later the surrealists in Paris opened the eighth international exhibition.

"Exposition inteRnatiOnale du Surréalisme, 1959–1960." Postcard-size announcements circulated toward the end of 1959 indicated, by the legend and by the photograph against which it was placed in relief, the notably erotic emphasis chosen for the exhibition. Anyone receiving one of those cards but unable to accept the invitation to attend the opening was left in no doubt about the orientation of the show. He had only to read, in the newspaper *Arts*, André Breton's article "L"Erotisme est le seul Art à la mesure de l'Homme." The catalog, *Boîte Alerte: Missives lascives*, confirmed that the latest international manifestation of the surrealist spirit had been placed under the aegis of D. A. F. Sade.

It is evident—Breton's remarks in Ferry's volume prove this—that the surrealists were not only taking a risk but were well aware of doing so, fully realizing that the nature of the gesture they were making lent itself only too easily to misrepresentation and misinterpretation. By 1959, it was unlikely that many would remember that, in France, rehabilitation of Sade's name—something for which Guillaume Apollinaire had already struck a blow[3]—owes almost as much to the efforts of the surrealists as the twentieth century's rediscovery of the work of Lautréamont. Few outsiders would realize it was no accident that the surrealists were among the first to seek to rescue Sade from the oblivion to which respectability had tried for so long to commit him, and among the first, also, to stress the relevance of his work for our time. Two of those who have done most to promote serious critical analysis of Sade's writings, Maurice Heine and Gilbert Lely, first displayed their interest while members of the surrealist group. Their efforts to lift the interdict weighing on Sade's name and their example of careful commentary found the fullest encouragement within the group, and betoken among surrealists something more than the need for sensationalism. It was of the latter, however, that surrealists stood accused in 1959, when their activities came to be reported across the Channel.

In a talk for a BBC Third Programme series, broadcast on January 18, 1960, A. G. Lehmann chose as his title "Surrealism, Love and the Marquis de Sade." In his comments, subsequently published in *The Listener*, Lehmann played up the sensational aspect of the Canadian poet Jean Benoît's gesture in branding himself with the four letters S-A-D-E, during a ceremony before an invited audience in the Paris apartment of the surrealist Joyce Mansour. He showed but little appreciation of the significance to be attached to this ritualistic act. It was left to a surrealist sympathizer and former participant in surrealism, Alain Jouffroy, to underscore its meaning in a very pertinent article:

> The act itself, which consists in branding oneself with the letters Sade, in a society as garrulous and as disinclined to make gestures as the one in which artists live at present in Paris, is obviously a challenge. A challenge to conformists, a challenge to forms of laziness, a challenge to sleep, a challenge to all forms of inertia, in life as in thought. It is very evident that such a ceremony, in absolute contradiction with the vulgarity peculiar to our time, can only be the object of derision in the conversation of our self-styled intellectuals. It is, though, a call to essentials, I mean to that mysterious axis about which human beings turn, and which the Tantric Hindoos call the *Kundalini*—the energy liberated by the sexual act, and which allows us to shatter for a few seconds the bolted doors of our circumstances.[4]

All in all, the most valuable contribution made by Lehmann to the BBC's "Art—Anti-Art" Series lay in the fact that his falsification of the surrealist case led, within a month, to a broadcast discussion on February 9, 1960 between representative surrealists, Robert Benayoun, Joyce Mansour, Nora Mitrani, and Octavio Paz, introduced by Jacques Brunius, and aired under the title "In Defence of Surrealism."

Making no attempt to place the latest surrealist exhibition in historical perspective, Lehmann was guilty of permitting his listeners to conclude that Sade had been discovered only recently by the surrealists, whose expression of respect in 1959 must therefore be interpreted as a sign of opportunism. Apparently, it was his hope that no one would recall either an essay by Paul Eluard that appeared in the eighth number of *La Révolution surréaliste* (December 1, 1926) under the title "D. A. F. Sade, écrivain fantastique et révolutionnaire," or the same author's "L'Intelligence révolutionnaire: Le Marquis de Sade," published in the sixth number of *Clarté* on February 15, 1927, or again Benjamin Péret's incidental tribute to Sade in his 1944 article in *VVV*, "La Pensée est UNE et indivisible," to say nothing of the influence of Sade on the same writer's *Les Couilles enragées* (completed in 1928), from which extracts appeared the following year with comparable texts by Louis Aragon (author of *Le Con d'Irène*, also completed in 1928), and appropriate photographs by Man Ray, under the innocent title *1929*. Even if Lehmann himself was unacquainted with all or any of these pieces of evidence that testify to the importance of Sade from the very beginnings of surrealism, he must still bear responsibility for having ignored a declaration in the *Manifeste du Surréalisme* that Sade "is surrealist in sadism" (p. 41) as well as Breton's insistence, in the same context, upon a "spirit of *demoralization*" (p. 30) unquestionably epitomized in the writings of *le divin marquis*.

The first surrealist manifesto explicitly associates the spirit of demoralization with the castle, mentioning the latter in relation to the theme of the marvelous. It is the marvelous, after all, that lends Gothic novels their special appeal for surrealists, so laying the foundation for romantic aspiration, as surrealists interpret this in the sense of a craving to see desire fulfilled. The spirit of demoralization may be traced back through Lautréamont, whose Maldoror is supremely a *sadique*, through Pétrus Borel, whose *Madame Putiphar* speaks of Sade as "that glory of France," through the Gothic romances, which owe their atmosphere of terror, in considerable measure, to the example set by Sade's work, right back into the writings of the Marquis himself. The subversive spirit certainly helps keep Sade alive for surrealists everywhere. Thus in his article "La Pensée est UNE et indivisible," Péret acclaims the author of *Les 120 Journées de Sodome* the only poet in eighteenth-century France, ascribing his poetic qualities to his violent opposition to the fundamental postulations of the Age of Enlightenment. Writing in *La Révolution surréaliste*, Eluard observed, "It is not surprising that all the hypocritical commentators on the divine marquis have always ignored the higher meaning of this man's writings, so as to fasten on to nothing but his legend which shocks their complete mediocrity and serves them as an easy pretext for defending their ever-outraged morality."

It is not merely as an example drawn from the literature of the past, however, that Sade deserves and receives attention from within the surrealist movement. Eluard's 1926 article sketches a second very important reason why surrealists admire the Marquis:

> For having wished to give civilized man back the strength of his primitive instincts, for having wished to free the imagination in love and for having struggled desperately for absolute justice and equality, the Marquis de Sade was shut up almost all his life in the Bastille, in Vincennes and in Charenton. His work has been thrown into the fire or turned over to the senile curiosity of pornographic writers who made it their *business* to change its nature. His name has become synonymous with cruelty and murder. All the *assis*[5] have slavered over this indomitable soul.
>
> There never was a man more supremely unhappy. He always accepted the challenge of conventional morality and always remained at the very center of the hurricane it unleashed against him. Revolution found him devoted body and soul.

Over the years, the themes isolated here from Eluard's first article on his life and work have found elaboration in the comments surrealists have made about Sade.[6] There is evidence aplenty of the inaccuracy of Lehmann's contention that, having lost its original impetus, surrealism in 1959 was looking to the name of Sade to give it an air of renewed vitality.

More reprehensible still is Lehmann's argument that the surrealists' supposedly sudden interest in Sade was evidence of a reorientation in surrealist aspirations:

> It would be perverse to mistake the exhibition of Erotica for a general invitation to get out and break the laws and codes of our society. Breton would consider it rather as a challenge to us to look on certain areas of our sensibility through new eyes. But once again it is impossible not to remember how much has been lost of the original purpose and sense of surrealism, the climate in which it was breaking new ground, speculating on marvellous discoveries thought to have been made, elaborating a wholly novel system of man. The moral of it all is plain. In place of that "certain sublime point" which dominated Breton's thought in the twenties, and was communicated to so many hopeful and brilliant young writers, there is now an appeal to imagination, to desire, to eroticism, to passion: that is to say to powers and appetencies valued as ends in themselves, not as clues to knowledge of a superior pattern of being. The Marquis de Sade was therefore entirely the right person to invoke at this moment.

It is not easy to tell who comes out the worse here, Sade or his surrealist admirer, both pictured in gaudily distorting shades. One is tempted to take issue with Lehmann from two directions at once. However, this is not the place to combat his views, which exemplify so blatantly the bad faith that the surrealists, with justification, have been able to blame in their critics. Lehmann's inaccuracies were laid bare in the "Defence of Surrealism," which significantly enough was not printed, either in *The Listener* or anywhere else.[7] All the same, it is appropriate to stress the fact that those speaking for surrealism during that broadcast identified defense of their cause with that of eroticism to the point where, in replying for themselves, they were defending Sade at the same time. In short, they were consistently pursuing a line of thought, where his work and example are concerned, from which surrealists have not deviated.

In view of the surrealists' fidelity to Sade, Lehmann's strictures do not carry the authority of viable criticism. To Lehmann Sade seemed "entirely the right person" for surrealism, because "it is impossible to extract from his works a coherent message or example." The very source of the attraction of Sade's name is that its magnetism draws minds and sensibilities already predisposed in certain directions. Even so, before hastening to draw doubtful conclusions regarding the nature of Sade's reputation among surrealists, we should note how applicable is a word Breton liked to use, *polarity*, when surrealist response to Sade is under consideration. This way, we see there is every reason to disregard A. G. Lehmann's reservations about the contradictions and ambiguities he appears to think himself among the first to notice. For Sade to begin to enjoy an incontestable reputation among surrealists, painters as well as writers, it is enough that, as Lehmann admits, he "set little store by conventional norms of sanity, or conventional artistic and moral ideas, or, significantly, by the approval of his fellow-men."

Even this, though, comes dangerously close to disparaging compromise, to making of Sade a rebel figure through whom the surrealists, especially in the early days, could project a satisfying self-image and exteriorize an urge to iconoclasm most useful in ensuring and maintaining a sense of unity within a group still seeking its way and urgently in need of making clear to the general public its anticonformity, its profound sense of alienation. To be sure, there is no lack of evidence that Sade has always been able to fill this role to perfection, whenever circumstances required it. No more striking example need be cited of surrealism's use of Sade's name in this connection, or of the predictable reaction of officialdom, than the experience of the Surrealist Group in England. The one and only issue of their magazine *Free UNIONS libres* carried, among other things, a translation of Péret's article "Thought is ONE and indivisible" (with minor cuts and one or two mangled sentences), four scenes from Alfred Jarry's play *Ubu Roi*, and an extract from Maturin's Gothic novel *Melmoth the Wan-*

derer (a favorite of Breton's, who named his Newfoundland dog Melmoth). Also among the material gathered within the covers of *Free UNIONS libres* was a poem of Patrick Waldberg's, in bilingual text, "Divin Marquis," and a translation of the celebrated passage from Sade's *La Philosophie dans le Boudoir*, "Frenchmen! One more effort if you want to be Republicans." Confiscated at the printer's during the 1939–45 war, the magazine was not released for publication until 1946.

It is difficult to overemphasize the importance surrealists attach to Sade's message of political revolt and to his example in asserting the necessity for total liberty of action, upon the social as well as the moral plane. In surrealist lore, Sade occupies a place at least as important as St Just, in his capacity as enlightened prophet of revolution, beyond all inculcated repressive controls. In this respect particularly, his work was no less a catalyst for surrealist thought during the twenties and thirties than Fourier's proved to be during the late forties, fifties, and sixties.[8] Buñuel's film *L'Age d'Or* (1930), for instance, is fully comprehensible only to someone acquainted with the work of Sade. To the surrealist, *L'Age d'Or* testifies, both Sade's message and example are eminently coherent.

Among surrealists, the word that carries weight is not *sensationalism* but *scandal*. Saluting the 1959–60 exhibition in N° 754 of *Arts*, Jouffroy accurately summarized the values to be recognized in the works shown when he chose as the title of his article: "By opposing eroticism to social order in the international exhibition, the surrealists remain faithful to scandal." In evolving out of Dada shock tactics, surrealist scandal continued to make public a deep sense of revolt. Yet surrealist revolt is of more profound significance than Dada iconoclasm, in its appeal for something other than present conditions allow. Hence Nora Mitrani's definition of scandal in the 1959 Eros catalog:

> The sudden unveiling, for purposes of provocation or defiance of that which society and conventional morality

tolerate only when camouflaged: the so-called shameful parts of the human body, the exploitation of man by man, the existence of torture, but also the too unbearable brilliancy of a person out of step with his environment.

From the time of Breton's early reference to the ideal human being as "a woman scandalously beautiful," we can observe developing among surrealists a myth of love with which the work of Sade, first impressions notwithstanding, is by no means unconnected. While some may feel we ought to set aside as supported by insufficient evidence the claim in Péret's *Anthologie de l'Amour sublime* that we are permitted to see in Sade's own debauchery "experiences tending toward the verification of hypotheses then taking shape in his mind" (p. 55)—hypotheses which Péret suggests indicate that Sade came to know "the temptation of sublime love" (p. 56)—we stand to learn much from an examination of the surrealists' interpretation of the conduct of key characters in Sade's novel.

Breton's inclusion of certain passages from *Juliette ou Les Prospérités du Vice* in his *Anthologie de l'Humour noir* calls for no special comment at this point. Like the other extracts presented in Breton's volume, these show black humor to be an instrument that makes it possible for man to affirm his defiance in the face of an oppressive universe that aims to turn us all into victims. Something calling for more emphasis is the manner in which surrealist scandal—in this respect analogous to the conduct most widely associated with the novels of Sade—marks a call for self-expression that, going far beyond self-indulgence into self-exploration, takes on poetic value in the surrealists' eyes.

When Aragon called love "an outlaw principle," in his *Le Paysan de Paris*, "an irrepressible sense of violation, contempt for interdiction and taste for confusion" (p. 63), he brought to light some essential characteristics of the surrealist view of the erotic, but in so doing accentuated its negative aspects to the detriment of the positive. Robert Desnos, author of the pseudonymously published erotic novel *La Papesse du Diable* and of the better-known *La Liberté ou l'Amour!*, indicated with greater subtlety the value Sade's heroes and heroines assume in surrealism. In his *De l'Erotisme* Desnos remarks, "All these heroes are haunted by the desire to bring into accord their outer existence and their inner lives."[9] Beyond question, it is reflection on these words that brings most enlightenment upon the nature of the fascination exercised over the surrealists' imagination by Sade's depiction of erotic drive. Sade's heroes, explains Desnos, "leave the earth for the ideal and are hardly ever content with a Deus ex Machina" (p. 79). Hence, Desnos observes, "All our present aspirations have been formulated in essence by SADE," whom he credits with having been the first to offer complete sexual life as the basis for a life of feeling and intelligence (p. 76).

Sade's principal characters personify rejection of the consolation offered by established religion, ridiculed by Péret in "La Pensée est UNE et indivisible," among other places. They present examples of the lucid assumption of a responsibility all their own, as they pursue to a logical conclusion a line of conduct in which, defying moral and social codes, they have placed their trust. In all this, they stand as valuable models for the surrealist, who sees in their situation a literary transposition of his own. Even when, like André Breton, he has the strongest private reservations regarding certain aspects of their behavior (homosexuality, notably), he continues to admire the self-reliance and dedication of purpose Sade instilled in the principal characters of the dramas played out in his novels. It was as a sign of respect for the creator of such characters that the 1959–60 exhibition was planned, as Jean-Louis Bédouin puts it, "to do nothing less than raise the question, the most radical question there is, of inner life and of man's being itself."[10]

It is in the direction to which Bédouin points that, with most promise of success, we shall be able to make an estimate of the motives that have led so many surrealists to follow Sade. In taking encouragement from Sade's example, they never once have risked being untrue to surrealism. On the contrary, the example they have found in Sade has helped clarify their poetic ambitions, sharpening the tools by which they have fashioned their poetry. Thus the correct point of departure is not this or that illustration of a technique which may be said to have originated in Sade —reference, for instance, to the scandalous amalgam of eroticism and humor so distinctively a feature of the verse of Joyce Mansour, or again mention of the elements that nourish Michel Leiris' novel *Aurora* or Radovan Ivsic's play *Le Roi Gordogane*—but rather acknowledgment of the importance taken on by Sade's kind of subversion in relation to a poetic program aimed at bringing about something Péret termed "a rectification of the universe."

As a force of resistance and upheaval, subversion is a fundamentally poetic element in surrealist endeavor. Thus a catalog of features showing this force in operation is valuable, really, only as an indicator of its vitality. Indeed, the poetics of subversion tend to grant the limits of this or that chosen medium little or no respect. The viability of the container is seriously questioned, because attention goes primarily—where surrealism finds purest expression, it goes exclusively—to content. A work like Péret's *Mort aux Vaches et au Champ d'Honneur*, for instance, represents violation of novelistic form in the interest of subversive poetry.

What this amounts to is the following. From where the surrealists stand, the gesture made by Jean Benoît on December 2, 1959, as the Eros exhibition was about to open, appears of just as much poetic significance as his painting.[11] His premeditated conduct—the Sade costume he designed had been two years in the making—evidences not an act of bravado or of self-advertisement but a *gravity* which at once commanded the attention of the surrealists as a token of responsibility. The same is true of his costume designed in homage to the celebrated nineteenth-century French necrophile, Bertrand, and a terrifying object created for the same occasion—the *Ecart absolu* show of 1965—a leather bulldog, wearing a collar studded with metal spikes and equipped with an erect human penis.[12]

In the surrealists' willingness to salue in others the influence of Sade—in Henri Raynal's *Aux Pieds d'Omphale*, for example, or in *Histoire d'O* (published over the name of Pauline Réage and attributed, in some quarters, to a surrealist who has chosen to conceal his identity)—we see further evidence of the close identification surrealism establishes between its aspirations and the example set by Sade. Like Sade, the surrealist advocates revolution. Thus for surrealists the most remarkable element in Sade's work may well be its alignment of the cause of revolution with that of desire. In the title of Desnos' early novel the words *liberty* and *love* are not mutually exclusive or even alternatives, but —in strictest accordance with surrealist thought—interchangeable. Love is one of surrealism's keys to liberty, just as liberty finds its purest expression in totally emancipated love.

It matters little that, linking the erotic principle with the instinct for liberation, surrealists offer a reading of Sade others may see as simplified to the point of distortion. The surrealists have long since given sufficient proof of their complete indifference to criticism directed against their unshakeable confidence in the validity of desire as the underlying motivating force of all worthwhile human activity. For them the world Sade depicts is one where desire is placed before moral and social constraint. It is, therefore, an exemplary fictional universe where violently anticonformist attitudes confront all that tends to combat the free expression of desire, and do so triumphantly.

"Les révolutions toujours en retard sur lui" ("Revolutions always late behind him"). In this verse, which brings to a close Gilbert Lely's poem "Sade," is communicated surrealism's undeviating confidence in the continuing pertinence of Sade's message and persistent faith in the necessity for our time to take instruction from it. This confidence finds repeated expression in surrealism and is confined to no one period in the history of surrealist activity:

> We believe in the revolt of Rimbaud, in that of
> Lautréamont and of Sade.
> We believe in the value of Poetry, of Love and of Liberty.
> We believe in the Surrealist Revolution.

This declaration, issued by the surrealist group constituted in Holland in 1960 shows well enough how much the name of Sade continues to fire the surrealists' enthusiasm, for the very reason that his name is associated in their minds with the cause to which they never cease to be dedicated. The Dutch surrealists followed the example of their elders in looking to Sade for inspiration. Almost twenty years before, the surrealists in England had cited from *La Philosophie dans le Boudoir:* "I come to offer you great ideas: they will be heard, they will be reflected upon; if they are not pleasing, at least a few of them will prove acceptable; I shall have contributed in a small measure to the approach of enlightenment, and I shall be content. . ."

One of the most important ideas surrealists in various parts of the world are sure they have heard is that poetry is neither a formal exercise with words nor a pastime in this or that alternative medium, but an explosive force. Enrique Gómez-Correa's collected poetic texts—covering the period 1935 to 1973 and including extracts from his 1940 essays "El marques de Sade e el amor considerado como un vicio esplendido"—bears the title *Poesía explosiva.*[13] Poetry, Sade taught the surrealists, is an explosion that takes place when and where subversion becomes revolution.

POETRY AND POLITICS
While it is evident that surrealists the world over interpret the work of the Marquis de Sade as authoritatively support-

ing their conviction that poetry retains its vitality only so long as it remains radically subversive, it still is not quite clear how, encouraged by the example of Sade, they come to understand poetry's close relationship to revolution. More exactly, perhaps, the significance attached by surrealists to the writings of the Marquis which, after all, do far more than merely toy with questions of sociological and political import, may be leading us to foresee his philosophy inspiring among surrealists revolutionary thinking of a certain order and poetic practice of a narrowly predictable kind. This assumption, in turn, may predispose us to anticipate seeing surrealist poetry committed to definite lines of development, to limited areas of activity, which supposedly impose upon the forms of poetic expression—the painted canvas no less than the written text—certain foreseeable characteristics. In reality though, to the extent that our anticipation takes this course it is liable to divert attention from poetic action, as surrealist ambitions give it impetus. In so doing, it will breed confusion and hold us back from real appreciation of the nature and scope of poetic activity in surrealism.

Let us begin modestly, with a remark made by the surrealist Jean Schuster, speaking on Bastille Day, 1966. Observing that rationalism, "generally regarded as an emancipating force," is, to surrealists, "the most thorough system for oppressing thought,"[14] Schuster seemed to have nothing very new to say. In fact he appears to have been content with repeating what we have heard often enough. Surrealism, he appeared to be reminding his audience, is an approach to language, designed to sidetrack reason, to sabotage rational conjecture, and to implement antirational methods in the creative process. Why then did he continue his address on the theme of surrealism and liberty not by discussing the liberating effects of surrealist principles, as these apply to linguistic expression, but by stressing surrealism's "radical and irremediable break with the differing ideologies of the Left?" And why did he insist, "This break is also at the basis of surrealism's criticism of these ideologies and of their historical application"? The answer is neither particularly difficult nor especially elusive. It comes down to this: surrealism's defenders really meant and continued into the sixties to mean what was said in a well-known declaration issued by the surrealist group in Paris on January 27, 1925:

> 1. We have nothing to do with literature;
> But we are quite capable, if need be, of making use of it like everyone else.
> 2. *Surrealism* is not a new or easier means of expression, or even a metaphysics of poetry;
> It is a means for the total liberation of the mind *and of all that resembles it.*
> 3. We are firmly determined to create a Revolution.

The 1925 *Déclaration* did not pretend to cover all surrealist intentions in its first three points, even as these intentions already had reached formulation (the word *poetry*, as it appeared in that text is noticeably ambiguous, after all). Even so, it indicated clearly how concerned the surrealists were from the beginning to promote revolution well beyond the bounds of literature. We should be following a false trail, if we believed surrealists to be practitioners of literature who succumb, now and again, to an apparently ungovernable impulse to unburden themselves of impertinent inflammatory opinions on political matters. Indeed, we understand better where the essence of surrealism lies by trying to discover in which ways the surrealists' outlook on politics helps cast light on their approach to poetry.

Looking again at Schuster's comments, we notice he spoke of breaking with the ideologies of the Left, making no mention of the Right. Lack of acquaintance with the history of surrealism would incline us, no doubt, to believe he implied some permissible indulgence for the Right. The truth is that, from the first, a pressing need to oppose a society built on reason, in which bourgeois values flourished, led the surrealists to promote revolutionary ideals by every means available. At the beginning, naturally, these ideals were not formulated with impeccable clarity in terms directly applicable to politics. Yet, although they remained vague initially, surrealist aspirations were openly and aggressively antagonistic to the existing social and political order. Publishing their first magazine, the Paris group called for "a new declaration of the rights of man" and titled the official organ of their movement *La Révolution surréaliste*. When *La Révolution surréaliste* (1924–29) was replaced by a second magazine, the latter's title also underscored surrealism's dedication to the cause of revolution: *Le Surréalisme au service de la Révolution* was to run between 1930 and 1933.

Even before 1930, the French surrealists had evidenced a strong attraction to the Left. (Of the first-generation members in France, Aragon, Breton, Eluard, Péret, and Unik joined the Communist Party in January 1927, but only Aragon and Eluard, in the end, were to choose in favor of communism.) However, so far as their dealings with the political opponents of the Right went, they manifested a certain amount of caution. More than one surrealist brought misgivings to discussions with the group that published the para-communist newspaper *Clarté*. This is to say that those who have recounted the history of surrealism's involvement with communism[15] have placed insufficient emphasis upon the following fact. Idealism, rather than deficient foresight, prompted the Paris surrealists to look, despite obvious dangers, for common ground with those directing *Clarté* and, through them, with the Party. Conditioned by enthusiastic responsiveness to dialectical materialism, the surrealists, Breton was to remark in *Entretiens* (p. 121), were guilty of "too much precipitation." Schuster put it more forcefully when he attributed their behavior to naiveté. Whether naive or merely precipitate, the early surrealists in France gave dramatic proof of their sincere wish to parallel their efforts in favor of poetic liberation with participation in a movement having the declared purpose of advancing social and political emancipation.

Time has shown that since the twenties the surrealists have never attempted to propose a system of political thought all their own. Their interest in revolutionary endeavor on the plane of political and social militancy has been consistently proportionate to their belief that such an endeavor increases man's prospects of attaining complete freedom. Political and social oppression, at all events, is regarded in surrealist circles as the equivalent of the limitations imposed on poetic expression through verse by rationally controlled language and rules of prosody. Accordingly, liberty in the field of political self-determination is considered an accompaniment to the freedom that is an essential prerequisite for poetry in the widest sense entertained by surrealists.

As surrealists see it, conformity to imposed opinion in matters of politics is no less reprehensible than conformity, in verse, to accepted custom with regard to ethical, moral, or aesthetic issues. For this reason, whenever a member of the surrealist group has elected to place fidelity to some political cause before his obligations to surrealism, he either has found it advisable to part company with the surrealists of his own accord, or has found himself repudiated by them. The surrealists have remained adamant on this subject, ever since finding out for themselves the consequences of seeking compromise between their program of poetic liberation and that program of social and political revolution we know as the version of Marxism defended within the Communist Party.

Essentially, surrealists in France were victims of a misunderstanding upon which agreement with communism appeared, at first, both practical and efficacious. In two years of organized and purposeful activity, following the appearance of Breton's first manifesto, members of the surrealist movement in France had concluded that poetry could not find complete liberation within the framework of complacent bourgeois society. So, in 1926, Breton's *Légitime Défense* asserted, "There is not one of us who does not wish power to pass from the hands of the bourgeoisie into those of the proletariat." However, in his very next sentence, Breton went on to insist upon the need for preserving independence of action: "In the meantime, it is no less necessary, in our opinion, for the experiments in inner life to go on, without any external control, naturally, even Marxist control."[16]

The line seemed to have been plainly drawn, to mark once and for all the point beyond which surrealists would refuse to be led. Yet when, the following year, Breton and several of his associates decided to enter the Party, the author of *Légitime Défense* took his text off the market, "out of loyalty to the Communist Party," as *Entretiens* explains (pp. 120–121). Despite this and other tokens of their readiness to submit to Party discipline, the surrealists were regarded with suspicion by those in command, ever distrustful of the bourgeois origins of their new French recruits. Moreover, the surrealists were found guilty of distracting preoccupations that reduced their efficiency in advancing the immediate purposes of communism in France, when they did not impede these altogether. These preoccupations, needless to say, grew out of the surrealists' determination to pursue their own purposes—those of poetic liberation—in their own way. In consequence, dissension was inevitable, and not long delayed.

Having sought to escape the servitude imposed by the class-thinking to which they were born, the French surrealists found themselves facing the alternative of substituting for submission to bourgeois values unquestioning obedience to communist imperatives. Before long, they had learned a painful lesson they would never forget. While the *Second Manifeste du Surréalisme* reaffirmed faith in the principles of dialectical materialism, Louis Aragon's surrender of independent creative action to Party policies inspired horror in those who continued to be faithful to the author of both surrealist manifestoes. In 1932, Aragon's exclusion from the surrealist camp publicly marked the abandon of hopes of reaching an understanding with the communists. Within six years, André Breton had co-signed *Pour un Art révolutionnaire indépendant.*

Appearing for tactical reasons over the signatures of Breton and Diego Rivera in Mexico, on July 25, 1938, *For an Independent Revolutionary Art* was written by Breton and Leon Trotsky. It characterized true art as that which "tries to give expression to the inner needs of man and of humanity today," and as, by definition, revolutionary. Looked at this way, art becomes, in surrealist perspective, synonymous with poetry. For revolutionary art, said Breton and Trotsky, aspires to "a complete and radical reconstruction of society," incidentally "releasing intellectual creation from the chains that impede its activity." One observer has asked, "Can Trotsky really have signed this document?"[17] But he quite rightly showed no surprise at Breton's having done so. The basis upon which the 1938 tract was erected is the one on which surrealists had wanted to build, from the first. Acknowledging that social revolution alone can "clear a path to a new culture," *Pour un Art révolutionnaire indépendant* expressed aversion for the ruling classes in contemporary USSR. The faith it went on to affirm is the one from which surrealist aspirations have never ceased to take flight—identification of the need for emancipating the spirit with "that primordial necessity," the need for emancipating man. And the conclusion drawn from this postulation is no less consistent with the surrealist posture: "It follows that art cannot consent without falling into decay to bend to any external directive and to fit meekly into the framework that some people believe they can assign it, for extremely short-sighted pragmatic ends."

Lest they be accused of indifference to political responsibility, Trotsky and Breton insisted they had no intention of pleading for so-called "pure" art, which they dubbed reactionary. "We consider that the supreme task of art in our time is to participate consciously and actively in preparing revolution." "Giving artistic incarnation to his inner world," the artist will make his contribution most effectively by emphasizing his individuality, they argued, not by stifling it in a cause to which he has abdicated the right to speak in his own name. All forms of artistic commitment, from social realism to Sartrian *engagement*, are rejected *a priori*. Meanwhile, confidence goes entirely to the revolutionary force that reflects individual poetic vision, such as gives the writings of Péret—an anarchist militant, as it happens, who took inspiration from Trotsky—a quality Breton and other surrealists have recognized very willingly as irreplaceable and inimitable.

The purpose behind *Pour un Art révolutionnaire indépendant* was clear enough to see: it appealed for promotion of revolution through art, or poetry, while guaranteeing art and poetry liberty in the face of "the usurpers of revolution." It marked the establishment of a Fédération internationale de l'Art révolutionnaire indépendant, more notable for its declared aims than for what it had the chance to accomplish in the short time before the war broke out in 1939: "*independence of art—for revolution; revolution— for the definitive liberation of art.*" In collaborating on the 1938 tract, Breton had reaffirmed that, as a surrealist, he identified political pragmatism and opportunism with rationalism, seeing them as equally limitative, so far as revolutionary action goes; just as rationalism appeared to him and his fellow surrealists to restrict thought, and to channel the poetic venture into unproductive byways. At the same time, he reaffirmed the surrealist belief that, if political and social freedom is a prerequisite for the liberation of the mind, it can never be the end to which all mental effort should be bent, since it does not, of itself, guarantee the mental freedom surrealists hope to see man attain thanks to poetry.

The collapse of France and the establishment of the Vichy Government, whose Censor deferred permission for Breton's poem *Fata Morgana* to be published,[18] made it necessary for several of the surrealists to flee France. Upon his release from internment in Martinique, Breton made contact with Aimé Césaire in Fort-de-France, where in April 1941, Césaire had founded his magazine *Tropiques*. In the review edited by Césaire, his group's sympathies with surrealism were manifest from the first. As Suzanne Césaire explained, "Thus, far from contradicting, attenuating, or diverting our feeling for revolutionary living, surrealism trains it on its target."[19] When we look back to the forties, most deserving of special attention, however, is that the surrealists then became fully convinced that political activism, aimed at ameliorating social structures and remedying or even eradicating their weaknesses, could not provide all the answers they were seeking. Indicative of their position is an article signed by Pierre Mabille in the last number of the surrealist magazine Breton helped launch during his wartime exile in New York: *VVV*. Concentrating on the *élan révolutionnaire*, Mabille explained that it

> is identical, for us, with the *permanent* will to ensure the triumph of life over death. It does not date from yesterday, it is the apanage of no party and tends toward the constitution of no ideal state. No one can make himself its guardian, none can enclose it within a closed system, it is limitless in time, it aims at all areas at once, that is to say it cannot be satisfied by an action directed solely toward a political, economic, religious, or artistic end. In this respect, while recognizing the decisive importance of economic factors in human evolution, we are mistrustful of a transformation touching only that side of the social problem; just as we consider that a simple change of diet is insufficient to change man.[20]

By the time Breton returned to France in 1946, it had become plain that reconciliation of the Marxist program, as summarized in the dictum "transform the world," with the ambition the surrealists had inherited from Rimbaud, "change life," could not be achieved simply by willingness on the surrealists' part to come to terms with this or that socio-political program for reform. As a result of their re-examination of the problem facing them, surrealists gave up their search for a solution in the political arena. They looked to another, alternative line of conduct, squarely faced in the catalog of the international surrealist exhibition of 1947, held in Paris to celebrate the reconstitution of the surrealist group in France.

In reality, no sudden change took place in surrealist policy with respect to the world about us. Looking back to 1935 and the preface Breton wrote then for his *Position politique du Surréalisme*, we can see he was already speaking of having been preoccupied for ten years with "bringing together surrealism as *a mode for creating a collective myth* with the much more general movement for liberating man which tends first of all to modify fundamentally the bourgeois form of property." Finding the price of this undertaking too high, the surrealists quite naturally fell back on their original program, underlined by Breton himself in the statement just cited. At almost twenty years' distance, two international surrealist exhibitions have offered their evidence of the surrealists' attempt to define a myth suited to our time. The article "Devant le Rideau," written by Breton to open the catalog of the 1947 exhibit, is of central importance in this connection. No less significant is the catalog *L'Ecart absolu*.

No reader of the French surrealist magazines could fail to notice how often reference is made to Saint-Simon, to the Abbé Constant, to Enfantin, and to Flora Tristan, during the fifties and sixties. Furthermore, Breton's last major poetic work was his *Ode à Charles Fourier* (1947), written in 1945. Prior to his stay in the United States, Breton had been interested in Fourier mainly as the advocate of social reform. Not until he purchased the 1846 edition of Fourier's complete works in New York, did he discover "the great poet of harmonious life" lauded in the *Ode*. For the next two decades, the influence of Fourier widened and deepened, not only upon Breton but also upon his entourage: the surrealist magazine which appeared only after Breton's death, *L'Archibras* (1967–68), was so called as a tribute to the author of *La Théorie des quatre Mouvements*.

The significance of surrealist revulsion before political activism and the surrealists' growing preference for the promises of nineteenth-century utopianism cannot be overestimated. Nor, though, must it be interpreted as a sign of the collapse of their hope of contributing, here and now, to improving man's situation. The specifically ideological tenor of the 1965 international exhibition, the surrealists insisted in a broadsheet, *Tranchons-en*, dated December 1965, was deliberately intended to "attack *directly* the most intolerable aspects of the society in which we live." Moreover, they pointed out, "Nothing having been able to reduce us by *assimilation* to a religious sect, to a political party or a literary coterie—or, over the years, to really break our unity and our capacity for renewal—those whom we disturb can no longer hope to drown surrealism in the confusion from which they derive profit and glory."

After a review of the evidence summarized above, to the objective observer the confusion to which reference is made in *Tranchons-en* is hardly likely to appear to be the creation of surrealism's detractors alone. To dispel it, we need to proceed beyond the theoretical positions which Breton, principally, has mapped out. We must go on to examine how, in practice, the surrealists have met the challenge of protecting the independence of poetry, while defending the cause of revolution.

The familiar polarity—art for art's sake–committed art—represents, to surrealist thinking, oversimplification of the choices open to the creative artist. Surrealists certainly condemn the former. But they are keenly sensitive, also, to the risks run by any artist whose paramount concern is to transmit a *message*. Consequently, one of the reasons for the unrivalled reputation enjoyed within the surrealist movement by Benjamin Péret is his success in being, at one and the same time, a revolutionary activist and a poet whose work testifies to enviable freedom both from rational restraint and from socio-political fervor.

At no time did Péret permit his political involvement to find an echo in his poetry. Indeed, his was the voice that rose in protest when the situation in France during the German occupation of the forties prompted several poets—including the former surrealists Aragon and Eluard—to lend their support to the Resistance and to preach fervent nationalism. Péret greeted the publication of a selection of their patriotic verse, *L'Honneur des Poètes*, with uncompromising opposition. His *Le Déshonneur des Poètes* appeared in 1945 to affirm the poet's right and obligation to keep his distance, and to preserve his poetic statement from all forms of contamination. Yet, throughout his life, Péret's determination to make clear his own opposition to established government and controls could not be questioned. The contributions he made to the anarchist newspaper *Le Libertaire* in 1952, criticizing the trade unions and analyzing the reasons for which they had ceased to militate for the cause of revolution, demonstrate that he never turned his back upon society and its problems.[21] Meanwhile, the title of his most violent collection of poems, published in 1936, just before he left for Spain, is self-explanatory: *Je ne mange pas de ce pain-là* (*I'd rather starve*). Péret was a surrealist writer who believed the poet must accept a meal ticket from no one. This is to say that he spoke out more clearly than anyone else on the subject of true revolution, as surrealists understand it. In *La Parole est à Péret*, a text subsequently taken up in his *Anthologie des Mythes, Légendes et Contes populaires d'Amérique,* he declared in 1942 that the status of poet places the person who claims it "on the fringe of society":

> The poet of today has no other resource than to be a revolutionary or not to be a poet, for he must forever plunge into the unknown; the step taken the day before in no way releases him from taking a step the following day, since everything has to be started over again every day and since what he acquired in the hour of sleep has fallen to dust at the moment of waking. For him there are no gilt-edged investments but risk and adventure renewed indefinitely. It is thanks to this alone that he can call himself poet and claim to take a

legitimate place in the very forefront of the cultural movement, where he can earn neither praise nor laurels, but strike
with all his strength to level the barriers raised time after
time by habit and routine.

Today he can only be damned. This malediction cast
on him by present-day society already indicates his revolutionary position; but he will come out of his obligatory reserve to see himself placed at the head of society when, completely turned upside down, it has recognized the common
origin of poetry and science and when the poet, with the active or passive cooperation of everyone, creates the exciting
and marvelous myths that will send the whole world to storm
the unknown.[22]

So long as the word "poet" is interpreted as identifying the writer satisfied with adopting or adapting traditional poetic forms to the expression of private thoughts
and feelings he has persuaded himself to treat as having
universal significance and appeal, Péret's statement has a
pretentious, not to say a ludicrous character. When, though,
his remarks are placed in the context of surrealist thinking,
they serve to guide us where we must go. They assist us in
understanding that the surrealist idea of revolutionary action
gains definition, not loses it, outside the framework of organized political thought. The key to surrealist revolution,
in other words, is still subversion, not this or that system of
political revolt. Looking back some thirty years to the poems
he wrote while a surrealist, Gui Rosey was fully entitled to
point out, in 1965:

> Not being among those who subscribe to the opinion that a
> poet "is no more useful to the good of the State than a
> bowler"—which plainly stated means still today that his place
> in the sun is certain only in the service of public interest, I
> reject this despicable compromise, opposing it, not to be
> behindhand, by openly wishing harm to the State, to all
> States, not excepting those that have gone to seed, said to be
> at the revolutionary forefront of the century.[23]

Rosey's words render explicit one of the implications of an
earlier group statement, the tract *Haute Fréquence*, of May

24, 1951. The latter gives prominence to a direct result of the surrealists' disinclination to place their revolutionary energies at the service of this or that political machine, declaring that surrealism "offers for prospecting anew ground sufficiently vast and magnetic for desire and liberty to recreate one another endlessly."

Haute Fréquence did not mark a noteworthy change of direction for surrealist ambitions. After 1951 surrealists did not suddenly cease to agree with *Pour un Art révolutionnaire indépendant* that "artistic *opposition* is today one of the forces that can contribute usefully to discrediting and ruining regimes in which, concurrently with the right of the exploited class to a better world, all sense of the grandeur and even of the dignity of man is engulfed." The surrealist view of how this ambition is to be reached has not been subject to any significant evolution, either, even though firmer stress gradually comes to be placed upon individual effort. The essential feature of surrealism's political iconoclasm emerges, beyond dispute, as its independence, born of the instinct to protect the poetic principle from infringements of any and every kind. Duly critical of the Marxist perspective as it has found political expression, Schuster asserted, while discussing "Le Surréalisme et la Liberté":

> Now what *we* believe it necessary to rehabilitate today is individual revolt, to break down at the same time the old bourgeois framework, to which individual revolt can always apply itself, whatever the evolution of the bourgeoisie, and the bureaucratization of that revolt, the negation of that revolt which the Stalinist conception of revolution has created.

Schuster did not mean that Stalinism represents "bad" communism, while some other manifestation of the same ideology might be termed "good," or even tolerable. At best, political partisanship, to him, as to all surrealists, betokens compromise; at worst, it means surrendering independence of action. So the subversive role surrealists take on is not seen in its full significance by anyone who has failed to consider the consequences of the viewpoint reflected in Schuster's words.

Whereas surrealists have been obliged to conclude that politics is not the field they can till most productively, poetry continues to enjoy their undiminished confidence. The true meaning of that confidence escapes us, unless we take seriously the surrealists' claim to be concerned with supplying "a means for the total liberation of the mind." Hence the special relationship poetry bears to revolution, as we hear a young American surrealist allude to it:

> Poems do not make revolutions any more than revolutions make poems. The function of poetry, in terms of revolution, is to destroy conventional and limiting associations and all the decrepit, stifling myths of capitalist civilization by liberating images of desire. The function of revolution, in terms of poetry, is to destroy oppressive social conditions through the self-activity of the masses, leading to a total human liberation, and thus to create a situation in which poetry is realized in life itself.
>
> Poetry serves revolution just as revolution serves poetry. An enemy of one is the enemy of the other.[24]

The interdependence of poetry and revolution has always been a major theme in surrealist doctrine. In the circumstances, and in view of the self-assured tone of the passage just cited, we are entitled to ask whether surrealism's theory is an empty one, following a course of self-defeating repetitiveness and having no practical results. It might well be so, if surrealism did not have its source in implicit trust in the marvelous, defined by Péret as "the heart and nervous system of all poetry."

It was Péret who most insistently demanded in the name of surrealism that poetry contribute to the liberation of mankind from rationalism. Significantly, it is also Péret whose writings bear witness most strikingly to the contribution expected of the marvelous in surrealist poetry. To an outsider, Péret's poetic approach may seem impertinent and, in a sense, it *is*, deliberately so. But to those in the surrealist camp, it is never irrelevant. On the contrary, to them it appears a truly revolutionary approach, put to the use for which it is eminently suited: the fuller emancipation of man. We can look to Mabille for an explanation of the phenomenon epitomized in Péret's work. In his article in *VVV* we read:

> The main value of surrealism seems to me to have been the reintroduction of the marvelous into daily possibilities. It has taught that if reality appeared deadly dull, this is because man did not know how to see, his glance being limited by an education deliberately designed to blind him and by an aesthetic censorship handed down from times past. It has taught that if man was deaf in a mute world, this is because he was deafened by the hubbub of the most silly kind of society, by the soporific leitmotifs repeated *ad nauseam* by our teachers. It has taught us to listen to the inner voice which, every minute, is capable of dictating the poem. (p. 36)

In Péret better than in anyone else, the inner voice, liberated by the method of automatic writing, dictated a vision of the marvelous. Reading Péret's texts, we grasp more readily the central importance of the poetic marvelous in surrealist revolutionary theory. Then we can turn for confirmation to what is said in *Tranchons-en*, for example, where the appetite for the marvelous is termed "inseparable . . . from the call for liberty," and the marvelous is called "the occult organizer of myths."[25]

Among surrealism's most treasured myths, of course, is that of the perfectibility of man's situation and of its amenability to improvement by revolutionary effort. The most original feature of the surrealist program for revolutionary action is thus its unswerving reliance on the ability of the marvelous to make of poetry a revolutionary weapon. It is the "seed of the marvelous," as Breton called it,[26] which germinates and flowers, through poetry, in revolt against acceptance and conformity. So it is that, in unremittingly giving precedence to poetry over politics, the surrealists have not chosen to turn away from revolution. The very contrary is the case; as a collective statement published in December 1964 lets us see. Surrealists recognize the transformation of the world as a "primordial task." However, they believe that a revolutionary struggle aimed at carrying out this task alone could "come down to pernicious conformism," not only because substitution of one form of political government for another is unlikely to bring improvement, but because of the unambitious limits it imposes upon man's needs. Resisting conformism, surrealists declared their interest in "a total reshaping of the sensibility." Instead of addressing ourselves to the destruction of this or that manifestation of servitude, they argue, we should mount an attack upon "the mental structure" which makes man passive before his social fate. Hence they preach "the violent irruption of everything within the individual which, from having been submitted too long to repression, remains today in a state of virtuality." No misunderstanding is possible, then: "A true revolutionary must transform man in his social and individual totality."

As is manifested by renewed interest in surrealism during the sixties, in countries as dissimilar as Czechoslovakia (Bratislova, Brno, and Prague), England (Exeter), Holland (Amsterdam), and the United States (Chicago and San Francisco), these are not empty words. The circumstances under which they came into print underline the importance that surrealists in France attach to the ideas they communicate.[27] Meanwhile, the closing phrases of the collective statement from which they come are too clear to foster misunderstanding: "SURREALISM HAS ALWAYS WANTED TO BE IN ITS OWN DOMAIN THE CATALYTIC AGENT OF REVOLT. . . ." That domain, surrealists have never forgotten, is the domain of poetry. For the domain of poetry is, to them, revolutionary action.

Alfred Schmeller describes as follows a picture, "The Battle of the Potatoes," painted in 1948 by Raoul Michau:

"An easily understood allegory: Potatoes armed with pikes and bars are forming a phalanx and waging a peasant's [sic] war under a sultry sky. Battle pictures from Ahdorfer down to the 19th century shine through. Not unhumorously, the rustling of banners is divested of heroic meaning. It is significant that the arms carried by these potato troops are their own shoots sprouting in the dark of the cellar, on that underground level to which the Surrealists like to descend."[28] Whoever Michau is, he is a surrealist only in Schmeller's imagination. For surrealists are not interested in "easily understood" allegories or even allegories rationally interpretable at the price of earnest attentiveness. They could never agree that the needs of subversive poetry can be met by such crude and inappropriate means.[29] Certainly, nothing in their approach to the revolutionary-creative act gives us to believe that the kind of allegorism attributed to "The Battle of the Potatoes" could possibly meet the demands summarized by André Breton on the occasion of the appearance of the first number of the Parisian magazine Le Surréalisme, même: "We wish to pursue, in the direction that a third of a century of obstruction and trickery has not managed to controvert, the quest for an always greater liberation of the mind."[30] There is a world of difference between Michau's ponderous symbol of revolt—to say nothing of the muddy thinking that inspired it—and the surrealist poetry of painters and graphic artists like Polish-born Hans Bellmer, the Dane Wilhelm Freddie, the Frenchman Pierre Molinier, J. H. Moesman from Holland, and Max Walter Svanberg from Sweden.

Not all those just mentioned have articulated their views on the function of art.[31] Bellmer, though, has demonstrated that definition of poetry in surrealist perspective is not the prerogative of surrealist writers only.[32] So have other leading surrealist artists, Magritte, for example, and André Masson.[33] What they have to tell us is summed up best, perhaps, in this observation taken from Eluard's Donner à Voir: "The vanity of painters, which is immense, has for a long time impelled them to install themselves in front of a landscape, of a picture, of a text as if in front of a wall, to repeat them. They did not hunger after themselves. They applied themselves. The poet, for his part, is always thinking of *something else*" (p. 73).

What is important, here, is not an instinct for evasion, leading the poet into acceptance of the traditional solution—withdrawal into the ivory tower—but refusal to submit to conditions which limit our freedom of action on every plane. This is why we hear Jean-Louis Bédouin declare:

> Starting from refusal of the ludicrous conditions imposed on man by constraints of every nature, surrealism is an impassioned search for "the powers of the mind," an unprecedented attempt to restore them to him. The idea that the limitations on all expression can be abolished thanks to appropriate methods guides it in the domain of poetry which is specifically, but not restrictively, its own. In life, it is a matter also of setting in motion the secret motives of being, so as to change this life, which is so to speak only conceded us, into a real life, worthy of being lived.[34]

And this, too, is why Robert Desnos could write, regarding his period of involvement in surrealism, "I have often asked myself what held us so closely together. Probably something that resembled the fellowship of those who are going to blow up a city in a spirit of revolt."[35]

The idea of poetry as an active force invests surrealist endeavor with its characteristic orientation, hence the following typical statement, borrowed from Eluard's *Donner à Voir*: "Surrealism, which is an instrument of cognition, and for that very reason an instrument as much of conquest as of defense, works at bringing to light the profound consciousness of man. Surrealism works at demonstrating that thought is common to all and, for that reason, it refuses to serve an absurd order, based on inequality, on deception, on cowardice" (p. 85). The important thing is that even when —as was the case with Bédouin, a moment ago—a surrealist gives the word "poetry" a narrower sense than usage generally demands in surrealism, he still says nothing that creates a conflict between the purposes to which he claims verse can be put and the goals embraced by the broadly subversive trends of surrealist poetry, as we have come to know them. In fact, listening to those who, because they are writers, are more inclined anyway to discuss the import of their work on a theoretical plane than surrealists primarily active in other media, we often find what they have to say capable of broadening and deepening our appreciation of the scope of the surrealist revolution.

Two examples illustrate this well enough. When speaking of his reasons for submitting to the attraction of surrealism, Jean-Jacques Lebel once commented: "Without calling upon psychochemistry, I think I can affirm that poetry has never meant to me anything but revolutionary behavior (a particular wavelength rather than a language)."[36] Such extension of the range of poetry, as a revolutionary means, beyond linguistic limits is far from uncommon in statements surrealists have made, even when they have been discussing individual collections of verse, as Eluard was doing in the *prière d'insérer* for Péret's *De Derrière les Fagots*, in 1934:

> One of the principal properties of poetry is to inspire in frauds a grimace that unmasks them and lets them be judged. Like no other, the poetry of Benjamin Péret encourages this reaction, as inevitable as it is useful. For it is endowed with that major accent, eternal and modern, which detonates and makes a hole in a world of prudently ordered necessities and of babbling old refrains. For it tends with its extra-lucid images, its images as clear as rock-water, evident like *the strident cry of red eggs,* toward a perfect comprehension of the unwonted and toward its use against the ravages of malignant exploitation by stupidity and a certain form of good sense. For it militates insolently in favor of a new *régime,* that of logic linked with life not like a shadow but like a star.[37]

Breton put it simply, in *Légitime Défense:* "It seems to me that revolt alone is creative." Almost twenty years later, Péret lent his support to Breton's declaration when he attacked the verse offered in *L'Honneur des Poètes*. In total consistency with the standards of poetry surrealism had taught him to respect and apply, Péret condemned the patriotic poems of the French Resistance, declaring in *Le Déshonneur des Poètes*, "Not one of these 'poems' rises above the lyrical level of pharmaceutical publicity" (p. 82). Return to the classical alexandrine, a noteworthy feature in the form of many of the poems in *L'Honneur des Poètes*, is an external sign of a dangerous instinct to conform which denies these texts any lyrical quality, so stripping poetry of its very *raison d'être*, because conformism has taken the place of revolution.

Publication of *Le Déshonneur des Poètes* could not but bring sharp criticism of Péret who, as a refugee in Mexico, appeared to have no right to condemn those who had stayed at home under foreign occupation. But just as Breton did in *Arcane 17* (written while he was in exile in the United States), Péret recognized nationalism as an emotion that lent itself to manipulation to counter-revolutionary ends. As such, it had to be opposed, at whatever cost to the surrealist who spoke out against it, as he would feel compelled to do against any other force operating against revolution and in favor of the status quo.

Breton makes it clear why Péret had no alternative but to denounce the concept of poetry illustrated in *L'Honneur des Poètes*, when he writes: "At the point we have reached, the poet or the artist could not be qualified as such, nor claim to lasting recognition, except so far as he has risen up against the specific forms assumed in our time by alienation in the non-clinical sense of the term." With these words opens one of the last public declarations Breton made before his death, and certainly one of the most important to anyone seeking to assign subversion and revolution their rightful part in surrealist effort: *A ce Prix*, a text written to introduce an exhibition of work by Jean-Claude Silbermann, *Enseignes sournoises*, held in 1964:[38]

From the philosophy of "Enlightenment," we absolutely must remember—consider established—that, from the
aspirations of mankind, everything opposes our inferring a
design, either intelligent or moral in nature, from which some
principle of order could stem. No permissible speculation
allows us to conclude a God to be necessary, even preserved
from the insane and despotic images imposed by established
religions. However, even if the supreme aberration of anthro-
pomorphism bedecked in the name of "God" were to be the
ultimate danger for the analogical process, it is no less true
that this process answers an organic need in man, and that, to
avoid coagulation into a disastrous entity—in consideration
also of the resources of Hegelian dialectic—it demands that it
not be held in suspicion or under restraint, but, entirely to the
contrary, that it be stimulated. *This is the price of poetry.*

Poetic surrealism to which Breton stressed that he
was devoting himself in the *Manifeste du Surréalisme* (p.
50), resists the idea of a universe dominated by a deity—
nationalism or any other: "Man proposes and disposes. It
rests with him alone to belong entirely to himself, that is to
say to maintain in a state of anarchy the band of his desires,
every day more formidable. Poetry teaches him how" (p.
31).[39] "We want, we will have, the beyond in our time,"
was Breton's assertion in the fourth number of *La Révolution surréaliste* (July 15, 1925).

With the same ideals in focus, Breton was to write in
A ce Prix that, since it is more and more widely admitted
nowadays that sexuality leads the world, all taboos and in-
terdicts must be raised: "Systematic sex education could
have no value except so far as it leaves intact the mainspring
of 'sublimation' and finds a means to overcome the attraction of 'forbidden fruit.' It can only be a question of initiation, with all this word presupposes that is sacred—outside
religions of course—and presupposing what the ideal con-
stitution of each human couple demands by way of a quest.
This is the price of love." Breton's remarks are certainly pertinent to the work of Silbermann, whose painting complements the poems in his *Au Puits de l'Ermite* (1959) and his

narrative *Le Ravisseur* (1966). More than this, though, they demonstrate that love and poetry follow a parallel course in surrealism. Both tend in the direction to which *A ce Prix* is leading us.

The ambition to "transform the world" and the ambition to "change life," Breton takes the opportunity to remind us, become one in surrealism, "one indivisible imperative." This explains the attack on Stalinism right in the middle of his preface to the Silbermann exhibit, with accompanying praise of Trotsky for proclaiming (in *Literature and Revolution*) that art must be free "contrary to all the required servilities of 'engagement'":

> At the moment when the silence maintained over the circumstances of Khrushchev's eviction betrays unprecedented embarrassment and instills uneasy feelings in the henchmen . . . the greatest attentiveness is obligatory, as also the greatest openmindedness with regard to possible events and the greatest degree of availability continue to be permissible. *This is the price of liberty.*

It is, says Breton, at the intersection of these three paths—poetry, love, liberty—that we find Jean-Claude Silbermann. At the same crossroads we come upon the subversive presence of revolutionary surrealism.

5

Surrealist Poetic Expression

MPLICIT in the poetics of surrealism is an unshakeable faith
in a special relationship existing between the poet—the
creative artist—and his audience: readers, spectators, or
listeners. The surrealist's poetic ambitions place this relationship on a footing where a distinctive reaction takes place
between the poet and his public. It was, beyond a doubt, to
this reaction that Paul Eluard alluded when, speaking in
England on June 24, 1936, on the occasion of the international surrealist exhibition held in London, he declared, "The
poet is the one who inspires much more than the one who is
inspired."[1] In the context of surrealist subversive endeavor,
the creator is by no means denied the privilege of inspiration, however. For he attains the status of poet, in the surrealists' estimation, when whatever he has to show or tell
stimulates in his audience a responsive creative activity to
which surrealist aims lend value. Surely it is in this sense
that we must attach significance to the surrealists' persistent
reiteration of Lautréamont's dictum, "Poetry must be made
by all, not one." Certainly, in surrealism the miracle of poetic exchange requires that the receiver be tuned to the correct wavelength, otherwise nothing has been gained by
beaming the radio signal in the first place.

Can it be that everything surrealists have been telling us just serves to mask banality? Does that phrase of Eluard's, offered above as exemplary of the surrealists' convictions, really give away the game, revealing surrealist poetry as not so very different, if indeed different at all, from poetic forms its practitioners have claimed to be outmoded and have proposed to replace? If it seems fair to raise these questions at this stage, it is above all because the nature of poetic exchange, as effected in surrealism, still lacks definition in our minds. We need to witness some practical application of their poetic principles if we are to see why surrealists have considered these fundamental to bringing about the revolution to which they have dedicated themselves. Examination of three complementary forms of surrealist expression will show how, above and beyond the technical concerns imposed by a given medium, the subversive poetics of surrealism take their effect.

Spectacle, Poetry, and Subversion
During the early days of cinema, it seems fair to say, the public at large generally agreed a film was successful to the extent that it proved faithful to observable reality. At all events, the success of the very first movies was measured, popularly, by the yardstick of familiarity. Why pay money to watch a movie of a train entering a station, or leaving it, when one could just as well witness the real thing, and free of charge, at the railroad station? One paid, and gladly, not for reality, but for the illusion of reality.

The special genius of Georges Méliès was that he reversed generally accepted propositions in the cinema, demonstrating the reality of illusion. He had only to film a falling wall, then run his strip of film backward, to invert the law of gravity, challenge his audience's sense of time sequence, and call into question the very function of cinema. It does not matter that Méliès—who, after all, accomplished other things as well—did all this inadvertently, when he projected one of his films after forgetting to rewind it. What counts is the following. Where we see illusion in the movies cease to be dependent on reality for authentication, while reality becomes, instead, the product of illusion, we are already—as the short subjects of Norman MacLaren testify—on the road to surrealism.

Now as Aragon asserted forcefully in *Le Paysan de Paris*, the key to the surreal is to be sought in the image:

> The vice called *Surrealism* is the disordered and impassioned use of the *image* as a drug, or rather the uncontrolled provocation of the image for itself and for what it brings in the domain of representation by way of unforeseeable perturbation and metamorphosis: for each image, each time, forces you to reconsider the whole Universe. (p. 80)

The word *l'image* embracing in French both the sense of *image* and of *picture*, extension of the theory of the liberative role of imagery to the plane of visual impression was not only quite a small step for the early surrealists to take. It was also a logical one—or so it seemed to Breton, when he began to speculate about surrealism and painting. And so, during the twenties the cinema too attracted surrealists in France, because it appeared to lend itself especially well to their purposes. "The cinema," wrote Antonin Artaud, "implies overturning values, a complete upset of optics, perspective, logic. It is more exciting than phosphorus, more captivating than love. One cannot devote oneself indefinitely to destroying its power to galvanize by use of subjects that neutralize effects and that belong to the theatre."[2]

Echoing Aragon's remarks, Artaud went on to comment, "The cinema is a remarkable stimulant. . . . The cinema has above all the properties of an inoffensive direct poison, a subcutaneous injection of morphine." In other words, Artaud wrote his scenario *La Coquille et le Clergyman* (1927) because he believed the cinema "possesses an element of its own, truly magic, really cinematographic," which "comes subterraneously from the images," not in logical sequence, but in the "mixture," "vibration," and "clash" of images. As he himself noted, this ambition over-flowed the framework of "simple narration," of the problems of music, usual rhythm, and aesthetics of the cinema, to raise the question of *"expression* in all its areas, and to its full extent."

Silent films had to aim at communicating with their audience visually. This, surely, is why misgivings about the usefulness of movies were not voiced with any degree of uniformity from within the surrealist movement until the introduction of sound, viewed by surrealists as having changed the nature of cinema radically. As surrealists now saw it, most movie-makers lost their way, once silent films had given place to talkies. Georges Sadoul, historian of the cinema and former surrealist, has recalled: "When sound came, we considered it with mistrust and even hostility. I remember long evenings spent with Jacques Prévert (the future writer of screen dialog) condemning not talkies (revealed by *White Shadows in the South Seas*), but the use of words, really inadmissible in a film."[3] As André Breton put it succinctly, "the silver wall" was "spattered with brains." Discussing "The Precocious Old Age of the Cinema" as early as 1933, Artaud affirmed: "Beyond the fact that, since talkies came in, the elucidations of the spoken word put a stop to the unconscious and spontaneous poetry of images, the illustration and completion of the meaning of images by words show the limits of the cinema." René Crevel and Paul Eluard had said substantially the same thing in December 1931, in the fourth number of *Le Surréalisme au service de la Révolution:* "Formerly silent and having become talkies, that is, struck with psittacism, the cinema reflects the nonsense, tall stories, ironical or sentimental vulgarities that make theatre houses preeminently disgusting places."

The point is not just that, from now on, a movie-house audience could enjoy the privilege of hearing a train arrive (or leave for that matter), as well as see it on the screen. It was not sound itself the surrealists opposed, but the restrictive role played by sound in confining films within realistic narrative tradition. The shift of attention was to them an alarming one. Film directors seemed, regrettably, bent on imitating stage directors, simply transferring theatrical aesthetics to a medium which, so long as it still was only that of pictures which moved, had promised discoveries to be found nowhere else. "For the theatre," wrote Artaud, who is best remembered for his theories of the theatre, "is already a betrayal." As early as January 1918, Philippe Soupault had noted in the magazine *SIC:*

> One day on a piece of waste ground in Vincennes an individual called Pathé presented to a group of rubbernecks a cinematograph invented by the Lumière brothers: man was endowed with a new eye.
> Those who from then on gave their attention to this extraordinary invention made a great mistake: they made the cinema the colorless mirror and mute echo of the theatre. No one has stopped making this mistake yet.

We know the surrealists' objections were leveled at certain trends in theatre above all, those having a guaranteed audience, outside France as well as in: psychological drama, notably. All the same, anyone interested in the various programs of surrealist revolt or in their interrelationship cannot fail to be struck by this fact: although they protested against contamination of cinema by theatre, the first surrealists by no means eliminated the theatre from their own creative activities.

If there appears to be a perplexing paradox here, it is resolved with least delay in the minds of those who recall how many surrealists of the first generation had begun by participating in Dada. Dada had taught them to appreciate the advantages of *manifestations*—public performances before an audience, directed against the latter's literary and artistic preconceptions and presumptions.

It is well known that the repetitive nature of *manifestations*, as Dadaists in Paris indulged in them, led Breton and several others to tire of an activity that by May of 1921 already seemed to Breton to have ceased being productive. Nevertheless, several of those who were to join Breton under the flag of surrealism shared his first-hand experience of the benefits that could be gained from demonstrations of an aggressive kind, carried out before an assembled audience. True, the surrealists were not to perpetuate the Dadaist custom of defiance by *manifestation*. Even so, when organizing and setting up their international exhibitions, held over a period of almost four decades, surrealists regularly were to take pains to create an atmosphere of mystery, shock, or surprise, the right ambience for stimulating wonder. In this way, they evidenced abiding faith in the part spectacle can play in making one's point, through an appeal directed at the eye.

Breton was to insist at the very beginning of his 1928 study *Le Surréalisme et la Peinture*, "The eye exists in an untamed state. . . . It presides over the conventional exchange of signals apparently required by the navigation of the mind. But who will draw up the scale of vision? There exists what I have seen many times . . . there exists also what I am beginning to see that is not *visible*." Trust in the primitive response of the eye, in its natural freedom from the influence of artistic sophistication and inherited tradition, links surrealist cinema and theatre—and of course painting, too—in one purpose. Thus the celebrated opening sequence of Luis Buñuel's movie *Un Chien andalou* (1928), culminating in the shot of an eyeball slashed by a razor, is indicative of the orientation of surrealist endeavor in the theatre, no less than it is of the direction taken by the surrealist cinema.

A comparable token of surrealist protest against inculcated aesthetic principles, far less well known, is the gesture that brings to a close the 1920 play *Vous m'oublierez* by Breton and Soupault. Advancing to the proscenium, the character named Parapluie (Umbrella) waves a flag like the ones used in France by railroad crossing keepers to warn road traffic to give way to traffic of another kind. In fact, so far as surrealism's attitude to the media of film and drama is concerned, the climax of this play is perhaps even more enlightening than the opening of *Un Chien andalou*. It concentrates attention visually, without serving identifiable narrative purpose by rounding off a plot (an element noticeably deficient in *Vous m'oublierez*) previously carried by dialog and now supposedly brought to a fitting conclusion.

The visual signal is capable of issuing a warning, even though the precise nature of the latter remains a matter of conjecture, and the reason why any warning should be necessary is not supplied explicitly through the spoken word. This is not to say that, from the outset, surrealists deliberately and consistently turned away from plot so as to concentrate upon unexplained visual effects, inexplicable ones even. However, it does seem worth noting that, in surrealism, aspects of theatrical spectacle which conventionally support plot and dialog, usually finding support in these, are no longer under obligation to play a role in imparting a message that reason has the right and capacity to interpret. Meanwhile, by his response to questions about the meaning of perplexing visual effects in movies he has made, Buñuel has shown time and again that the presence of such effects owes much more to the intrinsic appeal of the image itself than to its interpretable nature. Thus, for example, his continual preoccupation with ambiguity—it becomes more profound, not less so, after 1928—has more to do than symbolic intent with the presence of animals and insects in his films: the bear roaming the house in *El angel exterminador* (1962), shall we say, or the cockroaches falling on the piano keys, during a scene at the police station in *Les Charmes discrets de la Bourgeoisie*.

The ambiguity of Buñuelian cinema has as its equivalent in the theatre the ambiguity of the surrealist plays of José Pierre. Yet Buñuel does not presume to speak for anyone but himself, when he confesses to his interest in creating and maintaining ambiguity. For just like Artaud, he recognizes that the value of the image exceeds its possible symbolic signification. Speaking on the subject of "Sorcery and Cinema," Artaud once wrote, "The smallest detail and the most insignificant object take on a meaning and a life that belong to them alone. And this is so, outside the significative value of the images themselves, outside the thought they translate, the symbol they constitute." Both Buñuel and Artaud are responsive to what the latter calls "this sort of virtual power of images" and realize that the age of cinema coincides with the "precise moment when worn-out language is losing its power as symbol, when the mind is tired of representational play." To put it more simply, Buñuel agrees with Artaud that "Clear thought is no longer enough for us."

Buñuelian cinema finds in ambiguity one of its strongest links with surrealism. It is especially interesting that this should be so because Buñuel's trust in the ambiguous, fostered and sustained by means of cinematic imagery, helps explain the function of spectacle as essentially anti-realistic in the context of surrealism. At the same time, it helps us see why, in a movie significantly titled *L'Imitation du Cinéma* (1959), Marcel Mariën first extends his audience an invitation to interpret parts of his film in Freudian terms, and then deliberately explodes the myth of so-called Freudian images in a shot showing a gyrating labeled photograph of Freud disintegrating.

If Buñuel and Mariën—different enough, in all conscience, so far as their approach to the cinema is concerned—appear to have one belief in common, it is surely that of the inviolability of the filmic image, of its autonomy. The resistance put up by certain kinds of spectacle to domestication through interpretation according to familiar modes of thought, is especially precious to surrealists. Hence the statement of faith implicit in Breton's declaration that the eye exists in an untamed state. Hence, too, the recurrence of situations in the surrealist plays of Roger Vitrac that do not yield up "meaning" to reasonable thought. Reason has to take refuge in the idea that one or other scene of Vitrac's

Les Mystères de l'Amour (1923), for instance, must be a dream sequence, thus justifiably different from others, said to belong far more appropriately to the world of reality. Actually, though, what surrealists do is reaffirm the eye's right to see without interference from inculcated theory or acquired thought process.

It is surely instructive that, from his first surrealist manifesto onward, André Breton never wavered in his conviction that childhood is a privileged state. Contrasting the untutored response of the young child with our own, we can estimate our distance from paradise lost. We progress a long way with surrealism in theatre and film, when we see it as a persistent effort to reduce that distance. And such an effort promises a greater degree of success, surrealists are sure, when, in the journey back to lost paradise, one is able and willing to jettison heavy baggage acquired in the form of an education usually considered a necessary contribution to maturing the mind.

All this does not mean that surrealist plays and films appeal, or are meant to appeal, to brainless idiots. Yet it does suggest that surrealists tend to place their trust in movies and drama capable of weaning audiences of reliance upon reasonable interpretations as the key to appreciation. Obviously, Breton's statement about the nature of the human eye is, to say the least, tendentious. Indeed, its importance lies in betraying a need felt by all surrealists to be able to count on one of man's most valued gifts, sight, in a battle with intellect, a predisposition born of an imperious need to set receptivity on another track. It is evident that not all movies or plays meriting the appellation surrealist fall into this category. Nevertheless, one best grasps the contribution made in the pursuit of surrealist aims by many otherwise confusing experiments with film and dramatic form when one reflects on Breton's protest in *L'Amour fou* against "the extravagant overestimation of the known compared with what remains to be known,"[4] when one heeds the warning of the flag brandished at the close of *Vous m'oublierez*. Then a play like Georges Hugnet's *Le Muet* (1930), in which coincidence is taken well beyond the limits of credibility and plot is not coherent enough to inspire reason to confidence, earns a respect it could never command—and its author never sought—when judged by conventional theatrical criteria.

The tendentiousness of Breton's assertion regarding the eye typifies basic trends in surrealist dialectic. As such, it can and does draw ridicule. In spite of this, it illuminates surrealist endeavor, as the influence of surrealist aspirations may be traced through plays and films. Distinguishing sight from reasonable assessment of visual impressions, surrealists would take little or no interest in either theatre or cinema, if they did not locate the excitement of spectacle at a point between what we see and the interpretation placed upon it by reasonable minds. This is why one of surrealism's essential roles is to advocate severance of the connection between eye and brain, usually taken for granted as serving to link seeing and comprehending. The result would seem to be leading straight into unproductive chaos, if surrealism could be reduced to a game, perversely devised to eliminate reason and to do no more. But, treating reason as a negative force lending stability to an oppressive world, surrealists look upon its elimination as a very positive step indeed. And the consequences of their attitude are far-reaching. These come into focus when we ask how surrealism aims to keep eye and brain apart. What new connections are to be established, once reason has been discarded in film and drama? What about feeling, for instance?

One arrives at a very limited sense of the scope of surrealism, so long as the surrealists' contempt for sentimentality has not been recognized, so long as the significance of their mistrust of sentiment has not been grasped. To the surrealist mind, sentimentality denotes conformity, ultimate acceptance of social and ethical norms, compromise with and even capitulation to forces that infringe upon individual liberty. This is why love enthuses surrealists only when it finds expression as revolt, eminently represented in the spectacle of the two lovers in Buñuel's *L'Age d'Or* disrupting a public ceremony as they roll in the mud, in erotic embrace.

To surrealists, mad love as Breton called it, or sublime love, as Benjamin Péret spoke of it, is a passion undisciplined by reason, expressive of irrational impulses, and therefore assertive of freedom. Viewed from the angle of revolutionary surrealism, unsentimentalized love participates in establishing a new connection, more highly prized by surrealists than any other. It is one that rules out reason entirely, investing surrealist spectacle with a value rationality cannot gauge. The important thing is what happens when and where sight serves as the gateway to the marvelous, "heart and nervous system of all poetry" to other surrealists, as well as to Benjamin Péret.

Speaking on the theme of poetry and cinema at the University of Mexico in 1953, Buñuel referred to poetry as "mystery, all that completes and enlarges tangible reality." Artaud, as we have heard, spoke of "the spontaneous poetry of images." Both he and Buñuel confirm that to apply the test of poetic content, in whatever the genre under examination, means applying the only criterion recognized in surrealism, when artistic achievement comes to be weighed. Thus Buñuel's wish to have "an integral view of reality" goes with his desire to "enter the marvelous world of the unknown" and is, therefore, consistent with the etymological significance of surrealism as a higher sense of reality.

It is possible to expand Buñuel's reference to an integral view of reality by following out in his movies the consequences of his love for the instinctive and the irrational, which leaves its impression upon a film of apparently realist inspiration, *Los Olvidados* (1950). It is not so easy to trace the meaning of the marvelous in his writings, or in those of any other surrealist. Yet this fact has never stood between surrealists and use of the word which Péret, for one, actually took care (p. 33) not to attempt to define in *La Parole est à Péret*. Artaud, for example, asserted that "the object in film cannot be inferior to the film's power of action—and must partake of the nature of the marvelous." In the *Journal littéraire* Robert Desnos spoke on April 18, 1925 of the marvelous as "the supreme aim of the human mind since it gained possession of the creative power conferred upon it by poetry and the imagination." The marvelous assumes the character of an "admirable passport . . . for access to those regions where heart and mind liberate themselves at last from the critical and descriptive spirit that pins them to the ground." Time and again we notice how elusive is the meaning of the marvelous, as surrealists speak of it. Since they would contend that it is in the nature of the anti-rational to elude identification within the framework of reasonable language, the special interest presented by surrealist drama and film lies, in considerable measure, in their capacity for bringing us face to face with surrealist poetry through the spectacle of the marvelous.

A pertinent question now faces us. If silent films appear more likely to serve the cause of the marvelous than talkies, because dialog does not intrude to control our reactions to their images, then why not revert to silent movies, and why not at the same time limit stage performance to mime, with dialog suppressed altogether?

True, Vitrac did borrow techniques from the silent screen in his play *Poison* (1922). Nevertheless, surrealists soon made the discovery that words, after all, are not necessarily the impediment to examination of the marvelous they had feared at first. Inspired by Buñuel's example, they began to explore the potentialities of language and sound, in relation to investigation of the marvelous. In *L'Age d'Or*, to cite just one instance of Buñuel's use of sound-track to surrealist effect, the sight of the two lovers aging and suffering before us is offset by evidence of the marvelous permanence of love, in the form of a passionate dialog that continues without interruption, *voice over*. Something comparable is to be found in José Pierre's plays *Le Vaisseau amiral* (1967) and *Bonjour mon Oeil* (1968) in which, the playwright tells us, arbitrary punctuation contributes to "driving out the natural," and fanciful diction is to help the audience "only up to a certain point." José Pierre directs attention away from the familiar elements of stage action and dialog, toward a drama that may be concealed behind them, instead of being conveyed by means of these traditional ingredients. *Le Vaisseau amiral* reaches its climax as the backdrop opens on the darkened stage to reveal the flagship which lends this play its title, all lights burning. The flagship's siren, heard intermittently throughout, now blares louder than ever, and goes on doing so until not one spectator remains in the auditorium: there is nothing more to see, and the audience has been put to flight by what is audible.

The use of film collage that brings together visual elements—through the splicing of film clips, as practiced by Jacques Brunius—or unites unrelated sound-tracks, according to a method pioneered by Jindrich Heisler and Georges Goldfayn in their *Revue surréaliste*, is more than just the unpretentious counterpart of a much publicized pictorial technique having a significant influence upon surrealist painting and graphic art. They reflect a fundamental characteristic of surrealist expression. For surrealism consistently places the medium of choice second in importance to what we may term, provisionally, the message it is used to communicate.

The opening section of *L'Age d'Or*—an informative documentary about scorpions—is nothing other than a decoy, set to lure the unwary into the falsely reassuring assumption that, in this film, Buñuel asks of us only the submissive willingness to watch and listen without which didacticism would be ineffective. It appears to be, incidentally, a didacticism aimed at proving an unexceptionable point: that natural history is incontrovertible. Inspired, in contrast, by D. A. F. Sade's *Les 120 Journées de Sodome*, the closing sequence of the same movie gives new meaning to the instructional film, by presenting a chilling spectacle in which Sade's infamous Duke of Blangis is, to quote Buñuel's scenario, "evidently Jesus Christ," even though our inclination may be to deny, this time, that things are as they seem. As for Vitrac's play *Les Mystères de l'Amour*, its first tableau is brought to a close by the theatre manager's announcement, "Mesdemoiselles, mesdames et messieurs, le spectacle est terminé," and by the sight of a surrogate author, blood-spattered but howling with laughter. And this first tableau is succeeded by a second (missed by those who have taken the manager at his word), in which the play's hero, Patrice, has become Mussolini. Should we not wonder why?

At this point, there is a distinct possibility that confusion may result from use of the word "message" in connection with surrealist theatre and cinema. So far as we understand a rather involved statement of Artaud's, condemning a form of cinema he called "dramatic," it preaches rejection of deliberately engineered effects for which the movie medium is the chosen vehicle. In relation to surrealism, one cannot speak of the "message" communicated as being an effect totally encompassed within voluntary intention on the creator's part. Mariën's *L'Imitation du Cinéma* has forewarned us against making the mistake of assuming this to be the case, and also against the error of proceeding to reasonably deduced conclusions. If we were to try to handle Artaud's play *Le Jet de Sang* (published in 1925) this way, then results would be catastrophic. What is the message to reason, communicated in the following spectacle which, early on, follows an avowal of love between a young man and a young woman?

> A silence. We hear something like the sound of an immense wheel turning and setting off a wind. A hurricane breaks them apart.
> At this moment, we see two astral bodies come into collision and a series of legs of living flesh falling, with feet, hands, hair, masks, colonnades, doorways, temples, alembics, falling, but more and more slowly, as if they were falling in a vacuum, then three scorpions one after the other, and lastly

a frog, a beetle that comes to rest with heart-rending slowness, sickening slowness.

Whereas in *L'Age d'Or* the visual effect linking Sade's Duke of Blangis with Jesus is not difficult to interpret, the two instances of similar identification (Patrice=Mussolini, Dovic= Lloyd George) in Vitrac's *Les Mysères de l'Amour* elude reasonable explanation and, to this extent, come closer to communicating a sense of the kind of surrealist poetry conveyed by spectacle in *Le Jet de Sang*.

Spectacle would be valueless in the context of surrealism, if it were to serve only to reproduce the known, carefully respecting commonly accepted distinctions, if it merely rehearsed the familiar. As a surrealist makes use of it—as Aragon, for example, does in both his plays, *Au Pied du Mur* (completed in 1926) and *L'Armoire à Glace un beau Soir*, written in the winter of 1922–23—spectacle challenges the mind's meek acceptance of patterns of behavior that habit and convention have persuaded us to treat as normal, hence as real. In every instance, the surrealists' distaste for aesthetics is plainly reflected in refusal to present spectacle for its own sake. Indeed, surrealism's anti-aesthetic program, its unwillingness to be or to pass for mere amusement, may be said to find a logical conclusion in the theatre of Jean-Pierre Duprey, so far removed from dramatic presentation as we know it that it defies staging, calling instead for screen projection—on the inner screen of the imagination.

Duprey's writings in dramatic format confront us with an extreme but illuminating example of what becomes of consecrated form, under pressure from surrealist content. Theatre as dramatized presentation is inadequate to the task of communicating what Duprey's text has to tell us. (And this, we must bear in mind—recalling José Pierre's confession that he is not at all sure he knows what *Le Vaisseau amiral* means—is not necessarily only what Duprey wishes it to say.) Thus the familiar concept of theatrical spectacle does not give a fully satisfactory idea of the demands surrealism is capable of making upon the medium of drama. Even the cinema provides but a metaphor for the kind of projection needed, if Duprey's *La Forêt sacrilège* (dated August 1949) is to take effect. "The first and Only Scene" that makes up Part Three of the same author's *Derrière son Double* (1948) is conjured up by the curious central figure of the book, Monsieur H., "sorcerer without sorcery," whom we are permitted to watch "navigate in a film without actors." This strange film he projects on "the imaginary screen" which is nothing other than the top of the peaked cap belonging to a decapitated general.

Because in surrealism subversion is no mere adornment, being neither a matter of technical device nor of self-publicity, it touches plot, character delineation, the very idea of theatre itself. This explains why, paradoxical as it may seem at first, the means placed at the disposal of subversion appear fully adequate to the surrealist even when, on the plane of theatrical competence, they are woefully inadequate. Had this not been so, one wonders how the first-generation surrealists in France could have been so enthusiastic about the profoundly anti-dramatic plays of Raymond Roussel, when André Breton, for one, had to admit he could explain neither *L'Etoile au Front* nor *La Poussière de Soleils.*[5] In other words, surrealist subversion aims directly at the idea of drama as a means of communication, resting upon a basis of common trust in which playwright and his public share without reservation. Anything less demanding, anything calling for a less radical revision of our notion of what theatre serves to do, would be a betrayal of surrealism, a compromise that would offer more than a little justification for the widespread confusion in critical circles, as well as among the general public, concerning the true definition of surrealism. For it is the subversive principle which ensures that surrealism will be never *something added*—merely a constituent ingredient, subject to isolation and analysis at the whim of literary commentators. All this goes some way toward explaining the surrealists' attitude to the post-surrealist theatre of Antonin Artaud and the plays of Eugène Ionesco.

Considered from the point of view of theatre, surrealism's quarrel with Artaud now seems inevitable; the differences separating the two parties appear to have been insoluble. Whatever he said and did, Artaud never ceased to have faith in the theatre. Whatever the surrealists said and did during the later twenties and early thirties, they did not share that faith, and were not to find themselves doing so subsequently. They could never have agreed with Artaud in treating the drama as an object of respect. Meanwhile, from the surrealist standpoint, Ionesco's work presented a somewhat different problem, though a related one. To the extent that his *La Cantatrice chauve* was conceived as an "anti-play," it reflected the spirit of surrealism with which his other early writings for the stage apparently agreed also.[6] But to the extent that *Tueur sans Gages* gives substance to Breton's comments on the strangulation of revolutionary ideas and the individual's submission to general domestication, it represents denial of that spirit, or at least infidelity to it. It was as though Ionesco deliberately wished to invite criticism from within the surrealist circle.[7] The point at issue, then, is not whether, from outside the movement, the surrealists' treatment of Artaud and Ionesco may be judged right or wrong, permissible or unforgivable, but that, from within, no alternative reaction would have seemed consistent with the surrealists' subversive viewpoint on drama.

The important thing is that, like their ultimate rejection of Artaud (and of Roger Vitrac too), the surrealists' growing distaste for the dramatic work of Ionesco highlights what seems anomalous in their position on theatrical matters. Theatre presupposes a mode of direct communication with the public. Yet from its inception, surrealism shunned the compromise that seemed likely to attend "letting the public *come in*."

It would be oversimplifying to suggest that the best solution would have been for surrealists to exclude drama from their program of subversion. This would have been tantamount, after all, to arguing that, because a painting requires a spectator, they ought to have disregarded painting also. One solution, it is true, is abstention. This is the solution that proved acceptable to André Breton, who wrote no plays after he and Soupault had finished *Vous m'oublierez*, performed, incidentally, only once (on May 27, 1920) and within the framework of a Dada *manifestation*. Another of the solutions that have appealed to surrealists is more interesting, however. It is the one that attracted Jean-Claude Barbé and Robert Benayoun, each of whom has demonstrated his fidelity to surrealism by writing plays that defy staging, so firmly stressing the precedence of surrealism over theatre in the scale of priorities, just as Duprey has done.

Now the spirit of subversion asserts itself through an apparent contradiction. Does a play defined as unperformable still merit classification as theatre? If our answer to this question is unhesitatingly negative, then it betrays as prejudice an assumption that we never before may have had occasion to see challenged. On the other hand, if we are inclined to reply affirmatively, then we may well have begun to participate, albeit on a very elementary level, in the kind of subversion in which surrealists intend to implicate us.

If, now, we stand back from the question of theatre, keeping it to hand by holding on to the thread labeled "classification," we can remind ourselves of the celebrated *Déclaration* issued by the surrealists in Paris on January 27, 1925, in which they insisted they had nothing to do with literature but were quite capable, if need be, of making use of it. This statement directs our attention to the basic concern expressed through surrealism's attack upon literature as the destruction of rules, regulations, and customs that supposedly give dignity to modes of literary communication. Tradition, style, usage: none of these must be permitted to secure our respect for outdated classifications which, in their turn, impose the conditioned reflex of stock responses elicited by conventional means. So it is that surrealists may see their texts in dramatic format raided for techniques, for accessory effects, but never deprived of the originality they draw from their subversive origin.

Challenging the forces of literature entails a frontal attack that, on occasion, calls for use—that is, misuse—of forms of literature, so that subversive intent can take effect. And the results are clear to see. "I call tobacco that which is ear." These words of Péret's, pointing in the direction that surrealism takes from preference, help separate surrealist poetry from literature. Lured into mistaking surrealism for a mode of literary expression, critics blame it for not fitting into literary categories and complain when a surrealist adopts the form of drama yet does not produce something they can recognize as a play. On one level, certainly, the efficient implementation of subversion consists in turning the audience's preconceptions back upon them.

Through erosion of the consecrated forms of theatre, as understood in Western culture, surrealists promote release of the drama from traditional functions in which they have no confidence. Hence the act of borrowing a literary form, of appearing willing to submit to a traditional mode of communication, may be said to serve a dual purpose. Use of the word "theatre" first provides the surrealist with a password that gains him entry to the literary camp. Here he has no purpose other than, secondly, to plant a bomb and leave, well content in the knowledge that those among whom he has left his "play" will have trouble with it. Either it will explode in their faces or it will simply appear to them a dud.

The word *dud* may be understood here both in the way Webster interprets it, as slang for "a shell or bomb that fails to explode when it strikes," and as the *Shorter Oxford Dictionary* defines it: "a counterfeit thing." This way, one gains a better appreciation of how far drama historians, and stage directors too, stand from surrealism. To go beyond this point, we have to consider one other possibility, when speculating about what can happen to a surrealist text in dramatic form if it falls into the hands of literary experts. Sensing its potential danger, the more alert among the latter may try to render the bomb harmless. One serviceable method of disarming it, so it would seem, is to attach the play to a tradition, so giving it a *place*, assigning it a niche, in the evolution of dramatic form. Alternatively, the text may be denied serious attention because, as a play, it obviously does not *work*. This looks like being the most efficient method of bomb disposal, because, during its application, serious neglect of the conventions born of a traditional sense of drama, an inclination to flout these, can be cited as reason enough for setting the surrealist play aside as impertinent.

No surrealist could see any reason to object to such treatment, except so far as its intent and effect are to isolate surrealism in the theatre, to deny its presence, and to ignore the challenge it offers conventional modes of exchange that theatre traditionally represents. It would be a glaring error to assume surrealism, in its expression through theatre or any other of the consecrated literary genres, to be seeking the respectability of widespread recognition. It is important, in fact, never to lose sight of the surrealist attitude on this question. It is reflected in the following succinct statement in a letter from a Cuban surrealist—who is allowed to show his painting in the United States, but not his face—occasioned by the announcement of a symposium on Dada and surrealism, projected in New York City in 1968: "In the colloquium in N. Y. on surrealism, I thing it necessary to come out very STRONGLY against the idea that *surrealism*, its activity, belongs to 'history.' We've been talking about this colloquium here [in Paris]. After all, the museum 'curators' ought to be told we don't give a damn for them. We are opposed to surrealism's being *defused* to the advantage of 'bourgeois calm' (calm: see Vietnam) and of aesthetics."

Implicit in this statement is a perspective on history —literary history like any other—showing that the dual purpose mentioned above can be ascribed to the surrealist approach to literature, only at the risk of taking theatre more seriously than it is possible for surrealists to do. This fact in particular calls for emphasis, if surrealism is not to be viewed as standing on ground where it has no intention of going of its own accord or of allowing itself to be led. Liberation of form is not meant to benefit the theatrical mode, any more than the methods employed in surrealist painting—in some of which eminently respectable art historians have detected retrograde steps—are designed to advance painterly technique. In surrealism, it is the spirit that quickeneth. It remains always a matter of indifference whether the flesh of inherited literary form profiteth anything at all.

In an article titled "Comme dans un Bois," written for the special surrealist number brought out by *L'Age du Cinéma* in 1951, André Breton gave no sign of finding it difficult to ignore "the incontestably low quality of cinematographic production," deploring it "on a quite secondary, accessory plane." As he explained, "For my part it would mean being in conflict with myself, denying what conditions me in my own eyes, to appear unduly affected, as is customary, by the disappointments caused by the cinema as a means of expression that we have persuaded ourselves to believe better suited than any other to promoting 'true life.'"[8] "Comme dans un Bois" reaffirmed Breton's faith in the "magnetizing" function of cinema, specifying that "The *marvel*, beside which the merits of a given film are of little account, resides in the capacity granted anyone at all to abstract himself from his own life when he so desires, at least in large towns, as soon as he has passed through the soundproof doors that open onto the dark." For Breton agreed with Ado Kyrou's view that the cinema is "the best springboard from which the modern world will plunge into the magnetic, brilliantly black waters of the subconscious, of poetry, of dream."[9]

To the surrealist, the darkened auditorium in which

captivating cinematic images are to be projected holds infinite promise, so long as habitual preoccupations and the conditioned reflexes of habitual thought and inculcated prejudices have been left at the soundproof door. Darkness induces expectancy of a special kind when, as Kyrou does, one believes the cinema to be "in essence surrealist" because, in the dark, reality is "enriched with all its latent content," to which André Breton attached so much value. In the cinema, as elsewhere, surrealists follow their dream, a dream of *"mediation,"* according to Breton. Ever sensitive to those "perpetual solicitations" which, *Nadja* tells us, "seem to come from outside, and immobilize us a few seconds in front of one of those fortuitous arrangements, of a more or less new character, to which it seems that, by questioning ourselves thoroughly, we should find the secret in ourselves" (p. 19), surrealists are not reluctant to see in the cinema an instrument suited to "the *auscultation* of the imagination"—to borrow Breton's imagery—from which man will gain a greater understanding of the universe and of himself.

There can be no doubt that the film is regarded in surrealism as a potential means of exploration, possessing a precious virtue sensed by Artaud who, when writing *La Coquille et le Clergyman*, foresaw a cinema that would present "purely visual situations." Through the film, surrealists may hope to transport their public, as the title of one of Ernst's paintings has it, "inside sight." This means that the famous dichotomy with which surrealism confronts us, that of manifest content and latent content, is translated with particular acuity. Nowhere better than in movies do we grasp the meaning of Breton's assertion: "Surrealism is what will be." Nowhere is surrealist thought capable of being transmitted in purer form, when filmic images serve not so much to evoke the world we know but the world that still remains to be known. For the cinematic image does not affirm; it demonstrates. It does not persuade; it imposes conclusions the spectator cannot reject, if at all, until he has emerged from the darkness.

"But the real travelers," declared Baudelaire, "are those who leave for the sake of leaving." Within the program adopted by surrealists, the cinema has as its aim undermining the real, or at least breaking through the façade of visible reality so as to grant man privileged moments of a kind quite unknown to Marcel Proust. The process in question, we need to appreciate, has nothing to do with the aesthetics of film. Publishing his three surrealist scenarios, *Barre fixe*, *Paupières mûres*, and *Mtasipoj*, Benjamin Fondane asserted categorically, "It is not, consequently, to correct the cinema, to make it better (*let it not become an art; that is all we ask of it*) that we propose in our turn this mortar destined to ruin a certain form of cinema in people's minds, to bring another into the world." Hence the proposal made by Fondane, in anticipation of the treatment accorded theatre by Barbé and Benayoun and Duprey: "Let us open the period of unperformable scenarios."[10]

It was in the characteristically surrealist spirit of iconoclasm that Buñuel and Dalí put together the scenario of *Un Chien andalou*, directed against the form of vanguard cinema which addressed itself "exclusively to the artistic sensibility and reason of the spectators."[11] Similarly, resistance to preoccupations of an artistic order guided Henri Storck in devising his script *La Rue*, published in the surrealism issue of *L'Age du Cinéma*:

> The action of the film is set in the street. That is to say, the houses have been emptied of their contents and furniture and accessories clutter the middle of the street. We see also a drawing room completely set up, including its glass chandelier hanging in the middle of the street, the lady of the house presiding over an elegant reception.

So much the better, if irrational effects—the chandelier suspended over the street—catch the eye. Being seen, they exist on equal terms with the other elements of the décor which have been submitted to spatial displacement but retain their relationship to one another: everything is in its place, though on a plane unfamiliar in everyday experience. Such indifference to reasonable preconception, to habitual sights, and the reassurance of familiarity can even give rise to reluctance on the surrealist film-maker's part to utilize a written script, for fear that the act of notation will facilitate the intrusion of rationality. One of its co-directors has explained that *L'Invention du Monde* (1952) was conceived as "un poème en images": "The film was conceived as a poem in pictures and it was the analogies discovered between the pictures which entirely dictated the editing and the very articulation of the sequences. Instead of writing the scenario down, Zimbacca and I *drew* it entirely, using tracings."[12] According to the statement published by Bédouin and Zimbacca in the surrealism number of *L'Age du Cinéma*, their attempt to make a surrealist documentary stood "outside the latest-style classifications of ethnography and in perfect disregard for aesthetic ratings."

In effect, Bédouin and Zimbacca were attempting, through film, to draw their audience into a form of analogical play, so important to surrealists because it questions the stability of the everyday world, thus tending to unveil relationships of an unwonted nature. Bédouin and Zimbacca declared:

> *The Invention of the World* admits, as its basic hypothesis, the perenniality in the human mind of certain forms of association which permit us, as soon as poetic consciousness is awakened by one of them, to embrace by analogy all the others, and to be carried right away to the source of mythical thought. . . . In these conditions, only the poetic influx can *open* these forms and these symbols, considered as so many clusters of meaning closed in upon themselves. Only this can bring forth their multiple prolongations to organize them at last in a responsive chain reaction.

Because the surrealist cinema aims to invest the film with its essential character as a sequence of images, it invites audience participation of a distinctive kind. For the value of movies resides, now, in the significance to be attached to these images, considered from the angle of their interaction, of their analogical, poetic play. Noting as we go that two spokesmen for surrealism have stressed that "one forces locks, not images,"[13] we have no trouble relating the cinematic image to the image in the surrealist verbal poem, poetry being, to surrealists, a matter of optics. This explains the character of the verbal commentary supplied for *L'Invention du Monde*, which follows the evolution of primitive thought, as reflected in artifacts held by museums the world over. A press release points out, "Benjamin Péret here restitutes by his commentary the poetical images of primitive conception, founded on analogy, and at the same time delineates the sense and origins of the presented documents. By lending his voice to some of them, Benjamin Péret has reproduced their ritual significance, and by impersonating spirits and forces, expresses the dramatic side of the screenplay."[14] This is to say that the movie does not ask of its commentary an explanation for the visual images assembled but, rather, something notably similar to the *prose parallels* by André Breton, accompanying the twenty-two pictures in Joan Miró's *Constellations:*[15]

> My crest is a double crenelated rainbow traversed by lightning.
>
> . . . .
>
> Eyes take flight with the image that has risen out of matter, as the flower blossoms so that its seed may fall to germinate, grow, flower, fall, germinate, grow, flower, fall, germinate, grow, flower. . .

"I am," says Péret's text, "going to contemplate the other face of the world."

Like the rest of us, the commentator contemplates the other side of existence, mirrored in the images of *L'Invention du Monde* which speaks its own poetic language. It is not surprising, though, that "the key that sings in the lock" of the surrealist cinematic image should be, very often, the very key that permits entry to the world of the surrealist word poem. Certain passages in the scenario that Artaud called *La Coquille et le Clergyman* demand the same kind of responsiveness as appreciation of Philippe Soupault's poem "Le Nageur," in his *Georgia* (1926):

> je flotte visage perdu au milieu d'une heure
> sans secours sans appel
> je descends sans conviction des marches sans but
> et je continue sans regret jusqu'au sommeil
> dans les yeux des miroirs et dans le rire du vent
> je reconnais un inconnu qui est moi
> je ne bouge plus
> j'attends
> et je ferme les yeux comme un verrou

> [I float face lost in the midst of an hour
> without help no appeal
> without conviction I go down aimless steps
> and without regret I continue into sleep
> in the eyes of mirrors and the laughter of the wind
> I recognize an unknown man who is I
> I no longer move
> I wait
> and I close my eyes like the bolt on a door]

Again, the metamorphic landscapes of *La Coquille et le Clergyman* bring us in contact with a world in transformation under the weight of desire, similar to the one depicted by Aimé Césaire, in a poem, "Démons," from his *Soleil Cou coupé*, a 1947 collection named in tribute to Guillaume Apollinaire:

> Déjà la bête était sur moi invulnérable.
> Au dessous des seins et sur tout le ventre au dessous du cou et sur tout le dos ce que l'on prenait à première vue pour les plumes étaient des lamelles de fer peint qui lorsque l'animal ouvrait et refermait les ailes pour se secouer de la pluie et du sang faisaient une perspective que rien ne pouvait compro-

mettre de relents et de bruits de cuillers heurtées par les mains blanches d'un séïsme dans les corbeilles sordides d'un été trop malsain.

[Already the beast was upon me invulnerable.
Below the breasts and all over the belly below the neck and all over the back what one took at first for feathers were scales of painted metal which when the animal opened and closed its wings to shake off rain and blood created a perspective that nothing could impair of stale smells and of sounds of spoons rattled together by the white hands of a seism in the squalid baskets of a summer too unhealthy.]

The shift from concrete reality to the suggestive intangibles of Césaire's poem is paralleled in Artaud's script, with its close-up of the clergyman's head:

From inside his half-open mouth, in between his eyelashes something like a shimmering smoke emanates, piling up in a corner of the screen, forming a town scene, or extremely illuminated landscapes. In the end the head disappears completely and houses, landscapes, towns, mingling and untangling, form into a sort of unbelievable celestial firmament, lagoons, grottoes, with incandescent stalactites and beneath these grottoes, among these clouds, in the middle of these lagoons we see the silhouette of the ship which passes back and forth, black against the white background of the towns, white against the background of visions which suddenly turn black.[16]

Co-author of the film *Spiste Horisonter* (1950), Wilhelm Freddie explains: "Without apprehension I stand in the white, airless hall, where the laughter of children cascades down to me from the smooth walls, as letters of the alphabet from the dancing bell—letters which form words, sentences, meanings—whose pictures become the fittings of the walls, disappearing hastily, making me again naked. . . ."[17] Nakedness, stripping away all that holds us to the so-called real world is, in surrealism, but a prelude to regeneration, placing man on the threshold of a new experience. Thus, in Storck's 1952 scenario *Am-ster-dam*, the central figure "undresses and strips himself quite naked," when watching in a microscope "a battle between disgusting voracious insects." At such moments, man attains a new outlook upon the world. Perspective has surrendered its privileges, no longer shackling the imagination. Time has become, in Dalí's words, "the delirious surrealist dimension *par excellence.*" Commonly accepted relationships no longer hold good. In *Am-ster-dam:*

> The spectator observes a strange phenomenon, obtained by trick photography. The top of the character's body is detached from the bottom. While the trunk slips by among pedestrians who are fairly indifferent, the legs go walking on their own. Deciding that this absurd game has gone on long enough, the trunk whistles to the legs, which come rushing up like a dog but without enthusiasm. After making a show of refusing to rejoin the trunk, and trying to run away, the legs position themselves under the trunk, but obey in the end only before the master's anger.[18]

This logic in absurdity, a productive anti-logic, is characteristic of surrealist humor, in which gravity frequently joins forces with precision to depict a universe which is reached—as Lewis Carroll promised—when we pass through Pierre Mabille's "mirror of the marvelous," or look through the special stereoscope which permits us to observe Monsieur Phot.[19] In other words, the image in a surrealist movie or in a screenplay of surrealist inspiration is no more explicative than it is in a surrealist verbal poem. In each instance, the creator—the poet—acts, as Eluard put it, contagiously.[20] In *L'Invention du Monde* we hear Péret say, "They spring to the conquest of life all aquiver bursting forth from everywhere and shining from their daytime and nighttime faces." For and against, light and darkness cease to be contradictory, as the poet shows us he has reached that "certain point in the mind" to which Breton draws our attention in the *Second Manifeste du Surréalisme:*

Everything leads us to believe there exists a certain point in the mind from which life and death, real and imagination, past and future, communicable and incommunicable, high and low cease to be perceived contradictorily. Now, it would be pointless to look in surrealist activity for any other motive than the hope of determining that point. One can see fairly well from this how absurd it would be to attribute to it a solely destructive or constructive sense: the point in question is *a fortiori* that at which it ceases to be possible to brandish the one in the face of the other. (p. 154)

Faithful to the spirit of surrealism, Breton wrote in his poem "Vigilance" from a collection called *Le Revolver à Cheveux blancs* (*The Whitehaired Revolver*), "I hear the human linen tear like a great leaf/Under the fingernail of absence and of presence which are in league." The poet who inspires becomes, in consequence, self-inspired. This is the significance in surrealism of analogical play as applied, for example, in the composition of *Un Chien andalou*'s screenplay which resulted, Buñuel has reported, from the practice of "conscious psychic automatism," or again in the scenario of *Spiste Horisonter*, which is nothing more than a succession of notations relating to the images passing on the screen: "The shadows lie like huge, fateful draperies around their faces and the prayer that is uttered is the prayer of a red-hot sword."[21]

"For others, concern to nourish the soul on basic foods which are not rare, though indispensable to its stagnant mediocrity. I have wished to impose upon it luxurious, strange dishes, from the antipodes or the abyss," comment Breton and Schuster in their "Art poétique."[22] No more than any other form of surrealist expression does the film need to seek authority in reality. It would be as futile to look for a faithful image of everyday experience in surrealist cinema as for the heroine of *L'Age d'Or* to look for her own reflection in the mirror of her dressing-table, described as follows in Buñuel's shooting script:

Close-up of the mirror that reflects neither the woman nor the room but a beautiful sky with oval clouds, lazily drifting by in the sunset. In the foreground, the dry silhouette of a tree shaken by the wind. C-U side-face of the young woman and the mirror, but in such a way that one sees what the latter reflects. The woman with her hair tossed by the wind resting her face on her hands, lays her forehead against the mirror.

Breton testifies pertinently in an untitled poem from his *L'Air de l'Eau* (1934):

> C'en est fait du présent du passé de l'avenir
> Je chante la lumière unique de la coïncidence
> La joie de m'être penché sur la grande rosace
>   du glacier supérieur
> Les infiltrations merveilleuses dont on s'aperçoit
>   un beau jour qu'elles ont fait un cornet
>   du plancher
> La portée des incidents étranges mais insignifiants
>   à première vue
> Et leur don d'appropriation finale vertigineuse à
>   moi-même
> Je chante votre horizon fatal

> [It is all over with present past future
> I sing of the unique light of coincidence
> The joy of leaning over the great rosette of the
>   higher glacier
> The marvelous infiltrations about which one perceives
>   one fine day that they have made a horn of the floor
> The force of incidents strange but insignificant
>   at first sight
> And their gift for final appropriation vertiginous
>   to me
> I sing of your fatal horizon]

Breton's fatal horizon lies in the same direction as Freddie's eaten horizon. For, to the surrealist, liberation promises the infinite, admitting of no limitations.

SURREALISM, RADIO, AND GOONERY

It is no exaggeration to say that not a single area of creative expression is, *a priori*, immune to surrealist influence, protected from its consequences. The poetic subversion of surrealism is all-pervasive, because it exercises its magnetic attraction, in every case, from one of two directions. In the first place, the presence of surrealism makes itself felt as a consequence of deliberate intent, or at least of a general orientation in the sensibility of the creative artist. Subversive forces are released when and where the surrealist poet refuses to abide by rules and regulations, as he takes up a given artistic form for purposes of his own, when and where he declines to allow poetic expression, as he understands it, to be confined within prescribed limits customarily respected in the mode of his choice. Tracing the other direction from which the magnetic current of surrealism can be felt requires further reflection, not on the contagious role of the poet, this time, but on the surrealists' interpretation of the condition laid down by Lautréamont for the creation of poetry—that everyone participate in its production.

It is clear enough, now, that surrealist poetry can never be bound by classifiable modes of spectacle. On the contrary, the poetic element, as surrealism renders us sensitive to its presence, may impress itself upon us regardless of the degree of competence demonstrated in this movie or that play, or even in defiance of the supposed advantages resulting from technical command. We have only to recall Buñuel's ironic attitude toward film technique to appreciate that surrealists consider it an error to presume that poetry and professional skill go together. It is important, here, not to draw wrong conclusions—that only incompetence places the key to surrealism in the artist's hand. We must realize that surrealism is not the guaranteed result of applying a method. Something quite different calls for notice, in fact, before we can proceed any farther.

Surrealist poetry is capable of surfacing in the most unlikely places, in a potboiler like the movie *King Kong*, in an apparently sentimental love story like the film version of

Peter Ibbetson, in a play like Palau's *Les Détraquées*, which appears worthy of the Grand Guignol, or even in a reputedly absurdist piece of theatre like N. F. Simpson's *One Way Pendulum*. Surrealist spectacle, in other words, is the result of interaction between what is shown and what the audience —some of the audience, at all events—are capable of seeing in the presentation. Spectacle may be, to a greater or lesser extent, the creation of the spectator, a re-creation on the plane of responsiveness which treats the material presented as perhaps no more than the starting point, merely the exciting cause of poetic experience, as for instance André Breton did, when watching *Les Détraquées*. So much is this a feature of the surrealist experience that when Jean-Jacques Auquier and Alain-Valery Aelberts wrote their play *Cérémonial pour . . . Sade*, they intended from the first that it be performed and, doing so, anticipated not only the contribution of "the director's gesture" but also "the free and deliberate exercise of the imaginative *Book* that is in all of us."

"Exercise of the imaginative *Book*." This phrase suggests that the essence of surrealist poetry, in its intimate connection with spectacle, is located in imaginative release. Spectacle finds its *raison d'être* in poetry, while poetry takes shape for us as our imagination is stimulated. "Imagination," wrote Breton in his first surrealist manifesto, "alone gives me an account of what *can be*, and this is enough to raise a little the terrible interdict; enough too for me to abandon myself to it without fear of being mistaken . . ." (p. 17).

Reconsideration, now, of the process of poetic release, in which everyone is entitled—not to say obligated—to participate, brings appreciation of the important fact that the message of surrealism would be relatively limited in scope, if one had to think of it as communicated only when intentionally sent out on a particular wavelength. In fact, surrealism is not merely a matter of *emission*, it is just as much a matter of *reception* and, in some situations, the latter counts far more than the former. To the degree that the receiver is capable of decoding the message that has come in, it now communicates something of which the sender may continue to be quite unaware. Hence it is permissible to speak of some forms of surrealist communication as involuntary. Indeed, if we are to measure the full range of surrealist poetry, it is imperative to acknowledge surrealist effect as no less valid for having been attained unintentionally. We must recognize how apposite to some forms of surrealist creative activity are the following words from Breton's *Légitime Défense:*

> Once again, all we have is that we are endowed to a certain degree with the word and that, by it, something great and obscure tends imperiously to find expression through us, that each of us has been chosen and designated to himself from among a thousand to formulate that which, in our lifetime, has to be formulated.

At the same time, though, we must give due importance to a statement of Jean Schuster's, made some forty years later:

> The driving belt between the individual and the collective—and this is perhaps at the same time a vital gearwheel in surrealist activity, its most original characteristic—has been stretched, neither too tight nor too slack, once and for all. This being so, the means of ensuring the development of surrealism depend, in large part, upon the determination of each of us to force his own locks.[23]

Turning to a third form that may be taken by surrealist expression, radio, a form complementing drama and cinema, we have the opportunity to witness surrealism's invasion of a medium where imagination reigns supreme and where its benefits, in giving the surrealist an account of "what *can be*," are related directly to his determination to force certain locks, in preference to others in doors beyond which he expects to find nothing of interest.

In the main, two reasons have made it necessary to keep radio apart from film and theatre up to now. The first is a condition of the medium itself. While movies and plays avail themselves, if only to a minimal degree, of spectacle, the eye assisting the ear in eliciting response, radio eliminates visual spectacle and has to rely on sound alone in stimulating the imagination. The second reason is of a less general nature, having to do with the behavior of surrealists with regard to the radio medium. Whereas they have explored for themselves the surrealist potential of drama and film, they have not experimented with radio. In only one instance, in fact—Radovan Ivsic's play *Le Roi Gordogane*—has a surrealist text received broadcast performance.[24]

It would seem that the narrow restrictions imposed by the very nature of certain media, which have so confined surrealist experimentation with film and all but eliminated attempts to bring surrealism to the stage, have weighed even more depressingly upon the medium of radio. These restrictions are less technical in character than the result of commercial considerations which, in the case of radio, are paramount. In the circumstances, it is inevitable that surrealism has made little impression on radio and that no exception to this general rule may be noted, except in the form of surrealism which we have described as involuntary.

The series that ran on BBC radio for several years under the name "The Goon Show" was unique. As there is nothing that can quite compare with it, we cannot cite it as exemplary of involuntary broadcast surrealism. It deserves consideration, all the same, as conclusive proof of the surrealist potential of radio. Enjoying nationwide popularity, week after week it challenged listeners in the post-1945 period to say where they stood, affording ample opportunity for a variety of responses from those following the adventures of Neddie Seagoon:

Seagoon	Lady Marks—your late husband owned a banana plantation, yes?
Lady Marks	In South America.
Seagoon	That's abroad, isn't it?
Lady Marks	It all depends on where you're standing.[25]

In an episode of "The Goon Show" entitled *The Canal*, Neddie's father chides him thus: "Silence when you talk to me." Among other sound effects, *The Affair of the Lone Banana* calls for great heavy approaching footsteps, to be followed by Seagoon's greeting, "Ah Lady Marks, sit down" and by a comment to the listening audience from an indefinable but obviously demented character, regularly featured in the show, Eccles, "I bet you thought it was going to be me. Ha hum." Embroiled in an affair named after Napoleon's piano, Seagoon indulges in an aside, "Watch me turn the tables, listeners." Enjoyment of *The Dreadful Batter Pudding Hurler* demands of listeners visualization when visualization is patently unprofitable: "The ship was disguised as a train—to make the train sea-worthy it was done up to look like a boat and painted to appear like a train." Looking for *Napoleon's Piano*, arriving at the Café Tom (in Paris, of course), Seagoon proceeds to set the scene:

Seagoon	Inside, the air was filled with gorilla-smoke—I was looking for a man who might specialise in piano robberies from the Louvre.
	(*F. X.* WHOOSH)
Eidelburger	Gute evenung. You are looking for a man who might specialise in piano robberies from the Louvre?
Seagoon	How do you know?
Eidelburger	I was listening on the radio and I heard you say it.

Naturally, only an Eidelburger (an Idle Bugger) finds time to listen to the radio. What, then, are the advantages of doing so? "Meantime," interjects the Announcer, "for those of you cretins who want a happy ending, here it is":

(Grams	Soft Background Music, Very, Very Soft)
Harry	Darling—Darling, will you marry me?
Bloodnok	Of course I will, darling.[26]

The first thing one notices about "The Goon Show" is, no doubt, a readily identifiable spirit of mockery. It catches the attention, for instance, when—no doubt in memory of "Workers' Playtime," a wartime show which almost invariably seemed to emanate from remote corners of the British Isles (largely because it was broadcast so often from munitions factories)—*The Phantom Head-Shaver* is broadcast from an Arab Stench-Recuperation Centre in Stoke Poges. But there is far more to "The Goon Show" (a joyous corruption of the fatuous British military optimistic bray, "Good Show!") than irony directed at those who find something to sustain them in radio drama. From the very beginning, "The Goon Show" was a phenomenon that took its point of departure in denial of the convention of radio drama, finding its origin in a challenge to listeners to be attentive, in the old way, perhaps, but to things new. It was something far more significant than the equivalent of a play for reading. Sound effects, for example, took an active part in subverting radio drama, no longer serving to authenticate imagined events, except in defiance of naturalistic plot.

One of the prime virtues of "The Goon Show" was this: It gave precedence to language—to linguistic awareness—over plot, that ingredient of dramatic communication which language conventionally is assumed to have the obligation to serve. With the ending of *The Dreaded Batter Pudding Hurler* we have been exposed already to one significant consequence of the attitude from which Goonery was born: verbal collage—not of the unimaginative kind that Aragon finds so remarkable in Tristan Tzara's disastrous play *Mouchoir de Nuages*,[27] but bringing into incongruous proximity materials taken from two unrelated planes of expression. As practiced by Spike Milligan when writing his scripts, verbal collage results in the interplay of disconnected elements affording us a pleasure that could not be provided by meeting, in their normal affective environment, the materials he brings together. Isolating stock response from stock situation has the effect, here, of revitalizing statements, banal replies to banal questions, and so on, through relocation and by disrupting conditioned affective reactions. Hence, in Goon Show situations, characters who adopt stereotyped postures—and there is a rich variety of these—are allowed to do so only as those attitudes lend themselves to absurd effect, as a result of displacement. And it goes without saying that the effect obtained is heightened very frequently by the kind of piracy in which the Goons find satisfaction, when they borrow the voice of George Sanders or Dick Barton (the refined English radio detective) to *level* a certain concept of heroism or of exemplary patriotism, as much as to satirize a certain mode of suave villainy.

No one whose ethical standards are in keeping with surrealist principles need make any concessions, as he listens to shreds of noble feeling that hang in tatters from a Goon Show script.[28] Chasing the Phantom Head-Shaver, Bluebottle, who, for all we know, may *be* a bluebottle, cries in his Jiminy Cricket voice, "In I go—farewell! I go in for England," while the orchestra underlines his brainless fervor with a fanfare of trumpets.[29] And the spirit which (the story goes) made England great makes Neddie Seagoon—impersonated in maniacal style by a Welshman—the blundering clown he is: "Have a care, Latin devil—I am an Englishman. Remember, this rolled umbrella has more uses than one." The whole *Affair of the Lone Banana*, from which these stirring words come, is a mock celebration of the ludicrous empire-building syndrome. To the accompaniment of the "Harry Lime Theme," it reaches its climax in Peter Sellers' commentary, delivered in Dick Barton (Special Agent) tones:

> The Affair of the Lone Banana, Chapter Three. In the grounds of the British Embassy our heroes are dug in around the lone banana tree—the last symbol of waning British prestige in South America. They all anxiously await the return of Fred Nurke. Around them, the jungle is alive with revels—and nocturnal sounds—rain in places, fog patches on the coast. Arsenal 2—Chinese Wanderers 600.

It is because the center of gravity in a Goon Show script is never firmly located in plot, but is susceptible to displacement under the attraction of verbal magnetism, that we encounter so often a kind of *shift* such as allows the narrator in a dramatic plot to drift off into weather forecast and soccer results. Sometimes, it is true, one's impression is that of being bombarded with excruciating puns, as when Major Denis Bloodnok ("Military idiot, coward and bar") claims to be reading a book about the Scottish Regiments— *The Decameron*—or when Eccles proposes that he and Seagoon ("true blue British idiot and hero always") wait for the Phantom Head-Shaver to "come out," after Seagoon has told him the Phantom is "in the vicinity." But the significant fact, surely, is that word play of this kind is a symptom of a sensitivity to language with far-reaching consequences. Giving attention to words themselves, rather than looking through words at the thought they supposedly are meant to convey, the Goons are capable of redirecting our thinking, as during this exchange between Seagoon and the villainous Grytpype-Thynne:[30]

Grytpype-Thynne	So, Neddie, you managed to get your hands free.
Seagoon	Yes—they never cost me a penny, thanks to National Health!

This scrap of dialog in *The Hastings Flyer* is typical. For on many occasions the Goon Show scenario is reminiscent of the poems in Desnos' *L'Aumonyme*, turning homonyms to account in the reorientation of response:[31]

(F. X.	LONE CRICKET CHIRPING)
Bloodnok	Listen—what's making that noise?
Seagoon	Cricket.
Bloodnok	How can they see to bat in this light?
Seagoon	Major, a man's just climbed over the garden wall.
Bloodnok	A boundary! (*Aloud*) Well played, sir!

Now the use of words invites reflection upon the relation of language to expression and logical thought. What, after all, could be more logical than Bloodnok's surprise at a cricket match being held at night, while he and his associates are defending the Lone Banana Tree? Small wonder that this man, as his military rank testifies, successfully negotiated the hurdle of Staff College. When we listen to the Goons, we are made attentive to the nudity of a naked razor and have to consider the possibility of testing a watertight alibi by leaving it overnight in a fish tank. With this first step behind us, the second is easier to take. What can it be like, we wonder, to be Bloodnok, molested by a lobster "with a disgusting mind"? What is there to be seen "by the light of a passing glue factory"? What are the benefits to be derived from disguising oneself, like Fred Nurke, as a banana, or of wearing regulation-length lock-keepers' bathing drawers? And what are the satisfactions of owning a metal bowler hat (possibly of perforated bronze), a plasticine phonograph, a calibrated Turkish boot lathe, a portable volcano net, stained-glass corsets, an oiled groin-brush? Goonery, like the poems of Benjamin Péret, precipitates us right into *the crisis of the object* that Breton discussed at length, and on more than one occasion.[32]

Because the Goons recognize the ability of language to evade the limits of reasonable projection, they offer us the prospect of holding a celluloid baby, or playing a loaded sackbut from the kneeling position, of connecting a gas stove up to a horse (provided, that is, we get the right end, this time), of telling the time of day by our Order of the British Empire, of covering an enemy with a loaded finger or a tin of potted shrimps, or even of being, perhaps, part-inventor —with Seagoon—of the steam-driven explodable hairless toupée. And they make us witnesses to conversations like this one, from *The Hastings Flyer:*

Seagoon	That tricycle against the wall—whose is it?
Eccles	Mine—a present from an admirer.
Seagoon	Could you drive me to town on it?

Eccles   Oh, the tricycle ain't mine—the wall was the present.

Seagoon   Well, drive me there on that. . .

Eccles   Right—hold tight.

(Grams   Series of Sounds Played at Speed to Sound like Some Kind of Combustion Engine)

Bill   The sound you are hearing is Neddie and Eccles driving a wall at speed. We thought you ought to know.

Like the sound of a chirping cricket, the improbable noise of the wall's engine, given special stress by the program's announcer, makes its contribution to undercutting our sense of what is real. On the most elementary level, sound effects may either emphasize verbal associations or actually solicit these, as is the case in *The House of Teeth:*

Dr. Longdongle   No, gentlemen. I'll not be forestalled now. I'm near my goal.

(F. X.   FOOTBALL WHISTLE)

Bluebottle   Offside, he's too near his own goal.

In any case, the most important thing, always, is that sounds underline the fact that everyday language is, fortunately, but an approximation. If given the chance, words are likely to revolt. As Longdongle escapes, Bloodnok urges Seagoon to stick his head "out of the window," and the following is immediately audible: "HEAD BEING STUFFED THROUGH GLASS WINDOW." Sounds, then, help inculcate mistrust in language as a medium of reasonable communication, by confining audible signals within the bounds of lunatic literalness: as when, in the Lone Banana affair, Seagoon's admission that his nerves are strung up to breaking point precedes the sound of a fiddle string snapping and the cry "There goes one now." Alternatively, sound effects usher in anti-reasonable explanations. For example, tracking the Dreaded Batter Pudding Hurler, Seagoon flags down a taxi which sounds like bagpipes, not only when it comes to a halt but also when it is gathering speed once again. The Announcer intervenes with a comment, half non-explanation, half commercial: "Listeners may be puzzled by a taxi sounding like bagpipes—not only are they more musical, but they come in a wide variety of colours. See your local Bagpipe Offices and ask for particulars—you won't be disappointed."

Elsewhere the call for explanation is denied. In *The Affair of the Lone Banana*, for instance, a long vigorous symphonic finish, in the style of the "William Tell" Overture, terminates in an "EXPLOSION—FALLING GLASS, BITS & PIECES," while Milligan asks, "And why not?" When a fusillade of shots, punctuated by exploding bombs, signifies no more than a rain shower, the audience—whose only contact with what is going on is aural—must be prepared to discover that they can trust nothing they hear; or rather that they must not reserve trust for sounds which seem to confirm the familiar. The terrifying roar of a lion is identified as that of a man-eating tiger. A 1922 Jack Payne record of a one-step is attributed to another popular band, Geraldo's. Meanwhile, the very principle of stability becomes suspect when, as happens now and again, Big Ben strikes at varying speeds, sound distortion being used as a fitting background for subversive Goonery.[33]

Frequently rebuking those whose preconceptions impose upon them entirely commonsensical expectations, the sound track can confirm the impossible, granting it authenticity. In *The Affair of the Lone Banana* we hear:

Seagoon	One step nearer and I fire.
Moriarty	Fool—you can't shoot a banana! It's—
	(F. X. TWO PISTOL SHOTS)
Moriarty	Swine—it was *loaded*.
Seagoon	Of course—you don't think I'd threaten you with an unloaded banana?[34]

The pattern is significantly consistent. Words and sounds combine to parody logical action and reaction. This is why mimicry of the logic of rational discourse has its place here —at one place removed from conventional reality. When Seagoon makes a phone call and hears, in Churchillian tones (distorted) a voice that says, "Ten Downing Street here," he muses, "No, it couldn't be him—who would he want to throw a batter pudding at?" The logic of unreason finds expression everywhere, as it does so well in the Lone Banana episode:

Seagoon	Headstone, you say Fred Nurke disappeared whilst having a bottle of tea with his mother, Lady Marks.
Headstone	True—you might say he disappeared from under her very nose.
Seagoon	What was he doing there?
Headstone	It was raining, I believe.

In a world where Goonery runs wild, no one is ever at a loss for an answer, as this exchange from *The Canal* demonstrates:

Bloodnok	But how did you get past those turbanned devils of brown, the Arabs?
Seagoon	Arabs? What are Arabs doing in Lancashire?
Bloodnok	I can only put it down to the fog.

Nonsense—aggressive nonsense, not the placatory kind belonging to the respectable tradition of Lear and Carroll— outwits reason. Driving his snowplow train during *The Hastings Flyer* episode, Seagoon discovers that the steam boiler pressure has reached ninety-eight degrees.

Seagoon	Right—run my bath.
Moriarty	Don't be a fool—this is no time to take a bath, it's getting late.

Seagoon	Nonsense—plenty of time—according to the hairs on my wrist it's only half past ten.
Grytpype-Thynne	(disbelief) The hairs on your wrist say half past ten?
Seagoon	Yes.
Grytpype-Thynne	You must be mad.
Seagoon	Why?
Grytpype-Thynne	The hairs on my wrist say eleven-thirty.
Moriarty	Yes, he sets them by the hairs on Big Ben.
Seagoon	Still time for a bath. . .

This is a world where you know Napoleon's piano—the one he played at Waterloo, no less—to be worth ten thousand pounds because you have seen its bank book, and where an everyday act like smoking can become an entirely new experience. In *The Mighty Wurlitzer* Grytpype-Thynne offers Seagoon a statue of George the Third, but Neddie declines to accept one because they give him a headache. Seagoon also refuses a chopped liver cigarette, in *The Hastings Flyer*, because he always chops his own. During the *Napoleon's Piano* adventure, Seagoon will not take a gorilla because they hurt his throat. Later, though, he offers Eccles one:

(Grams	Gorilla fighting Another Gorilla [If You can't get the Right Sound Try Two Lions]. All stops abruptly.)
Eccles	Hey—dese gorillas are strong. Have one of my monkeys—they're milder.
Seagoon	And so for the rest of the voyage we sat quietly smoking our monkeys.

Eidelburger, perverse fellow, smokes only baboons.

The Goons develop the flexibility of verbal exchange beyond the range of practical necessity. In doing so, they uncover new possibilities for human activity: if there are under-footmen, then someone can be an over-footman. A new freedom is offered mankind: Seagoon will be neither forestalled nor fivestalled, and Bloodnok—albeit "in a moment of weakness"—is able to pick up a forty-ton chopper (which may or may not be interpreted, in its slang sense, as an overweight phallus). Radio, the medium of imaginative projection, becomes a means for projecting and realizing the impossible. Thus, the better to avoid detection in Calais, after stowing away on a cross-Channel ferry, Seagoon has only to slide down the ship's rope—in French.

Complementing this kind of implausibility, not contradicting it, is a special mode of dialog, setting the imagination on the slippery track of the anti-reasonable. In a prison cell, we hear the following:

Seagoon	Is there any other way out of here?
Eccles	Would you care to share my supper?
Seagoon	Ahh, how about that window up there?
Eccles	Oh, you can't eat that.

What is especially interesting about this example—by no means an isolated one, incidentally—is that no better explanation can be found for what goes on in situations of this sort than the following statement in the *Manifeste du Surréalisme:* "It is still to dialog that the forms of surrealist language are best adapted. Here, two thoughts confront one another; while the one is being delivered, the other attends to it, but how does it attend?" (p. 49). Breton goes on to remark that it is improbable that one thought lives entirely off the other, and he explains: "My attention, prey to a solicitation it cannot decently thrust aside, treats the opposing thought as an enemy; in ordinary conversation, my attention 'gets the better of it,' almost always by way of the words, the figures of speech it employs; my attention puts me in a position to turn these to advantage in my reply by changing their nature." Where the mechanism of dialog seems to have broken down, as when Seagoon and Eccles are in prison together, conversation as we usually know it has been replaced by an arrangement of parallel monologs, in which the *Manifesto of Surrealism* identifies the true nature of dialog, the kind of dialog, in fact, with which Breton and Soupault were experimenting as early as 1919, in their *Les Champs magnétiques:*[35]

Grytpype-Thynne	Where's Fred Nurke?
Seagoon	I don't know.
Grytpype-Thynne	So *that's* where he is.

It goes without saying that the elements noted here as presenting special interest, in the light of surrealism, are marshalled according to no system—surrealist or any other. They appear spontaneously and hence creatively. Above all, they intermingle to produce that "soaring upward" of which Harry (Seagoon) Secombe has spoken, "on the thermal currents of Milligan's imagination":[36]

Grytpype-Thynne	Ohhhh—come in—sit down. Have a gorilla.
Seagoon	No thanks, I'm trying to give them up.
Grytpype-Thynne	Splendid. Now Neddie, here's the money for moving the piano—there, five pounds in fivers.
Seagoon	Five pounds for moving a piano? Ha ha—this is money for old rope.
Grytpype-Thynne	Is it? I'd have thought you'd have bought something more useful.
Seagoon	Oh no—I have simple tastes. Now, where's the piano?
Grytpype-Thynne	Just a moment. First, would you sign this contract in which you guarantee to move the piano from one room to another for five pounds.
Seagoon	Of course I'll sign—have you any ink?
Grytpype-Thynne	Here's a fresh bottle.
Seagoon	(drinks) . . . ahhhh. Gad, I was thirsty.
Moriarty	Sapristi Nuckoes—do you always drink ink?
Seagoon	Only in the mating season.
Moriarty	Shall we dance?
(Grams	Old 1929 scratchy Guy Lombardo Record of 'Lover' Waltz)
Seagoon	You dance divinely.

Grytpype-Thynne	Next dance please! Now, Neddie, just sign the contract on the side of this horse.
Seagoon	Certainly.

(F. X.   SCRATCHING OF PEN UNDER SEAGOON AS HE
        SPEAKS NEXT LINE)

Seagoon	Neddie. . . Seagoon. . . A. G. G.
Moriarty	What's A. G. G. for?
Seagoon	For the kiddies to ride on . . . get it? A gee-gee . . . ha ha ha ha. . . (*Agonised silence*)
Grytpype-Thynne	You sure you won't have a gorilla?
Seagoon	No thanks, I've just put one out. Now, which room is this piano in?
Grytpype-Thynne	Ahemm. It's in the Louvre.
Seagoon	Strange place to put a piano.
Grytpype-Thynne	We refer to the Louvre Museum, Paris.
Seagoon	What what what what what? Ahhhh, I've been tricked—ahhhh.

(F. X.   THUD OF UNCONSCIOUS BODY HITTING GROUND)

Moriarty	For the benefit of people without television—he's fainted.

For the benefit of those who lack imagination, "There, there, don't take it so hard—it was only in thinks."

The distinction drawn in the *Anthologie de l'Humour noir* between "l'humour d'émission" and "un humour tout de réception" (p. 308) does not apply in the case of the Goon Show scripts. There is never any doubt that Spike Milligan's intent is humorous, whereas Jean-Pierre Brisset, whose writings prompted Breton to make the above distinction, wrote with the utmost seriousness. Humor is not of itself a letter of credit in the surrealists' eyes. To catch the surrealists' attention, Milligan has to have more to offer than a gift for amusing his public. Like that of Brisset (who claimed man to be descended from frogs because, under the microscope, spermatozoa look like tadpoles), his work takes on, in Breton's enthusiastic phrase, "great hallucinatory value" (p.

309) in that his use of language—again like Brisset's complex word play[37]—offers us "a succession of vertiginous verbal equations" leading to solutions that evade rational limitations. At the same time, taking the fullest advantage of his chosen medium, without consenting to let radio serve merely to echo familiar reality, Milligan's writing exploits sound effects in a way that promotes imaginative release, in defiance of reasonable logic and at the expense of stereotyped commonplace behavior in a commonsensical world. In these very ways, his Goon Show scripts demonstrate that radio is capable of giving authentic expression to the poetry of surrealism.

Conclusion

WHO IS TO PRESCRIBE the scale by which vision is to be measured? Breton's question on the very first page of *Le Surréalisme et la Peinture*[1] is of fundamental importance to anyone approaching the subject of surrealism without prejudice, because upon the answer surrealists bring to it depends not only what they see but also the intensity with which they see, and the value they attach to the things that claim their attention. Comprehension of the poetics of surrealism presupposes some understanding of what happens when surrealists reserve and exercise the right to set up their own scale of vision. The latter leaves them free to ascribe this object more value than that, and to see in the former, on some occasions or in certain circumstances, a meaning hidden from someone who does not bring to bear upon the world about him needs and desires (voiced or unvoiced, it makes no real difference) to which surrealist aspirations lend urgency, so leading Breton to open the second paragraph of *Le Surréalisme et la Peinture* with the following words: "To these different degrees of sensations correspond spiritual realizations precise enough and distinct enough for me to be allowed to grant plastic expression a value that, on the other hand, I shall never cease to deny musical expression."

Use of the word *expression* calls for no explanation in *Le Surréalisme et la Peinture*, because Breton sets expression through painting (*"l'expression plastique"*) on the same footing as verbal expression. Indeed, from the very beginning he argues that the visual images of painting, possessing great clarity and more rigor than those communicated by music, merit attention no less than verbal images. When he confides, "It seems to me that I can demand a great deal of a faculty which, above almost all the others, gives me an advantage over the real, over what is commonly understood by *the real*," he is alluding to the faculty of sight. The realm of painting, he notes, affords the individual an apparently limitless "power of illusion." This explains the confession Breton shows no reluctance in making: "So it is that it is impossible for me to consider a picture other than as a window about which my first concern is knowing *what it looks out upon*."

In consequence, academic painting has less hold over the surrealist's imagination than what is visible in the street outside the museums in which academic canvases can be viewed. As Breton states firmly, "to us, in this period, it is reality itself that is at stake." How to expand the realm of the real "to stupefying proportions"? How to bring to an end "the terrible struggle between lived experience and what is viable"? These are questions which, without for a moment assuming that definitive answers are to be found, the surrealist refuses to lose from sight. In order to continue to merit our trust, he believes, the eye must remain forever untamed, the images it reveals obstinately undomesticated, provocatively unassimilable by reason, speaking to us in that language which, the *Manifeste du Surréalisme* assures us, "has been given man so that he may make surrealist use of it."

Among the drawings done by René Magritte for Alain Jouffroy's *Aube à l'Antipode* is a bowler hat labeled "usage externe": "Not to be taken." Given the shape of the object in question, in which ambiguity hides beneath the common-place, this warning is by no means superfluous. In fact, it invests headgear with that equivocal air which strikes us everywhere in the universe painted by Magritte. The label attached on this occasion to a motif well known to those acquainted with his work (the derby hat appears in many of his pictures[2]) highlights our habit of limiting the applica-tion (*Usage externe:* "For external use") of so-called com-monplace things. The commonplace, after all, is that which has a foreseen use, presumably always foreseeable.

Generally one reserves for all hats, derby or not, an external use. As for poetry, is it not customary to ascribe it a private, so to speak internal, use? How, then, are we to understand Breton's gesture in labeling the correct use of language surrealist? How does one set about annexing the language that is shared by everyone to surrealism and its usages? We know that language, as Breton speaks of it in his second surrealist manifesto is but one aspect of *"human expression in all its forms"* with which surrealism proposes to deal. We have seen, too, that in order to take on that "anticipatory force" with which Breton wished to see it en-dowed, the poetic use of language must be free from all re-straint. This is why in *Les Pas perdus* Breton stressed the fundamental character of poetry as he was beginning to envision it—hence his insistence that "the word in itself" be brought under consideration and that "the reactions of words one upon another" be subjected to close study. Breton, therefore, was not slow to insist upon the internal use of the poetic logos, convinced that "It is only at this price that one could hope to return to language the full purpose for which it is intended, which, for some people, myself included, was to make cognition take a big step forward, to exalt life in that measure." In a reply to an inquiry conducted by the newspaper *Le Figaro*, he was soon affirming, "Poetry would hold no interest for me if I did not expect it to suggest to a few of my friends and myself a particular solution to the problem of our lives."

These important statements in *Les Pas perdus* give us to understand that, essentially, in order to be worthy of the surrealist label, poetry must adapt itself—whatever the appearances may be to those who accuse surrealism of incoherence, impertinence, or incomprehensibility—at the same time to external and to internal use. This accounts in notable measure for the haughty tone adopted by the surrealist poet: "I have noted with satisfaction," remark Breton and Schuster in their "Art poétique," "that my rapture kept me at a distance from the common herd." And this accounts, also, for the unity of surrealist poetry and for its diversity of expressive form. Escaping "the habitual glass retort of disasters," it turns aside from "the solemn geographies of human limits" toward those countries which, Paul Eluard assures us in his *Les Yeux fertiles* (*Fertile Eyes*) "are mine/ Because I do not know them."

Only with ironical intent does Magritte seem to confirm certain prejudices, in which good taste plays its limitative role, when he shows us yet another derby hat. In fact, with the assistance of humor he does so arbitrarily and in such a way as to do violence to the very prejudices he appears to share. The object we normally identify as destined invariably to protect the head adapts itself perfectly—where size is no impediment—to protecting the womb, as soon as its internal use is admitted. Removing it, we place both womb and head in danger of impregnation if, like Eluard, we recognize that "Les verges de l'ouragan/Cherchent leur chemin par chez toi." The interpretation that reason and good taste place on these words, as they elect to understand them in the sense they find least exceptionable ("The hurricane's rods/Seek their way to your house"), do not exhaust the surrealist potential of Eluard's poetic statement. For a *verge* is a penis as well as a rod, and surrealism does not stop short of postulating a pregnant head.

Notes

Introduction

1. Photographs appear in *XXe Siècle* No. 3 (June 1952), in the 1955 edition of André Breton's *Les Manifestes du Surréalisme* published in Paris by Le Sagittaire, in Robert Lebel, *Sur Marcel Duchamp* (Paris & London: Editions Trianon, 1959; New York: Grove Press, 1960), and in Arturo Schwarz, *The Complete Works of Marcel Duchamp* (New York: Abrams, 1969).

2. Hans Bellmer, *Die Puppe* (Carlsruhe O/S: Th. Eckstein, 1934). A French edition, *La Poupée*, of this volume of photographs of a child's doll—sometimes partially clothed, sometimes nude, but invariably with a sexually precocious expression, not to say a look of depravity, its torso and limbs rearranged with total disregard for anatomy—appeared in Paris with Editions GLM a year before the Gradiva Gallery opened. Raymond Borde has made a film about Molinier's work, with a commentary by Breton. See Raymond Borde and André Breton, *Pierre Molinier* (Paris: Le Terrain Vague, n.d. [1964]).

3. Presumably the lighthouse is lit up (*allumé*). In French *allumeuse* is the word for *tease*, and has the strongest sexual force. Hence Francis Picabia could offer, as a portrait of American Woman, a picture of a light bulb, on the cover of the sixth number (New York, July 1917) of his magazine *391*: the photograph of an incandescent bulb, cut out of a publicity catalog, touched up with white gouache and India ink.

4. André Pieyre de Mandiargues, *Les Incongruités monumentales* (Paris: Robert Laffont, 1948), p. 31.

5. The photograph in question appears in the first issue of *Le Surréalisme, même* (1956), p. 46, and bears the legend, "Document communiqué par le professeur Jacques Millot."

6. The surrealists' rejection of traditional standards of beauty led them from the very beginning to give special attention to the example set

211

by Isidore Ducasse, self-styled Comte de Lautréamont, in whose book *Les Chants de Maldoror* (of which a few copies were distributed among critics in 1869 before an edition appeared, after the author's death, in 1874) they were especially responsive to images like: "Beau comme la rencontre fortuite, sur une table de dissection, d'une machine à coudre et d'un parapluie" ("Beautiful as the chance encounter, on a dissecting table, of a sewing machine and an umbrella"). The influence of Lautréamont persists. Guy Cabanel, who did not join the surrealist movement until the fifties, writes in one of his poems, "Beau comme un intestin dans l'eau" ("Beautiful as an intestine in water").

7. Havelock Ellis reproduces a document reporting on how women employed at the turn of the century in clothing factories derived autoerotic satisfaction from operating their sewing machines. Technological progress from treadle machines to electric models is not without its disadvantages, apparently.

8. André Pieyre de Mandiargues has written a story, "Le Passage Pommeraye," on themes implicit in this interpretation of Lautréamont's image. See his collection of tales *Le Musée noir* (Paris: Robert Laffont, 1948). A translation of this tale appears in J. H. Matthews, *The Custom-House of Desire: A Half-century of Surrealist Stories* (Berkeley: University of California Press, 1975).

9. See André Breton, "Hommage à Max Walter Svanberg," *Médium: Communication surréaliste* Nouvelle Série, No. 3 (May 1954): 2. The third issue of *Médium* was dedicated to Svanberg's work as painter and graphic artist.

10. *En Avance du Bras cassé* dates from 1915. Man Ray's portrait photograph of Duchamp as Rrose Sélavy, executed in 1921, is reproduced in Schwarz, *The Complete Works of Marcel Duchamp*, p. 487. Duchamp contributed a *mannequin*, Rrose Sélavy, to the 1938 International Surrealist Exhibition held in Paris. It consisted, like all the other *mannequins* on display, of a dressmaker's dummy, a lifesize female wax figure. Duchamp's was dressed down to the waist only, and wore his own clothes. It stood near the street sign Rue des Lèvres, the Street of Lips. See the photograph in *The Complete Works of Marcel Duchamp*, p. 505, as well as in Man Ray, *Les Mannequins—Résurrection des Mannequins* (Paris: Jean Petithory, 1966).

Chapter 1—THE NINETEENTH-CENTURY HERITAGE

1. Louis Aragon, *Entretiens avec Francis Crémieux* (Paris: Gallimard, 1964), pp. 16–17.

2. Of the writers named by Aragon, three—Borel, Forneret, and Lautréamont—figure in Breton's *Anthologie de l'Humour noir*. Forneret is represented also in Péret's *Anthologie de l'Amour sublime*. Paul Eluard published an article in *Clarté* No. 5 (January 15, 1927), "L'Intelligence révolutionnaire: Pétrus Borel," in marked contrast with the entry "Borel (Joseph Pétrus)" to be found in the *Grand Dictionnaire Universel Larousse*. So far as Lautréamont is concerned, the reputation he was to enjoy from

the first among the surrealists is completely at odds with the assessment of his work by reputable literary commentators of the day like Marcel Arland, Jean Cassou, Joseph Delteil, Jean Hytier, Maurice Maeterlinck, Albert Thibaudet, and Paul Valéry. See Paul Eluard, "Le Cas Lautréamont," *La Révolution surréaliste* No. 6 (March 1926). Two surrealists, Georges Goldfayn and Gérard Legrand, were to offer the first edition, with commentary, of Lautréamont's *Poésies*. Dated 1960, their edition appeared in Paris with Le Terrain Vague in 1962.

3. Eluard's "Le Miroir de Baudelaire" is reproduced in his *Donner à Voir* (Paris: Gallimard, 1939).

4. André Breton, *Manifestes du Surréalisme* (Paris: Jean-Jacques Pauvert, n.d. [1962]), p. 184. All page references to Breton's surrealist manifestoes are to this edition.

5. Maurice Nadeau, in his *Histoire du Surréalisme* (Paris: Aux Editions du Seuil, 1945), arbitrarily dates "la période héroïque du surréalisme" from 1923 to 1925. Translated by Richard Howard as *The History of Surrealism*, Nadeau's study was published in New York by Macmillan in 1965.

6. J.-D. Maublanc, *Surréalisme romantique* (Paris: La Pipe à l'Ecume, 1934). During the thirties, Herbert Read also raised the question of surrealism's relations with romanticism, dealing with the matter in the context of English literature, and with polemical ends. See J. H. Matthews, "Surrealism and England," *Comparative Literature Studies* 1, 1 (1964): 55–72, and Paul C. Ray, "Sir Herbert Read and English Surrealism," *The Journal of Aesthetics and Art Criticism* 24, 3 (1966): 401–13.

7. Julien Gracq, *André Breton: quelques aspects de l'écrivain* (Paris: J. Corti, 1948). Cf. E. L. T. Mesens' preface, on the cardinal points of surrealist painting, in the catalog *De vier hoofdpunten von het surrealisme* (on Magritte, Ernst, Tanguy, and Miró) (Antwerp: Zaal Comité voor Artistiecke Werking, April 1956). Mesens quotes in English from his preface in "Homage to René Magritte," *Surrealist TransformaCtion* 2 (October 1968): 10–11.

8. See the chapters on Gracq and Fourré in J. H. Matthews, *Surrealism and the Novel* (Ann Arbor: The University of Michigan Press, 1966). The surrealist Annie Le Brun is the author of a study called *Les Châteaux de la Subversion*, as yet unpublished.

9. As quoted by Bernhild Boie and reported in Ferdinand Alquié, ed., *Entretiens sur le Surréalisme* (Paris: Mouton, 1968), p. 92.

10. Benjamin Péret, *Anthologie des Mythes, Légendes et Contes populaires d'Amérique* (Paris: Albin Michel, 1960), p. 15. Péret's introduction appeared originally as *La Parole est à Péret* (New York: Editions surréalistes, 1943).

11. Benjamin Péret, *Anthologie de l'Amour sublime* (Paris: Albin Michel, 1956), p. 57.

12. Pierre Mabille, *Le Miroir du Merveilleux* (Paris: Les Editions de Minuit, 1962). Mabille's much shorter essay, *Le Merveilleux* (Paris: Les Editions des Quatre Vents, 1946), is recommended only for day trips into the territory of the surrealist marvelous.

13. Paul Eluard, "Du Désir." This text, written in response to a questionnaire sent out by the Yugoslav surrealist Marco Ristic around

1932 remained unpublished until 1963, when it appeared in Paul Eluard, *Le Poète et son Ombre*, Robert D. Valette, ed. (Paris: Seghers), p. 22.

14. See Man Ray, *Les Mannequins—Résurrection des Mannequins* (Paris: Jean Petithory, 1966). Man Ray's photographs are of dressmaker's dummies, clothed or decorated by fifteen surrealist artists. They confirm that the *mannequin*, as surrealists speak of it, is the dressmaker's dummy whose magic presence first caught their imagination in the early painting of Giorgio de Chirico.

15. René Crevel, "La Grande Mannequin cherche et trouve sa peau," *Minotaure* 5 (1934): 18–19. For further details see p. 43 below.

16. Pablo Picasso, *Le Désir attrapé par la Queue* (Paris: Gallimard, 1945).

17. André Breton, *Les Vases communicants* [1932] (Paris: Gallimard, 1955), pp. 106–107.

18. Aragon, *Entretiens avec Francis Crémieux*, p. 22.

19. André Breton, *Entretiens: 1913–1952* (Paris: Gallimard, 1952), p. 21.

20. André Breton, *Nadja* [1928] (Paris: Gallimard, 1949), p. 19.

21. André Breton, "What Tanguy veils and reveals," *View* 2 (May 1942).

22. *En Rade* is the subject of a chapter in Matthews, *Surrealism and the Novel*.

23. *Médium* Nouvelle Série, No. 1 (November 1953): 1, 11–13.

24. J.-K. Huysmans, *A Rebours* [1884] (Paris: Fasquelle, 1961), p. 83.

25. André Breton, *L'Art magique* (Paris: Club Français du Livre, 1957), p. 36.

26. Tristan Tzara, "Essai sur la Situation de la Poésie," *Le Surréalisme au service de la Révolution* No. 3–4 (December 1931): 17.

27. Robert Desnos, *La Liberté ou l'Amour!* [1927] (Paris: Gallimard, 1962), p. 25.

28. See Georges Duthuit, "Où allez-vous Miró?" *Cahiers d'Art* No. 8–10 (1936): 262.

29. "The man warns you that he detests the past and the present. He has come only for the future. He is creating a void in himself. Of what he was, of what he is survives only a frenzied hunger for imagination. He closes his eyes so that no too immediate a sight will interpose itself between the future and the palms of his hands" (Paris: Editions de la Nouvelle Revue Française, 1929), p. 18.

30. Aragon, *Entretiens avec Francis Crémieux*, p. 20.

31. See, for instance, Breton's *Nadja*, certain photographs by Man Ray, and Yves Tanguy's object *De l'Autre Côté du Pont* (1936). Cf. José Pierre, "Le Gant et son Rôle dans l'Oeuvre de Klinger et de Chirico," *Le Surréalisme, même* No. 1 (1956): 131–39.

32. Emile Zola, *Oeuvres complètes* (Paris: Cercle du Livre précieux, n.d. [1966–69]), IV, 162. All references are to this edition of Zola's works.

33. *Ibid.*, p. 710.

34. Louis Aragon, *Le Paysan de Paris* [1926] (Paris: Gallimard, 1961), pp. 116–17.

35. See the discussion following J. H. Matthews, "Zola et les sur-réalistes," *Les Cahiers naturalistes* 24–25 (1963): 109. It should be noted that the transcript of this discussion, supposedly unedited, suppresses Mesens' protest at the irrelevant mention of Cocteau, in the context of surrealism, by Henri Mitterand.

36. For further details, see J. H. Matthews, *Theatre in Dada and Surrealism* (Syracuse, N.Y.: Syracuse University Press, 1974), pp. 81–83.

37. Jean Malrieu, "Tentative de Description," in his *Préface à l'Amour* (Marseilles: Cahiers du Sud, 1963).

38. Emile Zola, *Oeuvres complètes*, VI, 345.

39. *Ibid.*, II, 576.

40. Bibliothèque Nationale, Nouvelles Acquisitions, Fonds fran-çais, MS 10307, folio 14.

41. The Dane Wilhelm Freddie, one of the finest erotic artists of surrealism (he spent more than a week in jail on charges of pornography in 1937), has painted a picture of Zola and his mistress, *Zola og Jeanne Rozerot* (1938). Freddie has also created an object entitled *Zolas skrivebord* (*Zola's Writing Desk*). Both the object and the painting are reproduced in Gherasim Luca, *et al.*, *Wilhelm Freddie* (Copenhagen: Bjerregård-Jensen's Bogtrykkeri, 1962) and in the catalog *Where has Freddie been?* (London: Acoris, the Surrealist Art Centre, 1972), where *Zola og Jeanne Rozerot* appears in color reproduction. In this catalog *Zolas skrivebord* is dated 1936, while *Wilhelm Freddie* dates it from 1937. The date when the object was made remains speculative: an additional photograph in *Where has Freddie been?* which shows the artist at work (making or remaking it?) has, in the background, the canvas *Min kone ser på benzinmotoren, hunden ser på mig*, which was completed in 1940. So far as we are concerned, the important feature of *Zolas skrivebord* is not its date but the fact that it incorporates a dressmaker's dummy, laid horizontal on a wooden tripod. Upon the dummy rest an inkwell, with pen, and a revolver.

42. See Herbert Read, "Realism and Superrealism," expanded in his *Surrealism* (London: Faber and Faber, 1936), and "A Further Note on Superrealism" (reprinted from the *New English Weekly*), both in his *A Coat of Many Colours* (London: Routledge, 1945). Commenting on his lack of success in imposing "superrealism," Read was to remark: "But I do not propose to abandon the word 'superrealism' altogether; I propose rather to make a distinction between superrealism in general and Surrealism in particular, employing the first word for the tentative and historical mani-festations of what has now become a conscious and deliberate artistic prin-ciple. And those tentative and historical manifestations of superrealism I shall identify with some of the essential characteristics of romanticism— but of romanticism understood in a certain strict and not too comprehensive sense." "Introduction" to his *Surrealism* [1936] (London: Faber and Faber; New York: Praeger, 1971), pp. 21–22.

Chapter 2—The Emergence of Surrealism

1. Michel Sanouillet, *Dada à Paris* (Paris: Jean-Jacques Pauvert, 1965), p. 126.

2. Philippe Soupault, *Profils perdus* (Paris: Mercure de France, 1963), p. 166.

3. All the letters quoted are reproduced in Sanouillet, *Dada à Paris*, pp. 440–53.

4. Performance of Apollinaire's play *Les Mamelles de Tirésias* during 1974, within the framework of celebrations marking the fiftieth anniversary of the *Manifesto of Surrealism* at two American institutions of higher learning, the Pennsylvania State University and Hofstra University, is symptomatic. The practical reasons for selecting Apollinaire's play over a surrealist one (surrealist plays being thought to be, in general, unperformable) evidently found encouragement, in both instances, in the subtitle "drame surréaliste" which Apollinaire gave *Les Mamelles de Tirésias*.

5. André Breton claims in *Entretiens* (p. 23), that their first meeting took place May 10, 1916, the very day after Apollinaire's trepanation.

6. Soupault's contribution to the "Homage to André Breton" at the Institute of Contemporary Arts, London, in January 1967, provoked the broadside "Hola!" signed in the name of the surrealist movement by Gérard Legrand, José Pierre, and Jean Schuster, February 15, 1967.

7. André Breton, *Les Pas perdus* [1924] (Paris: Gallimard, 1949), pp. 25–45.

8. André Breton, *Anthologie de l'Humour noir* (originally 1940), definitive edition (Paris: Jean-Jacques Pauvert, 1966), pp. 409–12.

9. The picture in question, "Peinture" (1950), is reproduced in the catalogue of the D'Arcy Galleries' show, *Surrealist Intrusion in the Enchanters' Domain* (November 1960–January 1961), p. 97. It also appears, full page and in color, in Sarane Alexandrian's *L'Art surréaliste* (Paris: Fernand Hazan, 1969), p. 89, in the translation, *Surrealist Art* (New York: Praeger, 1974).

10. Like all the other poets from Mayoux onward whose testimony is presented here, Dhainaut wrote down his impressions of Apollinaire in 1963, in correspondence with the author.

11. For the word *poncif*, translated here as *stereotype*, Anna Balakian offers *platform* ("The Heresy of Innocence: a meditation on the fiftieth anniversary of the first surrealist manifesto," *The American Pen* 4, 3 [Summer 1974], reprinted in *Shantih* 3, 2 [Fall–Winter 1975]). In André Breton, *Manifestoes of Surrealism* (Ann Arbor: The University of Michigan Press, 1972), p. 40, the word is rendered as *pattern*. This translation of the surrealist manifestoes, by Richard Seaver and Helen R. Lane, is not only inaccurate but—as the version provided of the passage cited here amply testifies—based on a fanciful interpretation of French grammar. All translations from Breton's manifestoes in the present volume are my own.

12. Benjamin Péret, "La Pensée est UNE et indivisible," *VVV* No. 4 (February 1944): 10, translated as "Thought is ONE and indivisible," *Free UNIONS libres* (1946): 3.

13. Robert Champigny's analysis of the *Manifeste du Surréalisme*, originally published in *PMLA*, reappears in his *Pour une Esthétique de l'Essai* (Paris: Lettres Modernes, 1967), pp. 7–28.

14. Breton made this statement within the body of his *Second Manifeste du Surréalisme* (p. 211).

15. The original edition of Vaché's *Lettres de Guerre* appeared in Paris under the imprint Au Sans Pareil, in 1919. In 1949 it was reprinted in Paris by K éditeur, with four texts by Breton, the original 1919 introduction, the pertinent section of "La Confession dédaigneuse," from *Les Pas perdus*, the pages from the *Anthologie de l'Humour noir* on Vaché, and "Trente Ans après," dated 1948.

16. The fact that Lautréamont has received considerable attention of late does not reduce the importance of the role played by the surrealists in bringing his work to general notice. It is not unfair to say that this contemporary of Rimbaud's was discovered by the surrealists in France.

Chapter 3—A LANGUAGE OF INTELLIGENT REVOLT

1. Benjamin Péret, "La Soupe déshydratée," *La Nef* No. 63–64 (March–April, 1950), 'Almanach surréaliste du Demi-Siècle': 54.

2. Benjamin Péret, "La Pensée est UNE et indivisible," *VVV* No. 4 (February 1944): 11.

3. Benjamin Péret, *La Parole est à Péret* (1943) in his *Le Déshonneur des Poètes* précédé de *La Parole est à Péret* (Paris: Jean-Jacques Pauvert, 1965), p. 32.

4. Annie Le Brun, "L'Humour noir," in Ferdinand Alquié, ed., *Entretiens sur le Surréalisme* (The Hague: Mouton, 1968), pp. 99 100.

5. The fact deserves mention that we are not facing, in the *Anthologie de l'Humour noir*, evidence of a betrayal of surrealist thought, or a sudden reversal in Breton's own thinking. An earlier poem, "Vigilance" (from *Le Revolver à Cheveux blancs*, 1932), pointedly alludes to "the assent torn from me."

6. My review of Christian Bussy's *Anthologie du Surréalisme en Belgique, Symposium* 27, 3 (Fall 1973): 284–86, does no more than open up the question.

7. One typical gesture will serve to illustrate the independence of surrealists in Belgium. The second issue of the French surrealist magazine *L'Archibras* (October 1967) carried a prominent notice informing all who held letters written by André Breton that, in his will, Breton had expressed the wish that none of his letters be published until fifty years after his death. Without delay appeared in Holland, no publisher's name being mentioned, André Breton, *5 Lettres* (letters written to the following Belgian surrealists: one each to Camille Goemans, Marcel Mariën, René Magritte, and two to Paul Nougé). The pamphlet bore the publication date MMXVI. Printing supposedly was completed on September 28—the fiftieth anniversary of Breton's death. It should be noted that all the recipients of *5 Lettres* belonged to the surrealist group in Brussels. The Surrealist Group of Hainaut, founded in Mons by Fernand Dumont, looked to surrealism in France far more than did surrealists in the Belgian capital. For further details see J. H. Matthews, *The Custom-House of Desire* (Berkeley: University of California Press, 1975).

8. Paul Nougé, *Journal (1941–1950)* (Brussels: Les Lèvres Nues, 1968), p. 26.

9. See the interview granted Christian Bussy, reproduced in Bussy, *L'Accent grave,* published in Brussels under the imprint Les Lèvres Nues, in the series "Le Fait accompli" No. 19–20 (April 1969). All Les Lèvres Nues publications are published by Marcel Mariën, editor of the magazine *Les Lèvres Nues.*

10. See *ibid.,* which is unpaginated.

11. "La grande Question," in Paul Nougé, *Histoire de ne pas rire* (Editions de la revue *Les Lèvres Nues,* 1956), p. 65.

12. Paul Nougé, *Fragments,* Deuxième Série (1926–41), published in Brussels under the imprint Les Lèvres Nues, in the series "Le Fait accompli" No. 17 (February 1969), final fragment.

13. Paul Nougé, *Fragments,* Première Série (1923–29), published in Brussels under the imprint Les Lèvres Nues, in the series "Le Fait accompli" No. 13 (November 1968). Neither series of *Fragments* is paginated.

14. Letter dated March 2, 1929. The pertinent paragraph is reproduced in *Histoire de ne pas rire* (p. 79) and bears comparison with the following poem in Nougé's *Clarisse Juranville: Quelques Ecrits et quelques Dessins* (Brussels: René Henriquez, 1927):

Ils ressemblent à tout le monde
Ils forcèrent la serrure
Ils remplacèrent l'objet perdu
Ils amorcèrent les fusils
Ils mélangèrent les liqueurs
Ils ont semé les questions à pleines mains
Ils se sont retirés avec modestie
en effaçant leur signature

[They look like everyone else
They forced the lock
They replaced the lost object
They loaded the rifles
They mixed the drinks
They have scattered questions by the handful
They have withdrawn modestly
erasing their signatures]

15. Three numbers of *Distances,* plus a supplement, appeared between February and April of 1928. *Distances* took the place of the magazine *Cependant,* which never appeared. Hence Nougé's text published as No. 7 of the "Le Fait accompli" series in August 1968, under the title *Annonce de Cependant,* may be regarded as an unpublished announcement of *Distances.* It confirms that, as Nougé confided in Bussy, Valéry had taught him "a certain disdain for literature for literature's sake."

16. "L'Expérience souveraine," preface to an exhibition of photographs by Raoul Ubac (Brussels, May 1941), reproduced in Nougé, *Histoire de ne pas rire,* p. 125.

17. "La dernière Apparition," appears on p. 29 in the section "L'Ecriture simplifiée" of Nougé's poetic collection *L'Expérience continue*

(Brussels: Editions de la revue *Les Lèvres Nues*, 1966). With other selections from "L'Ecriture simplifiée," "La dernière Apparition" was originally published in the fourth issue of Mariën's magazine *Les Lèvres Nues* (January 1955), without indication of the date of composition. It was written some time between 1922 and 1953, probably in the early twenties.

18. "L'Occasion et les Sortilèges," in Nougé, *Histoire de ne pas rire*, p. 291.

19. Nougé *Fragments*, Première Série.

20. Paul Nougé, *Notes sur les Echecs* (Brussels: Les Lèvres Nues, 1968), pp. 81–84.

21. Extracts from this study appeared in the fifth number of *Le Surréalisme au service de la Révolution* in Paris on May 15, 1933. *René Magritte ou les Images défendues* was published in Brussels by Les Artistes associés in 1943. Additional texts appear in the version offered in Nougé, *Histoire de ne pas rire*. Further notes on the function of the object in Magritte's painting have appeared as *Pour illustrer Magritte*, published under the imprint Les Lèvres Nues, in the series "Le Fait accompli" No. 34–35 (April 1970).

22. Nougé appears to disagree with most surrealists on the role of scientists. He was by profession a biochemist. We find him writing in his undated "Notes sur la Poésie" (*Histoire de ne pas rire*, p. 164), "one may wonder if what is no doubt essential to the scientific approach, that is to say the spiritual habits it sets in motion, could not be of a nature to furnish us with an image, fairly crude no doubt, but valid all the same, of the poetic approach we have just indicated."

23. From a 1927 letter to Magritte, in Nougé, *Histoire de ne pas rire*, p. 218.

24. This text in *ibid.*, p. 20, is dedicated "Pour A. B." Its first paragraph, the one cited here, is reproduced in the statement "Pour garder les Distances," written by Nougé, Lecomte, and Camille Goemans on May 20, 1925.

25. This statement is taken from Nougé's lecture at the Charleroi Bourse (January 20, 1929), published as *La Conférence de Charleroi* (Brussels: Le Miroir fidèle, 1946). An English translation by Felix Giovanelli ran in *View*, December 1946 and Spring 1947. The slightly abridged translation was issued as a pamphlet entitled *Music is Dangerous* (Chicago: Surrealist Research & Development Monographs Series, No. 6 (1972).

26. From "La Messagère (paroles de femme sur petit fond d'orchestre)," written in 1927 and published in the eighth number of *Les Lèvres Nues* (May 1956).

27. "L'Epreuve poétique" (1936), in Nougé, *Histoire de ne pas rire*, p. 114.

28. "Récapitulation" (1941), in *ibid.*, p. 143.

29. From the section headed "Les Moyens de la Poésie" in the undated text "Notes sur la Poésie," in *ibid.*, p. 166.

30. See Michel Leiris, *Grande Fuite de Neige* (Paris: Mercure de France, 1964, no pagination), where we find "la causalité s'enfuit à tire-d'aile" ("causality flies swiftly away") being replaced by "la *cause-alitée*, principe des causes malades, détraquées" ("*cause confined to its bed*, principle of sick causes, causes out of order"). Breton qualifies great poets as

auditifs in his "Silence d'Or" (1944), reprinted in his *La Clé des Champs* (Paris: Les Editions du Sagittaire, 1953), p. 80.

31. Paul Nougé, *Subversion des Images* (Brussels: Les Lèvres Nues, 1968), p. 10. The photographs in this volume and the accompanying text are all by Nougé himself.

32. In *Clarisse Juranville: Quelques Ecrits et quelques Dessins* the texts are Nougé's, the drawings Magritte's. The prefatory note is dated September 7, 1927. The following year some of Nougé's poems were set to music by Souris, the score of one of them being published in the third number of *Distances* (April 1928) beneath the title "Une Page de Clarisse Juranville."

Subsequently, Nougé published his "Nouvelle Géographie élémentaire" (1928), presenting it as a marginal note by Mlle Juranville in a school geography book. See *Variété* (June 1929) (special number, hors série, 'Le Surréalisme en 1929'): 16–17.

33. Published under the pseudonym Ganchina in *Les Lèvres Nues* No. 6 (September 1955): 18–26.

34. See Nougé's *Journal*, entries for June 13 and June 10, 1941. See also *L'Invention de la Force* (1928), published under the imprint Les Lèvres Nues, in the series "Le Fait accompli," No. 31 (January 1970).

35. *Le Jeu des Mots et du Hasard* (Brussels: Editions de la revue Les Lèvres Nues, 1955)—fifty-five boxed playing cards.

36. From "La Publicité transfigurée," written in 1925, presented at a *Correspondance* concert (February 2, 1926), to percussion accompaniment arranged by André Souris.

Chapter 4—Subversion and Revolution

1. It should be noted that Nougé terminated his diary in 1950. He made no attempt to publish the *Journal*, which was brought out on Mariën's initiative the year after its author's death.

2. André Breton, "Introduction," in Jean Ferry, *Le Mécanicien et autres contes* (Paris: par les soins des Cinéastes Bibliophiles, 1950), reissued by Gallimard in 1953. Breton's prefatory essay is reprinted in his *La Clé des Champs*, pp. 213–23. The passage quoted here occurs on p. 220.

3. Apollinaire called Sade the "freshest mind that has ever existed." See his introduction to *L'Oeuvre du marquis de Sade* (Paris: Les Maîtres de l'Amour, 1909), reprinted in his *Les Diables amoureux* (Paris: Gallimard, 1964). The phrase cited here falls on p. 194 in the Gallimard edition.

4. Alain Jouffroy, "Un Acte surréaliste: L'Exécution du Testament de Sade," *Arts* No. 754 (December 23–29, 1959), reprinted in his *Une Révolution du Regard* (Paris: Gallimard, 1964), pp. 34–37. The paragraph quoted here closes Jouffroy's text. A photograph of the costume worn by Benoît appears in Jouffroy's book. Two more photos appear in the surrealist Robert Benayoun's *Erotique du Surréalisme* (Paris: Jean-Jacques Pauvert, 1965), pp. 217 and 218.

5. "Les Assis" is the title of a poem by Rimbaud which caricatures

those who haunt library reading rooms and, by extension, all sedentary figures.

6. The most elaborate tribute to the life and work of Sade that has come from within surrealism is Alain-Valery Aelberts and Jean-Jacques Auquier's *Cérémonial pour saluer d'Eruption en Eruption jusqu'à l'infracassable Nuit la Brèche absolue et la Trajectoire du marquis de Sade* (Brussels: privately printed, 1970), the subject of a chapter in J. H. Matthews, *Theatre in Dada and Surrealism* (Syracuse, N.Y.: Syracuse University Press, 1974), pp. 253–71.

7. Transcripts of the telediphone recordings of A. G. Lehmann's talk and of "In Defence of Surrealism" were made available to the author through the kind cooperation of Miss Leonie Cohn of the British Broadcasting Corporation's Talks Department. Octavio Paz authorized citation of some of his remarks made during the latter program—in which he places stress on the surrealist attitude toward eroticism—in a review of his *Selected Poems* (trans. Muriel Rukeyser), published in *Comparative Literature Studies* 2, 1, (1965): 97–103. Cf. the surrealists' *Lexique succinct de l'Erotisme* (Paris: Eric Losfeld, 1970).

8. Having dedicated their eighth international exhibition to Sade, the surrealists dedicated the eleventh, *L'Ecart absolu* (Paris: Galerie de l'Oeil, December 1965), to Charles Fourier.

9. Robert Desnos, *De l'Erotisme considéré dans ses manifestations écrites et du point de vue de l'esprit moderne* (Paris: Editions "Cercle des Arts," n.d.), p. 78. This text appears to have been written during the twenties, when Desnos was still a member of the surrealist movement.

10. Jean-Louis Bédouin, *Vingt Ans de Surréalisme (1939-59)* (Paris: Denoël, 1961), p. 300.

11. In his *Le Surréalisme*, published in 1966 in the *Histoire générale de la Peinture* put out by Editions Rencontre in Lausanne, the surrealist José Pierre speaks of the "incomparable poetic charge" common to Benoît's painting, his *Exécution du Testament du marquis de Sade*, and his *Le Nécrophile*. In Pierre's volume Benoît's work is illustrated by a color photograph of Benoît in his Sade costume, pulling the trolley carrying the brazier used during the ceremony.

12. In José Pierre's *Le Surréalisme: dictionnaire de poche* (Paris: Fernand Hazan éditeur, 1973), Benoit's work is illustrated by a front-view color photo of *Le Nécrophile*, reproduced, presumably, from the catalog *L'Ecart absolu*, where the same photo appears full page. Two photographs of *The Necrophiliac* with accompanying description by Benoît, appear (pp. 82–84) in the Canadian magazine *Exile* 2, 2–3 (1975), as do three photographs of *Maldoror's Bulldog* (pp. 85–87) and pictures of other Benoît objects.

13. Enrique Gómez-Correa, *Poesía explosiva* (Santiago de Chile: Ediciones "Aire Libre," 1973). Like other surrealist publications in Chile, this one bears the imprint Mandrágora. Co-founder with Gómez-Correa of the Chilean surrealist group mandrágora, Braulio Arenas translated into Spanish Lautréamont's *Poésies* and, in 1948, Sade's *Dialogue entre un Prêtre et un Moribond*.

Gómez-Correa's status as Consul General of Chile in Guatemala gives piquancy to the title of his collected poems. Two years before *Poesía explosiva* appeared, on July 6, 1971, Jean Schuster was condemned by the Chambre du Tribunal Correctionnel de Paris to a fine of one thousand francs for publishing in No. 4 (hors série) of the surrealist magazine *Coupure*, confiscated by the police, the articles in *La Cause du Peuple* which had led to the imprisonment of Le Dantec and Le Bris. Thus *Coupure* became the first collective surrealist publication to be brought to court in France. Surrealists elsewhere have not always been so lucky. In Japan Takiguchi Shūzō and Fukuzawa Ichiro were both arrested in 1941, charged with being surrealists, and jailed. In Czechoslovakia, surrealism was banned officially in 1939. Upon the death of one of the promoters of surrealism in Czechoslovakia, Karel Teige, his apartment was subjected to a police search in 1951, many of his manuscripts being confiscated. Also confiscated by the Czech police were copies of the catalog of an exhibition *Imaginatouní malířstiví 1930–1950*, forced to close in 1964 after only one day.

The liberal policies of Dubcek's democratization movement made it possible for an important exhibition of surrealism to be held in Brno (March), Prague (April), and Bratislava (June), during 1968, under the title *Princíp Slasti (The Pleasure Principle)*. The occasion was marked by the redaction of an important statement, *La Plateforme de Prague*, drawn up in collaboration by French and Czechoslovak surrealists during the month of April. The Russian invasion of August 21 brought surrealist activities in Czechoslovakia to an abrupt halt. On September 30, 1968, *L'Archibras* issued in Paris a special number (No. 5, hors série), "Réalité politique et Réalité policière," in which *La Plateforme de Prague* was reproduced, the names of twenty-one Czech signatories having been prudently removed from the end of the document.

14. Jean Schuster, "Le Surréalisme et la Liberté," in Alquié, ed., *Entretiens sur le Surréalisme*, reprinted in his *Archives 57/68: batailles pour le surréalisme* (Paris: Eric Losfeld, 1969).

15. Details are to be found in Maurice Nadeau, *Histoire du Surréalisme* (Paris: Editions du Seuil, 1945), and Victor Crastre, *Le Drame du Surréalisme*. For evaluations of the surrealists' dealings with the Communists, see Robert S. Short, "The Politics of Surrealism, 1920–1936," *The Journal of Contemporary History* 1, 2 (1966): 'The Left-Wing Intellectuals between the Wars, 1919–1939': 3–25; and especially the chapter "In the Arena: Surrealism and Politics," in Herbert S. Gershman, *The Surrealist Revolution in France* (Ann Arbor: University of Michigan Press, 1969), pp. 80–116.

16. André Breton, *Légitime Défense* (Paris: Editions surréalistes, 1926). This publication embodies Breton's reply to attacks leveled at the surrealists for political ineptitude in Pierre Naville's *La Révolution et les Intellectuels* (Paris: Gallimard, 1926).

17. Gershman, *The Surrealist Revolution in France*, p. 105. José Pierre, *Position politique de la Peinture surréaliste* (Paris: Le Musée de Poche, 1975), shows less surprise than Gershman (p. 31) regarding Trotsky's involvement. Noting, however, that *Pour un Art révolutionnaire indépen-*

dant synthesizes Breton's reflections over the period from 1926 (the date of *Légitime Défense*), Pierre does not dismiss the possibility that the tract was written mainly by Breton (p. 30). Arturo Schwarz has published an *André Breton, Leone Trotsky* (Milan: Edizioni Savelli, 1974). Marguerite Bonnet's "Trotsky et Breton" appears as an appendix to Trotsky's *Lénine* (Paris: Presses Universitaires de France, 1970).

The text of *Pour un Art révolutionnaire indépendant* appears in French in *London Bulletin* No. 6 (October 1938) and in translation in No. 7 (December 1938–January 1939) of the same magazine.

18. Written in December 1940 and intended for publication in Marseilles shortly thereafter, *Fata Morgana* appeared in Buenos Aires (Editions des Lettres Françaises) in 1942. An English translation by Clark Mills came out in the magazine *New Directions* in 1941. The *New Directions* text was accompanied by a reproduction of the Censor's stamp bearing the date February 1941 and the manuscript notation "deferred until the final conclusion of peace." Mills's translation and the accompanying stamp, taken from the manuscript of Breton's text, appear in the English version of *Fata Morgana* put out by Black Swan Press (Chicago) in February 1969.

19. Suzanne Césaire, "Le Surréalisme et nous," *Tropiques* No. 8–9 (1943). Césaire's *Cahier d'un Retour au Pays natal* appeared originally in Cuba. Before its republication in Paris by Présence africaine in 1956, it came out in New York in 1944, under the imprint Editions Hémisphères. For the occasion, Breton wrote his article "Un grand Poète noir," *Hémisphères* No. 2–3 (Winter 1943–44): 3–11, in which we read, "The poetry of Césaire, like all great poetry and all great art, has the highest value in the power of transmutation it embodies and which consists in producing, from the most discredited materials, among which must be counted ugliness and servitude themselves, something one knows very well not to be gold any more, the philosopher's stone, but certainly liberty." Césaire had written, "En Guise de Manifeste littéraire," in the fifth number of *Tropiques*, "Because we hate you, you and your reason, we claim kinship with dementia praecox, with flaming insanity, with tenacious cannibalism. . . . Adapt yourselves to me. I'm not adapting myself to you."

20. Pierre Mabille, "Le Paradis," *VVV* No. 4 (February 1944): 36. Mabille's statement represents what we may term the orthodox surrealist viewpoint. See for instance Breton's statement "Misère de la Poésie" of 1932 [reproduced in Maurice Nadeau, *Documents surréalistes*, (Paris: aux Editions du Seuil, 1948), pp. 208–16], his *Position politique du Surréalisme* (Paris: Editions du Sagittaire, 1935), his "Visite à Léon Trotsky" dating from 1938 (reprinted in his *La Clé des Champs*). Dissident views held by the Bureau International du Surréalisme Révolutionnaire, were to have found expression in a bimonthly magazine called *Le Surréalisme révolutionnaire*, published in Paris by an international editorial committee. The first number appeared, dated March–April, 1948. It included, among other texts, an essay signed by René Passeron, "Introduction à une Erotique révolutionnaire," marked for continuation in the second number, which never came out.

21. Péret's texts for *Le Libertaire* were published subsequently, together with G. Munis' "Les Syndicats contre la Révolution," in a volume pre-

sented by the surrealist Jehan Mayoux, *Les Syndicats contre la Révolution* (Paris: Le Terrain Vague, 1968). Mayoux's preface drew attention to the timeliness of this publication which appeared the year of the student revolt in France. For surrealist reaction to the social disturbance of 1968, see the special number (No 4, hors série) of *L'Archibras*, subtitled *Le Surréalisme en 18 juin 1968*. The surrealists' unreserved approval of student revolt finds expression in this important document. No less important is Schuster's testimony to his conviction that surrealism helped precipitate the events of summer 1968.

Solicited by questionnaire, Schuster wrote "Mai 1968" when asked to single out the most important political and social event of the sixties. Invited to assess events outside France, he wrote under the same heading, "La révolution étudiante." He refused, however, to comment on literary events of note, observing, "There are never any events in literature." Questioned about circumstances which might have contributed to advancing the surrealist cause since 1960, he wrote simply "oui—Mai 1968." To a query about the special contribution that surrealism had made in the sixties, he answered, "The surrealist group, in the twenties, in the thirties, in the forties, in the fifties, and in the sixties directly and indirectly prepared for May 1968. That is total revolution—to change life—transform the world—today the surrealist group is working so that May 1968 may resume as quickly and as effectively as possible." Response, dated November 17, 1968, furnished in connection with J. H. Matthews, "Surrealism in the Sixties," *Contemporary Literature* 2, 2 (Spring 1970): 226–42.

22. See Benjamin Péret, *Anthologie des Mythes*, pp. 30–31. It should be noted that when Péret speaks of the common origin of poetry and science, he understands the word *science* in the sense of *knowledge*, as Breton speaks of *connaissance* as *cognition*. There is no question of concluding that in *La Parole est à Péret* we can detect an attitude in conflict with Péret's habitual mistrust of scientific procedures.

23. Gui Rosey, "Leçon d'Hommes, Leçon de Choses," preface to his *Seconde Ligne de Vie* (Paris: José Corti, 1965), pp. 13–14.

24. Franklin Rosemont, "Revolution by Night: Surrealism Here and Now," in his *The Morning of a Machine Gun* (Chicago: Surrealist Editions, 1968), p. 8. The history of the Surrealist Group in Chicago evidences a quite frantic effort to reconcile their wish to follow at the same time André Breton and Herbert Marcuse, while still responding to the call of American radicalism. See their magazine *Arsenal: Surrealist Subversion*, their contribution to *Radical America*, and *Surrealist Intervention*, papers presented by the Surrealist Group in Chicago at the second international TELOS conference, November 1971.

25. Mention of the tract *Tranchons-en* is not intended to divert attention from other equally important documents like Mabille's *Le Merveilleux* and *Le Miroir du Merveilleux*, and especially Breton's article "Le Merveilleux contre le Mystère," *Minotaure* No. 9 (October 15, 1936), reprinted in his *La Clé des Champs* (1953).

26. From an address by André Breton before a meeting of the Rassemblement Démocratique Révolutionnaire on December 12, 1948.

27. The title speaks for itself: "L'Exemple de Cuba et la Révolu-

tion—Message des Surréalistes aux Ecrivains et Artistes cubains," *La Brèche: Action surréaliste* No. 7 (December 1964): 103–104. The statement is dated Summer 1964.

28. Alfred Schmeller, *Surrealism*, text trans. Hilde Spiel (London: Methuen, 1956), Se 52. It is difficult to understand why Schmeller assumes the potatoes to be in a cellar. The reproduction of Michau's painting clearly shows a cloud-laden sky overhead.

29. Writing on "The Rose and the Revolver" in the first number of *Yale French Studies* (Fall-Winter 1948): 106–11, the surrealist Nicolas Calas, author of *Towards a Third Surrealist Manifesto*, declared, "If surrealism distorts symbols it is because, on the social level, there is a need to reach negation through distortion. On the poetic level, the existing order can be both criticized and transcended. Surrealism aims at increasing insights, at revealing conflicts rather than smothering them under wreaths of flowers."

30. Quoted by Gilbert Ganne, "Qu'as-tu fait de ta Jeunesse?" *Arts* No. 560 (March 21–27, 1956). *Le Surréalisme, même* ran from 1956 to 1957, five numbers in all.

31. On Freddie see Gherasim Luca, *et al.*, *Wilhelm Freddie* and especially the Acoris catalog *Where has Freddie been?* which details Freddie's experiences with police cencorship. See Borde & Breton, *Pierre Molinier* (Paris: Le Terrain Vag·ie, n.d. [1964]) on Molinier. It has stills from Borde's film. On Moesman see Her de Vries, Jak van der Meulen, Laurens Vancrevel, *Moesman* (Utrecht, privately printed, 1971). As for Svanberg, see André Pieyre de Mandiargues, *et al.*, *Max Walter Svanberg: Grafik* (Malmø: Lilla Antikvariatet, n.d.), and José Pierre, *Max Walter Svanberg et le Règne féminin* (Paris: Le Musée de Poche, n.d. [1975]).

32. Hans Bellmer, *Petite Anatomie de l'Inconscient physique ou L'Anatomie de l'Image* (Paris: Le Terrain Vague, n.d., [1957]). See the review of this work by Jean-Louis Bédouin in *Le Surréalisme, même* No. 3 (Autumn 1957): p. 16. See also Hans Bellmer, *Vingt-Cinq Reproductions 1934–1950*, with texts by Nora Mitrani, *et al.*, (Paris: no publisher's name, 1950).

33. René Magritte, *Manifestes et autres Ecrits* (Brussels: Les Lèvres Nues, n.d. [1973]). André Masson, *Anatomy of my Universe* (New York: Curt Valentin, 1943).

34. Jean-Louis Bédouin, "L'Affaire Gurdjieff: Force et Faiblesse de la Volonté de Puissance," *Médium: Communication surréaliste* Nouvelle Série No. 3 (May 1954): p. 17.

35. Robert Desnos, "Déposition," *Les Cahiers du Mois*, 1926.

36. Jean-Jacques Lebel, from a statement broadcast in Warsaw, communicated by Lebel and reproduced in J. H. Matthews, ed., *An Anthology of French Surrealist Poetry* (London: University of London Press, 1966), p. 112.

37. The text of this *prière d'insérer* appears in Paul Eluard, *Le Poète et son Ombre*, (Paris: Seghers, 1963) pp. 106, 107. The phrase "the strident cry of red eggs" is taken, of course, from one of the poems in *De Derrière les Fagots* (Paris: Editions surréalistes, 1934).

38. Accompanied by a *chronique critique*, titled *Quand j'étais Pomme de Terre*, written by José Pierre, *A ce Prix* appeared in a limited

edition, without publisher's name or date, in 1964. It was reprinted in the definitive edition of Breton's *Le Surréalisme et la Peinture* (Paris: Gallimard, 1965), pp. 407–09.

39. In linking *bande* with anarchy, Breton evidently is alluding to the anarchist gang led in France by Bonnot.

Chapter 5—SURREALIST POETIC EXPRESSION

1. Paul Eluard, "L'Evidence poétique," in his *Donner à Voir*, p. 81.

2. All quotations from Artaud's writings are borrowed from his *Oeuvres complètes* (Paris: Gallimard, 1962), III.

3. Georges Sadoul, "Souvenirs d'un Témoin," *Etudes cinématographiques* No. 38–39 (1965): 21–22.

4. André Breton, *L'Amour fou* [1937] (Paris: Gallimard, 1957), p. 61.

5. See André Breton, "Fronton Virage," in Jean Ferry, *Une Etude sur Raymond Roussel* (Paris: Arcanes, 1953), p. 12. It is true that acquaintance with Roussel's novels had predisposed the surrealists in favor of his theatre. All the same, the incomprehension of the audience, confronted with *L'Etoile au Front*, could not but delight Breton and his friends. Roussel himself has reported that when one of his "adversaries" cried out, "Hardi la claque," during the second act, Robert Desnos, in whom the playwright identified one of his "partisans," replied "Nous sommes la claque et vous êtes la joue." See Raymond Roussel, *Comment j'ai écrit certains de mes Livres* [1935] (Paris: Jean-Jacques Pauvert, 1963), p. 32.

6. See Francis Valobre's article "A Tout rompre," in *Médium: Communication surréaliste* Nouvelle Série, No. 3 (May 1957): 7.

7. Robert Benayoun, "Eugène Ionesco ou le Pélican," *BIEF: Jonction surréaliste* No. 6 (April 15, 1959): no pagination.

8. See *L'Age du Cinéma* No. 4–5 (August–November 1951). The text of "Comme dans un Bois" reappears in Breton's *La Clé des Champs*, pp. 241–46.

9. Ado Kyrou, *Le Surréalisme au Cinéma* (Paris: Le Terrain Vague, 1953; rev. ed., 1963), p. 9.

10. Benjamin Fondane, *Trois Scénarii* (Brussels: Les Documents internationaux de l'Esprit nouveau, 1928).

11. Luis Buñuel, "Notes on the Making of *Un Chien andalou*," in Frank Stauffacher, ed., *Art in Cinema* (San Francisco: The Museum of Art, 1947).

12. Information graciously provided by Jean-Louis Bédouin, in a letter to the author dated April 26, 1963.

13. André Breton and Jean Schuster, "Art poétique," *BIEF: Jonction surréaliste* No. 7 (June 1, 1959): no pagination.

14. Press release on the occasion of the showing of *L'Invention du Monde* within the framework of the Edinburgh Festival. It was particularly fitting that Péret, author of *Histoire naturelle*, should have been asked to provide a commentary for *L'Invention du Monde*. *Histoire naturelle* combats

the scientific explanation of life—the elements and the evolution of forms—in favor of a rigorously anti-rational poetic interpretation. For further information on this little-known privately printed text, see J. H. Matthews, *Benjamin Péret* (Boston: Twayne, 1975), pp. 42–54.

15. See André Breton, *Poésie et Autre* (Paris: Club du Meilleur Livre, 1960).

16. *La Coquille et le Clergyman* was published originally in No. 170 (November 1927) of *La Nouvelle Revue Française*, where it was preceded by Artaud's essay "Cinéma et Réalité." Artaud subsequently repudiated the film made of *La Coquille et le Clergyman* by Germaine Dulac. Both the screenplay and "Cinéma et Réalité" appear in the third volume of his *Oeuvres complètes*.

17. The scenario of *Spiste Horisonter (Eaten Horizons)* appears in Gherasim Luca, *et al.*, *Wilhelm Freddie* (Copenhagen: Bjerregård-Jensen's Bogtrykkeri, 1962), pp. 97 and 98.

18. The screenplay of *Am-ster-dam* was published in the first number of the French magazine *Bizarre* (May 1955).

19. See Joseph Cornell's film script *Monsieur Phot (see through a Stereoscope)* (Flushing, N. Y., privately printed, 1933).

20. "The poet acts as a contagious phenomenon. Comprehension of the poem comes only after." Cited by André Delattre, "Personal Notes on Paul Eluard," *Yale French Studies* (Fall–Winter 1948).

21. In the catalog *Where has Freddie been?* each notation is reproduced beside the relevant frame in *Spiste Horisonter*. The translation of the scenario provided appears to have been taken from a French version of the text. The English version used here is the one by Wm Petersen in Luca, *et al.*, *Wilhelm Freddie*.

22. For elaboration of the concept of surrealist poetry as an antipodean venture, see Alain Jouffroy's surrealist verse collection *Aube à l'Antipode*, written between 1947 and 1948 and published integrally by Le Soleil noir (Paris) in 1966, a "diary of dawns that have appeared at the antipodes of 'real' life."

23. Jean Schuster, "A l'Ordre de la Nuit, Au Désordre du Jour," *L'Archibras* No. 1 (April 1967): 4.

24. The Yugoslav Ivsic began writing his play in 1943, during the German occupation. Reading the text at the end of 1954, Breton invited its author to join the surrealist movement. *Le Roi Gordogane* was broadcast on April 18, 1956, on the Chaîne Nationale of the Radiodiffusion-Télévision Française. It was published in 1968 in Paris, under the imprint Editions surréalistes.

25. The first of a series called "Crazy People" (with Michael Bentine) was broadcast on May 28, 1951. On June 22, 1952, the series was re-titled "The Goon Show." Leaving the show on November 11, 1952, Bentine committed suicide not long afterward. The final "Goon Show" program, *The Last Smoking Seagoon*, was aired on January 28, 1960. The author of the scripts was Spike Milligan. Neddie Seagoon was played by Harry Secombe. The other voices were shared by Milligan and Peter Sellers. Two volumes of *Goon Show Scripts* have been published by the Woburn Press in London.

26. Like Milligan's father, Bloodnok bears the title "Ind. Arm. Rtd."

27. Louis Aragon, "Petite Note sur les collages chez Tristan Tzara et ce qui s'en suit," in his *Les Collages* (Paris: Hermann, 1965), pp. 141–49.

28. Understandably, Jacques B. Brunius has emphasized this point in his article "The Goon Show," *Le Surréalisme, même* No. 2 (Spring 1957): 86–88. In the photograph of the three Goons, Milligan, Secombe, and Sellers, reproduced with Brunius' text, only Milligan is accurately identified.

29. Whatever he looks like, Bluebottle is "a cardboard cut-out liquorice string hero," given to curiously functional exclamatory sounds.

30. The Hon. Hercules Grytpype-Thynne, "a plausible public school villain and cad." The Goons invariably take pleasure in undermining the British caste system.

31. The results are not always of necessity intentional, by the way. *Napoleon's Piano* offers French listeners indecency as a bonus:

Seagoon	Two glasses of English port-type cooking sherry and vite.
Throat	Two glasses of sherry and vite *[vit]* coming up.

32. See, to begin with, André Breton, "La Crise de l'Objet," dated 1936, in his *Le Surréalisme et la Peinture* (Paris: Gallimard, 1965), pp. 275–80. Breton's text might well have been written as a commentary on the objects listed here.

33. An appropriate analogy is not so much the inclusion of a cage of live hens among the exhibits of the *Surrealist Intrusion in the Enchanters' Domain* show at the D'Arcy Galleries, New York, as the recording, audible in the Galleries during the show, of the *Marseillaise*, agonizingly and inaccurately picked out with one finger on a piano. (When speaking of the Goons, one dare not write "picked out on a piano with one finger"). It was tempting to leave uncorrected the typo that interestingly changed one of my sentences to read, "The terrifying roar of a loan is identified as that of a man-eating tiger."

34. Moriarty, "French scrag and lackey to Grytpype-Thynne," is of noble descent: Comte Toulouse-Moriarty of the House of Roland.

35. See especially the section called "Barrières" in André Breton and Philippe Soupault, *Les Champs magnétiques* (Paris: Au Sans Pareil, 1920). Cf. the plays *Vous m'oublierez* and *S'il vous plaît* which appear in the reprint of *Les Champs magnétiques* (Paris: Gallimard, 1967).

36. Harry Secombe, "Backword," *The Goon Show Scripts* (London: The Woburn Press, 1972), p. 190.

37. On Brisset's use of language which reached, as Michel Foucault has put it, "the extreme point of linguistic delirium," see Foucault's preface to the volume that brings together both Brisset's *La Grammaire logique* and his *La Science de Dieu* (Paris: Tchou, 1970). See also Mary Ann Caws, "Jean-Pierre Brisset et la Grammaire des Grenouilles," *Nineteenth-Century French Studies* (Fall 1972): 43–50.

CONCLUSION

   1. A translation of *Le Surréalisme et la Peinture* appeared as *Surrealism and Painting* with Icon Editions, New York, in 1972.

   2. In a photograph taken in 1938, next to his painting "Le Barbare," Magritte wears a derby. See Patrick Waldberg, *René Magritte* (Brussels: André De Rache, 1965), p. 13.

Index

TOWARD THE POETICS OF SURREALISM

was composed in 12-point Linotype Palatino and leaded one point,
with display type in Alphabet Innovations and Avalon Shadowed
Helvetica foundry by Dix Typesetting Co., Inc.;
printed offset on 55-pound Lock Haven Offset
by Vicks Lithograph and Printing Corporation;
Smyth-sewn and bound over boards in Columbia Mills Triton
by Vail-Ballou Press, Inc.;
and published by

SYRACUSE UNIVERSITY PRESS

Syracuse, New York 13210